W9-BND-592

IMPORTANT NOTICE

THE HALLIFORD EDITION OF THE WORKS
OF THOMAS LOVE PEACOCK

VOLUMES IX AND X

IT was originally intended to issue Volume VIII
(containing the *Four Ages of Poetry*, the *Memoirs
of Shelley*, Letters, Diary, Unfinished Novels, etc.)
together with IX and X. The publication of
Volume VIII has, however, been deferred in the
hope that it may yet be possible to trace the
original MSS. of Peacock's letter to Hookham,
dated April 9, 1811, and of the unfinished novel
which has been called *The Lord of the Hills*. Both
of these MSS. were in the possession of the late
Dr. Richard Garnett, probably not long before his
death in April 1906; and a text of both subsequently appeared in his volume of Peacock's
Letters, etc., privately printed for the Bibliophile
Society of Boston, U.S.A., in 1912. Inquiries in
England and America have hitherto been unsuccessful, and the editor and publishers would be
grateful for any information as to the present
ownership of these two MSS.

THE HALLIFORD EDITION
OF THE WORKS OF
THOMAS LOVE PEACOCK
EDITED BY H. F. B. BRETT-
SMITH & C. E. JONES

This volume contains a portrait of Peacock's eldest daughter, Mary Ellen.

1858

MARY ELLEN

Eldest daughter of Thomas Love
Peacock and joint - author of
Gastronomy and Civilization.

From a drawing made in 1858
by an old friend.

THE WORKS OF
THOMAS LOVE PEACOCK
VOLUME NINE

CRITICAL
& OTHER ESSAYS

AMS PRESS, INC.
New York
1967

Reprinted with the permission of
CONSTABLE & CO. LTD.

AMS Press, Inc.
New York, N.Y. 10003
1967

Manufactured in the United States of America

PREFATORY NOTE

TO VOLUMES IX AND X

THERE is evidence among the family papers
that Peacock, in his old age, contemplated
the collection of some at least of his mis-
cellaneous writings, but the intention was
never carried out, and the two volumes now
submitted to the public contain articles
which have hitherto been accessible only in
the files of magazines and reviews, where
most of them appeared either anonymously
or signed with initials not those of the
author. In addition to these, Peacock's
criticism of the opera and his unpublished
writings on gastronomy have been fully
illustrated in appendices, in the latter of
which the editors have made liberal use of
manuscripts in private ownership. The
translation of *Gl'Ingannati*, published in
1862, and now so scarce that only five
copies have been traced, is also reprinted.
In the main, however, these volumes represent the bulk of Peacock's journalistic

work, which has been practically unknown to modern readers.

All journalism is to some extent ephemeral, but the subjects chosen by Peacock have stood the test of time ; gastronomy and music, classical and French literature, Lord Byron and Tom Moore, even the American constitution and the treatment of our London bridges by officialdom, are themes which are still continually before the public. We still fear, like Peacock, that " we have brought chemistry into our kitchens, not as a handmaid but as a poisoner," * nor have we ceased to find, among professed critics, that " the oracle shakes his head, and the profane take for granted that there is something in it." †
Readers who already know their Peacock will recognise many such typical turns of thought and phrase, as well as the recurrence of the author's cheerful and familiar prejudices against gas, paper currency, universities, modern poetry, and the conferment of " the most Christian distinction of knighthood " upon Jews and Parsees. There are a number of pleasant passages also which recall the classical examples of wit in the novels and the acknowledged prose. Most of these must be left to the discoverer, but in witness of good faith a

* IX. 394. † IX. 337.

PREFATORY NOTE

couple shall be cited here : the reminiscence of *The Four Ages of Poetry* in Peacock's remark that " the light of the kitchen fire was probably the brightest spot in the dark ages," * and the evident suggestion and foreshadowing of *Nightmare Abbey* in Pigault le Brun's account of the soliloquy of M. de Roberville,† contemplating (in a *fiacre*) the renunciation of an ungrateful world in favour of philosophic solitude. It is too long to quote ; but if de Roberville, shut up in his library, with a damask dressing-gown, a velvet cap, and a young and pretty housekeeper, was not responsible for Scythrop's similar seclusion with a dressing-gown of striped calico, a nightcap, and Celinda, we are grievously mistaken.

* IX. 366.   † IX. 279.

CONTENTS

MOORE'S EPICUREAN

MOORE'S EPICUREAN *

THIS volume will, no doubt, be infinitely acceptable to the ladies " who make the fortune of new books." Love, very intense ; mystery, somewhat recondite ; piety, very profound ; and philosophy sufficiently shallow ; with the help of

> —new mythological machinery,
> And very handsome supernatural scenery ;

strung together with an infinity of brilliant and flowery fancies, present a combination eminently calculated to delight this very numerous class of readers. It is a production in the best style of M. de Chateaubriand.

In the reign of the emperor Valerian, Alciphron, a young Epicurean philosopher, is elected chief of that school in the beginning of his twenty-fourth year, a circumstance, the author says, without precedent, and we conceive without probability.

Youth, however, and the personal advantages that adorn it, were not, it may be supposed,

* *The Epicurean.* By Thomas Moore.

among the least valid recommendations to a sect that included within its circle all the beauty, as well as wit, of Athens, and which, though dignifying its pursuits with the name of philosophy, was little else than a pretext for the more refined cultivation of pleasure.—pp. 1, 2.

Here is a circumstance, which, the author says, never before occurred ; which, therefore, according to his own showing, never occurred at all, excepting in fiction ; and which most assuredly never did or could occur, followed by very goodly reasons to show that it must naturally and necessarily have occurred always. For if women were the electors, and youth and its personal advantages the recommendations of a candidate, it is not easy to perceive how a simple elderly gentleman, like Cicero's Patro, who had no better recommendation than that of being qualified for his office, could have had any chance against such a competitor as Mr. Moore's hero.

The character of the sect had indeed much changed since the time of its wise and virtuous founder, who, while he asserted that Pleasure is the only Good, inculcated, also, that Good is the only source of Pleasure.—p. 2.

Alciphron should have added, that Epicurus did not bandy about the two words like a shuttlecock, but took the trouble of explaining very clearly what he meant by both.

4

MOORE'S EPICUREAN

The purer part of this doctrine had long evaporated, and the temperate Epicurus would have as little recognized his own sect in the assemblage of refined voluptuaries who now usurped its name, as he would have known his own quiet garden in the luxurious groves and bowers among which the meetings of the school were now held.—p. 2.

This is a great misrepresentation of the character of the later Epicureans.

Many causes, besides the attractiveness of its doctrines, concurred at this period to render our school the most popular of any that still survived the glory of Greece. It may generally be observed, that the prevalence in one half of a community of very rigid notions on the subject of religion, produces the opposite extreme of laxity and infidelity on the other ; and this kind of re-action it was, that now mainly contributed to render the doctrines of the garden the most fashionable philosophy of the day. The rapid progress of the Christian faith had alarmed all those who either from piety or worldliness were interested in the continuance of the old established creed ; all who believed in the deities of Olympus, and all who lived by them. The consequence was, a considerable increase of zeal and activity throughout the constituted authorities and priesthood of the whole Heathen world. What was wanting in sincerity of belief, was made up in rigour ; the weakest parts of the Mythology were those of course most angrily defended, and any reflections tending to bring Saturn or his wife Ops into contempt, were punished with the utmost severity of the law.—pp. 2, 3.

MOORE'S EPICUREAN

As a light touch of satire, glancing from the past to the present, all this is very well ; but the concluding sentence, if intended to be at all taken as the assertion of an historical fact, is decidedly incorrect.

In this state of affairs, between the alarmed bigotry of the declining faith, and the simple and sublime austerity of its rival, it was not wonderful that those lovers of ease and pleasure who had no interest, reversionary or otherwise, in the old religion, and were too indolent to inquire into the sanctions of the new, should take refuge from the severities of both in the shelter of a luxurious philosophy, which leaving to others the taste of disputing about the future, centered all its wisdom in the full enjoyment of the present.—pp. 3, 4.

With respect to the alarmed bigotry of the declining religion (the Athenians never called it a faith), there never was a religion from first to last so little tinctured with bigotry ; the persecutions of the Christians by the Roman emperors originated in political motives ; they were persecuted as Jacobins and Radicals, not as Infidels : though religion was of course then, as now, called in to subserve, as far as it would go, the cause of political supremacy ; and with respect to "the simple and sublime austerity," they are words which involve a great quantity of misrepresentation, employed as they are here, antithetically to the bigotry of the

6

ancient mythology, and the luxurious philosophy of the Epicureans.

The sectaries of the garden had, ever since the
death of their founder, been accustomed to dedicate
to his memory the twentieth day of every month.
To these monthly rites, had for some time been
added, a grand annual festival, in commemoration
of his birth. The feasts given on this occasion by
my predecessors in the chair, had been invariably
distinguished for their taste and splendour, and it
was my ambition, not merely to imitate this
example, but even to render the anniversary now
celebrated under my auspices, so brilliant as to
efface the recollection of all that went before it.—
pp. 4, 5.

Here follows a description of a very gay
festival, much more Vauxhallian than Attic,
such, the author says, as Athens seldom,
he should have said never, witnessed. But
as soon as it is over, the hero is troubled
with a qualm, to which we recollect no
parallel ; but to which an authentic case
which we remember to have somewhere
read, of a South-Sea Missionary, furnishes
a remarkable converse.

This pious brother was one of three, who
went forth to be shining lights to the Austral-
asian gentiles. One night he was troubled,
not by a dream of a ghost, but by what
was to him a much more astounding phæ-
nomenon, a process of reasoning which
went to syllogise him out of his conviction

of the immortality of the soul. The dismayed brother applied in deep tribulation to the saint, who finally turned out to be the Abdiel of the party, for a refutation of the intrusive syllogisms. Brother Abdiel told him, the refutation was to be found in the Scripture ; but the doubting Thomas shook his head and said, if his reason erred so grossly in this point, he could not trust it in any, even in the reception of the evidence of his faith ; and that if his reasoning were correct, his labours and privations among savages were miseries incurred for nothing. Brother Abdiel was inexorable in refusing to put down the fiend by argument instead of by faith, and brother Thomas took the first opportunity of returning to Europe, in a state of reprobation.

The third saint of this hopeful party turned out no better than a Belial. He took to wife a native girl, who not only would not walk with him in the path of life, but actually made him a backslider, even unto idolatry. She converted him to her own religion by a process which was so far less sinful than brother Thomas's, that reason had certainly nothing to do with it ; but he was so lost to grace as to assure brother Abdiel, that, if he would pursue the same course of inquiry, he would arrive at the same conclusion.

MOORE'S EPICUREAN

We suspect the volume before us is a composite plagiarism from the adventures of these worthies. The hero begins very like brother Thomas, with a qualm of dissent from his sect's doctrines on the subject of immortality, and ends by being converted from his philosophy, as the result not of any process of reasoning, but of the same cogent passion which converted brother Belial.

That very night my triumph, my happiness, had seemed complete. I had been the presiding genius of that voluptuous scene. Both my ambition and my love of pleasure had drunk deep of the cup for which they thirsted. Looked up to by the learned, and loved by the beautiful and the young, *I had seen in every eye that met mine either the acknowledgment of triumphs already won, or the promise of others still brighter that awaited me.* Yet, even in the midst of all this, the same dark thoughts had presented themselves ; the perishableness of myself and all around me, every instant recurred to my mind. Those hands I had pressed—those eyes in which I had seen sparkling a spirit of light and life, that should never die—those voices, that had talked of eternal love—all, all, I felt were but a mockery of the moment, and would leave nothing eternal but the silence of their dust !

Oh ! were it not for this sad voice,
   Stealing amid our mirth to say,
That all, in which we most rejoice,
   Ere night may be the Earth-worm's prey :
But for this bitter—only this—

MOORE'S EPICUREAN

> Full as the world is brimm'd with bliss,
> And capable as feels my soul
> Of draining to its depths the whole,
> I should turn Earth to Heaven, and be,
> If bliss made gods, a deity !—pp. 12, 13.

A garden deity, of course.

This picture of an Epicurean, the chief of his school in Athens, divided between self-congratulation on his *bonnes fortunes*, and lamentations over his own conviction of the truth of his sect's dogma of the mortality of the soul, could only have been hazarded by a confident reliance on the profound ignorance of every thing truly classical, which characterizes the vast majority of the reading public, and especially of that portion of it which our author especially addresses.

After this he goes to sleep, and dreams a dream. He sees " a pale venerable man, with a taper in his hand," standing before him, " like a messenger from the grave."

After a few moments of awful silence, during which he looked at me with a sadness that thrilled my very soul, he said, "Thou who seekest eternal life, go unto the shores of the dark Nile—go unto the shores of the dark Nile, and thou wilt find the eternal life thou seekest."—p. 16.

The Epicurean, who is a seeker of eternal life, is also a believer in dreams. He therefore determines to visit the land of the Pyramids, gives himself leave of absence

10

with as much *nonchalance* as if he had been the chairman of a bubble company, and sets sail for Alexandria, " A.D. 257, furnished with recommendatory letters to all parts of Egypt ! "

So far all we have seen of our Epicurean exhibits him as a *bon vivant*, a gay deceiver, a seeker after eternal life, and a believer in dreams. We do not mean to say, that among the *soi-disant* Epicureans scattered throughout the Roman Empire in the third century, there may not have been many such gentlemen ; but we do mean to say, that the later Epicureans, of whom we have any authentic knowledge, were very differently-compounded persons : and as our hero is the *élite* of his sect, we conceive that the best known specimens of his class should have sat for his picture. As it is, we cannot think it possible that such a person as is here represented could have been elected chief of his school in Athens, unless we could suppose that the Athenians had forestalled us in our own system of virtual representation, and had carried it to a pitch of perfection, which, until we revived it in the eighteenth century, had been lost almost as hopelessly as the art of making mummies.

At Alexandria our philosopher lives very jovially, with intermittent fits of his qualm, till he is startled and shocked by unveiling a skeleton at a banquet. The poor young gentleman is " wholly unprepared for such a spectacle : " he had neither sufficient knowledge of ancient customs to look for it, nor sufficient philosophy to endure it. Yet the custom of introducing skeletons, either natural or artificial, at banquets, having passed from the Egyptians to the Greeks, and from the Greeks to the Romans, long before the time of our hero, without any other recorded effect on the guests than that of a stimulus to present enjoyment in consideration of the brevity of life, his surprise and discomposure on the occasion form two more new and curious traits in the character of our Epicurean. It strikes him, at the same time, that if this were what his dream had sent him to look for, the pale venerable man had adopted a very original method of keeping his promise-to-pay : very original, at any rate, in those days, though quite in accordance with our more enlightened practices.

He now becomes satisfied that he shall not find immortality in Alexandria, and determines to look for it in Memphis, having some very cogent reasons for supposing that the key to it is under the Pyramids.

At Memphis he begins as usual, by amusing himself with the lions, and indulges himself in a number of most un-

MOORE'S EPICUREAN

Attic conceits, of which the following are specimens :—

I stood before the Pyramids of Memphis, and saw them towering aloft, like the watch-towers of Time, from whose summit when he expires he will look his last.—p. 37.

This is a very infelicitous conceit. The peak of a pyramid must be an uncomfortable dying-bed even for Time. If we attempt to make a picture of this figure, we must imagine the old gentleman dying on tip-toe, and finishing his terrestrial career by rolling down the side of the Pyramid into the sand.

The sun half sunk beneath the horizon, was taking calmly and gloriously his leave of the Pyramids, as he had done evening after evening for ages, till they had become familiar to him as the earth itself. On the side turned to his ray they now presented a front of dazzling whiteness, while on the other, their great shadows, lengthening to the eastward, looked like the first steps of night, hastening to envelope the hills of Araby in their shade.—p. 40.

Here we have night in the novel attitude of stepping from west to east, a most extraordinary image to present itself either to a philosopher or a mythologist.

In another place we have the Libyan desert like a sea, and Time standing by it like a tide-waiter.

13

MOORE'S EPICUREAN

Memphis, still grand, though no longer the un-rivalled Memphis, that had borne away from Thebes the crown of supremacy, and worn it undisputed through so many centuries, now softened by the moonlight that harmonised with her decline, shone forth among her lakes, her pyramids, and her shrines, like a dream of glory that was soon to pass away. Ruin, even now, was but too visible around her. The sands of the Libyan desert gained upon her like a sea ; and among solitary columns and sphinxes, already half sunk from sight, Time seemed to stand waiting, till all, that now flourished around, should fall beneath his desolating hand like the rest.—p. 42.

The sands of the Libyan desert gaining on Memphis like a sea, is an impressive though not original image, but the picture is altogether spoiled by the figure of Time standing waiting. Has Mr. Moore forgotten that time and tide wait neither for men nor sands? The very essence of the idea of Time is steady, incessant, interminable progression. If he has any business in the place, it is as an agent, himself silently impelling the progress of desolation, not waiting till the sands have done their work, in order to begin his. And as Memphis was still a flourishing city at least four centuries later than our very curious specimen of an Epicurean, Time must have stood waiting for no inconsiderable portion of himself.

14

Again, the hero being alone in a skiff on the inundation of the Nile :—

Absorbed in such thoughts I rowed on, scarce knowing whither I went, till, startled by finding myself within the shadow of the City of the Dead, I looked up, and saw rising in succession before me pyramid beyond pyramid, each towering more loftily than the other, while all were out-topped in grandeur by one, upon whose summit the moon seemed to rest as on a pedestal.—p. 51.

This looking up just in the nick of time to catch the moon on the peak of the great pyramid, strikes us as a very petty straining after pantomimic effect, and as throwing away, for the sake of a tricksy phantasy, all the real sublimity of the picture of the City of the Dead by moonlight, standing (by aid of the inundation) on the margin of the waters. And we may, perhaps, be permitted to wonder how he could be startled from his reverie by finding himself in the shadow, when, according to his own showing, he was still in the full moonlight.

We think Mr. Moore must admit, in his cooler moments, that these are very foolish freaks to play with Time, and the Sun, and the Moon, and the Pyramids. The truth is, the sublime is beyond his grasp ; and, in aiming at it without adequate power, he only achieves, as many worthy aspirants have done before him, a pompous seizure of its close neighbour the ridiculous.

At Memphis, Alciphron falls violently in love with a young priestess, whom he sees in a temple at " the great festival of the Moon." We shall extract the entire passage, in which he describes the commencement of his disease.

On the waters all was life and gaiety. As far as eye could reach, the lights of innumerable boats were seen, studding, like rubies, the surface of the stream. Vessels of all kinds, from the light coracle, built for shooting down the cataracts, to the large yacht that glides to the sound of flutes,—all were afloat for this sacred festival, filled with crowds of the young and the gay, not only from Memphis and Babylon, but from cities still farther removed from the scene.

As I approached the island, I could see, glittering through the trees on the bank, the lamps of the pilgrims hastening to the ceremony. Landing in the direction which those lights pointed out, I soon joined the crowd ; and, passing through a long alley of sphinxes, whose spangling marble shone out from the dark sycamores around them, in a short time reached the grand vestibule of the temple, where I found the ceremonies of the evening already commenced.

In this vast hall, which was surrounded by a double range of columns, and lay open over head to the stars of heaven, I saw a group of young maidens moving in a sort of measured step, between walk and dance, round a small shrine, upon which stood one of those sacred birds that, on account

of the variegated colour of their wings, are dedicated
to the moon. The vestibule was dimly lighted,
there being but one lamp of naphtha on each of the
great pillars that encircled it. But having taken
my station beside one of those pillars, I had a
distinct view of the young dancers, as in succession
they passed me.

Their long graceful drapery was as white as
snow, and each wore loosely, beneath the rounded
bosom, a dark-blue zone, or bandelet, studded,
like the skies at midnight, with little silver stars.
Through their dark locks was wreathed the white
lily of the Nile—that flower being accounted as
welcome to the moon as the golden blossoms of
the bean-flower are to the sun. As they passed
under the lamp, a gleam of light flashed from their
bosoms, which I could perceive was the reflection
of a small mirror that, in the manner of the women
of the East, each wore beneath her left shoulder.

There was no music to regulate their steps;
but, as they gracefully went round the bird on the
shrine, some by the beat of the castanet, some by
the shrill ring of the sistrum—which they held
uplifted in the attitude of their own divine Isis—
harmoniously timed the cadènce of their feet;
while others, at every step, shook a small chain of
silver, whose sound, mingling with those of the
castanets and sistrums, produced a wild but not an
unpleasing harmony.

They seemed all lovely; but there was one—
whose face the light had not yet reached, so downcast she held it—who attracted, and, at length,
rivetted all my attention. I knew not why, but
there was a something in those half-seen features,
a charm in the very shadow that hung over their

imagined beauty—which took me more than all the out-shining loveliness of her companions. So enchained was my fancy by this coy mystery, that her alone, of all the group, could I either see or think of—her alone I watched, as with the same downcast brow she glided round the altar gently and aërially, as if her presence, like that of a spirit, was something to be felt, not seen.

Suddenly, while I gazed, the loud crash of a thousand cymbals was heard ;—the massy gates of the temple flew open, as if by magic, and a flood of radiance from the illuminated aisle filled the whole vestibule ; while, at the same instant, as if the light and the sounds were born together, a peal of rich harmony came mingling with the radiance.

It was then—by that light, which shone full upon the young maiden's features, as, starting at the blaze, she raised her eyes to the portal, and, as suddenly, let fall their lids again—it was then I beheld what even my own ardent imagination, in its most vivid dreams of beauty, had never pictured. Not Psyche herself, when pausing on the threshold of heaven, while its first glories fell on her dazzled lids, could have looked more beautiful, or blushed with a more innocent shame. Often as I had felt the power of looks, none had ever entered into my soul so far. It was a new feeling—a new sense— coming as suddenly as that radiance into the vestibule, and at once filled my whole being—and had that vision but lingered another moment before my eyes, I should have wholly forgotten who I was and where, and thrown myself, in prostrate adoration, at her feet.

But scarcely had that gush of harmony been

heard, when the sacred bird, which had till now stood motionless as an image, expanded his wings, and flew into the temple ; while his graceful young worshippers, with a fleetness like his own, followed, —and she who had left a dream in my heart never to be forgotten, vanished with the rest. As she went rapidly past the pillar against which I leaned, the ivy that encircled it caught in her drapery, and disengaged some ornament which fell to the ground. It was the small mirror which I had seen shining on her bosom. Hastily and tremulously I picked it up, and hurried to restore it ;—but she was already lost to my eyes in the crowd.

In vain I tried to follow ;—the aisles were already filled, and numbers of eager pilgrims pressed towards the portal. But the servants of the temple prevented all further entrance, and still, as I presented myself, their white wands barred the way. Perplexed and irritated amid that crowd of faces, regarding all as enemies that impeded my progress, I stood on tiptoe, gazing into the busy aisles, and with a heart beating as I caught, from time to time, a glimpse of some spangled zone, or lotus wreath, which led me to fancy that I had discovered the object of my search. But it was all in vain ;— in every direction, files of sacred nymphs were moving, but nowhere could I see her whom alone I sought.

In this state of breathless agitation did I stand for some time,—bewildered with the confusion of faces and lights, as well as with the clouds of incense that rolled around me,—till, fevered and impatient, I could endure it no longer. Forcing my way out of the vestibule into the cool air, I hurried back through the alley of sphinxes to the shore, and flung myself into my boat.—pp. 43-49.

He now rows away to the City of the Dead, where he sees two female figures, muffled up and veiled, land from a boat, and comforts himself with the prospect of curing his passion by a *bonne aventure* among the tombs. He follows the new comers till they disappear into a pyramid by a concealed opening, which he detects, " with infinite promptitude," and dips after them into subterranean passages, till he gets into a " chapel," where he again discovers the lady of his love, watching over a lifeless female form, in a crystal shrine, on an altar of granite.

The lamp, by which the whole of the chapel was illuminated, was placed at the head of the pale image in the shrine ; and between its light and me stood a female form bending over the monument, as if to gaze upon the silent features within. The position in which this figure was placed, intercepting a strong light, afforded me, at first, but an imperfect and shadowy view of it. Yet even at this mere outline my heart beat high,—and memory, as it proved, had as much share in this feeling as imagination. For on the head changing its position, so as to let a gleam fall on the features, I saw, with a transport which had almost led me to betray my lurking place, that it was she—the young worshipper of Isis—the same, the very same whom I had seen brightening the holy place where she stood, and looking like an inhabitant of some purer world.

The movement by which she had now given me an opportunity of recognising her was made in raising from the shrine a small cross * of silver, which lay directly over the bosom of the lifeless figure. Bringing it close to her lips, she kissed it with a religious fervour ; then turning her eyes mournfully upwards, held them fixed with an inspired earnestness, as if at that moment, in direct communion with heaven, they saw neither roof nor any other earthly barrier between them and the skies.

What a power hath innocence, whose very help-lessness is its safeguard—in whose presence even passion himself stands abashed and turns wor-shipper at the altar which he came to despoil. She who but a short hour before, had presented herself to my imagination as something I could have risked immortality to win—she whom gladly from the floor of her own lighted temple, in the very face of its proud ministers, I would have borne away in triumph, and defied all punishments, both human and sacred, to make her mine—she was now before me, thrown, as if by fate itself, into my power—standing there, beautiful and alone, with nothing but her innocence for her guard ! Yet, no—so touching was the purity of the whole scene, so calm and august that protection which the dead seemed to extend over the living, that every earthlier feeling was forgotten as I gazed, and love itself became exalted into reverence.

Entranced, indeed, as I felt in witnessing such a scene, thus to enjoy it by stealth seemed a wrong, a sacrilege—and rather than let her eyes meet the flash of mine, or disturb by a whisper that sacred silence in which Youth and Death held

* A cross was, among the Egyptians, the emblem of a future life.

communion through Love, I would have let my
heart break, without a murmur, where I stood.
Gently, as if life depended upon every movement,
I stole away from that tranquil and holy scene—
leaving it still tranquil and holy as I found it, and,
gliding back through the same passages and windings
by which I had entered, regained the narrow stair-
way, and again ascended into light.

The sun had just risen, and, from the summit
of the Arabian hills, was pouring down his beams
into that vast valley of waters,—as if proud of the
homage that had been paid to his own Isis, now
fading away in the superior light of her lord. My
first impulse was to fly from this dangerous spot,
and in new loves and pleasures seek forgetfulness
of the scene which I had witnessed. " Once out
of the circle of this enchantment," I exclaimed, " I
know my own susceptibility to new impressions
too well, to doubt that I shall soon break the spell
that is around me."

But vain were my efforts and resolves. Even
while I swore to fly, my steps were still lingering
round the pyramid—my eyes still turned towards
the secret portal, which severed this enchantress
from the world of the living. Hour after hour
did I wander through that City of Silence,—till
already it was noon, and under the sun's meridian
eye, the mighty pyramid of pyramids stood, like a
great spirit, shadowless.

Again did those wild and passionate feelings
which had, for a moment, been subdued into
reverence by her presence, return to kindle up my
imagination and senses. I even reproached myself
for the awe that had held me spell-bound before
her. " What would my companions of the Garden

say, did they know that their chief—he whose
path Love had strewed with trophies—was now
pining for a simple Egyptian girl, in whose presence
he had not dared to give utterance to a sigh, and
who had vanquished the victor without even knowing her triumph ! "—pp. 58-63.

He now determines to watch at the entry
for her forthcoming, and executes his resolution like one who well knows what belongs
to a watch; for he sleeps like an ancient and
most quiet watchman, till some time after
moon-rise of the following night. He lets
us, however, into an important secret in the
art of watching, for he went comfortably to
sleep in the confidence that " his heart, if
not his ear, would still be on the watch."
We wish we could imagine what sir Hugh
Evans, who was so much astonished at
Pistol's " hearing with ears," would have
said of a philosopher who supposed that
when he was too fast asleep to hear with
his ears, he should be able to hear with his
heart—

> As Rosicrusian virtuosis
> Can see with ears and hear with noses.

Such are the frippery impertinences which
ladies and lady-like gentlemen call " beautiful ideas ! "

He refreshes himself with dates and dried
fruits from his boat, which he always keeps
victualled for a day's voyage, furnishes him-

self with a lamp from the same store, and determines to re-enter the pyramid in quest of the fair unknown. He is very nearly deterred by a sound which he takes for an ill omen, but his love overcomes his superstition, and he gets into " the chapel " again.

We wish Mr. Moore would tell us what is the Attic word for a chapel.

He finds nothing in the chapel but the crystal shrine and the mummy : he is awed thereby.

We must stop to enumerate. The exclusive love, the omen, and the awe, form three more new traits in the character of our Epicurean.

He discovers an outlet from the chapel, which leads him through narrow windings into a catacomb, at the end of which he finds a well, where, having occasion for both his hands, he finds, at the same time, very opportunely, that his lamp fits his head like a helmet. He gets down part of the well, by a hundred morsels of iron steps, then clambers through an aperture, and goes down a spiral staircase, almost as deep as Bottom's dream, which had no bottom ; then passes through two iron gates, which open at the touch of his finger, and close with a din as if all the echoes which had been due to all the noises made from the beginning of the world were being paid off

MOORE'S EPICUREAN

by a run (this is not Mr. Moore's image, but our own, after his fashion). He then walks into an illuminated alley, very like the dark walks of Vauxhall since they have been lighted by order of the Surrey magistrates, where he finds odoriferous thickets flourishing without daylight or fresh air, like the peaches in sir George Mackenzie's economical hot-house, which were very good peaches, wanting nothing but taste and colour, very like turnips in semblance, and no doubt almost as good in substance, excepting that no rhetoric could prevail on a pig to eat one. In this alley he hears some mellifluous music, consisting of " a harmony tapering into a spire of female tones, towering high and clear over all the rest ; " and at the peak of this spire he thinks he can " spy his Thisbe's voice."

We wish Mr. Moore would tell us where our Athenian got his notion of a spire, in the sense in which the word is here employed.

He proceeds into a veritable dark walk, where he smells the damp of death-vaults, sees phantoms flitting, and is mystified by a blue flame which writes the following verses on the wall—

> You, who would try
>   Yon terrible track,
> To live or to die,
>   But ne'er to look back—

MOORE'S EPICUREAN

You, who aspire
    To be purified there,
By the terrors of fire,
    Of water and air,—

If danger, and pain,
    And death you despise,
On—for again
    Into light you shall rise ;

Rise into light
    With that Secret Divine,
Now shrouded from sight
    By the Veils of the Shrine !

But if—

Here the letters faded away into a dead blank, more awfully intelligible than the most eloquent words.

A new hope now flashed across me. The dream of the Garden, which had been for some time almost forgotten, returned to my mind. " Am I, then," I exclaimed, " in the path to the promised mystery ? and shall the great secret of Eternal Life *indeed* be mine ? "

" Yes ! " seemed to answer, out of the air, that spirit-voice which still was heard crowning the choir with its single sweetness. I hailed the omen with transport. Love and Immortality both beckoning me onward—who could give a thought to fear, with two such bright hopes in view ? Having invoked and blessed that unknown enchantress whose steps had led me to this abode of mystery and knowledge, I plunged into the chasm.—pp. 75, 76.

MOORE'S EPICUREAN

After this he goes through fire and water, in a manner not very dissimilar to that which the frequenters of the Italian Opera must remember to have seen achieved by signor Garcia and madame Bellocchi, in the " Flauto Magico " of Mozart. The opera and the corresponding portion of the work before us are both drawn from the same source, Terrasson's Romance of " Sethos," which his French biographer says contains " des détails curieux sur les initiations." From these " détails curieux " Mr. Moore has helped himself liberally ; and by turning the absurd into the monstrous, and the improbable into the impossible, he passes his hero through a process of half-burning, half-drowning, and half-hanging, from which his life is only saved by availing himself, on each occasion, of a fantastical means of escape which a single moment would have placed beyond his grasp, and his apprehension of which is nothing less than a miracle. He is landed from the three several elements in which he has escaped the several perils of suspension, combustion, and submersion, in a sunless Paradise—a subterranean garden lighted by a composition of golden moonlight, and some other light (gas perhaps), where he finds shrubs and flowers, and, amongst other marvels, verdant turf.

We recommend Mr. Moore to try the

experiment of growing a pot of grass in his cellar before he again amuses the public with similar fantasies.

Nor were there wanting inhabitants for this sunless Paradise. Through all the bright gardens were wandering, with the serene air and step of happy spirits, groups both of young and old, of venerable and of lovely forms, bearing, most of them, the Nile's white flowers on their heads, and branches of the eternal palm in their hands ; while, over the verdant turf, fair children and maidens went dancing to aërial music, whose source was, like that of the light, invisible, but which filled the whole air with its mystic sweetness.

Exhausted as I was by the trials I had undergone, no sooner did I perceive those fair groups in the distance, than my weariness, both of frame and spirit, was forgotten. A thought crossed me that she, whom I sought, might be among them ; and, notwithstanding the awe with which that unearthly scene inspired me, I was about to fly, on the instant, to ascertain my hope. But in the act of making the effort, I felt my robe gently pulled, and turning, beheld an aged man before me, whom, by the sacred hue of his garb, I knew to be a Hierophant. Placing a branch of the consecrated palm in my hand, he said, in a solemn voice, " Aspirant of the Mysteries, welcome ! "—then, regarding me for a few seconds with grave attention, added, in a tone of courteousness and interest, " The victory over the body hath been gained !—Follow me, young Greek, to thy resting place."

I obeyed in silence,—and the Priest, turning away from this scene of splendour, into a secluded path, where the light faded away as we advanced, conducted me to a small pavilion, by the side of a whispering stream, where the very spirit of slumber seemed to preside, and, pointing to a bed of dried poppy-leaves within it, left me to repose.— pp. 85-87.

After a good deal of mystification, in the course of which the hero begins to wish himself safe back in his boat, and has " his very soul chilled " several times over, the Hierophant makes his appearance, and expounds to him the doctrine of the immortality of the soul, in a sort of figurative predication, which contains nothing more than what Alciphron and his brother Epicureans must have laughed at fifty times over, and which it certainly was not worth his while to go through a good singeing and ducking for the sake of having preached to him, as something new, below the level of the sea. He shows himself somewhat restive under the process, but a phantasmagoric glimpse of his fair enchantress, in a veil made of something like a meteor, which gradually becomes transparent, reconciles him to his locality. We cannot follow him through all the mummeries of his initiatory process. He is finally admitted into the Sanctuary, where the mighty secret is to burst upon him, in a blaze of light, from behind the mystical Veil.

MOORE'S EPICUREAN

While, with an imagination thus excited, I stood waiting the result, an increased gush of light still more awakened my attention ; and I saw, with an intenseness of interest which made my heart beat aloud, one of the corners of the mighty Veil slowly raised up. I now felt that the Great Secret— whatever it might be—was at hand. A vague hope even crossed my mind—so wholly had imagination resumed her empire—that the splendid promise of my dream was on the point of being realised !—p. 128.

But, instead of the Great Mystery, a female form slips out from under a corner of the curtain, and placing the end of a riband gently in his hand, says, in a tremulous whisper, " Follow, and be silent."

He follows her accordingly, leaving the Mighty Mystery to expound itself to his vacant place. She conducts him through a long series of zig-zags and inclined planes, up and down which they go shooting like arrows, in a mechanical car, to the foot of an old ascent of innumerable stairs, from whence they emerge into day-light in a ruined temple, on an island in Lake Mœris.

The young lady, who turns out to be his beautiful unknown, faints away ; and, on her recovery, inquires for the " venerable Athenian " whom she had brought with her out of the bowels of the earth. It seems that a Philosophic Chairman of twenty-four was quite out of her calculation of the

MOORE'S EPICUREAN

Athenian character. She is alarmed at finding that the supposed old gentleman is a young one ; but, having no time to lose, she exclaims, " To the Nile, without delay ! " Alciphron hails one of the boats which ply on the lake for hire, and

without a word, a look, that could alarm, even by its kindness, or disturb that innocent confidence which she now placed in me, led her down by the winding path to the boat.

Every thing looked smiling around us as we embarked. The morning was now in its first freshness, and the path of the breeze might be traced over the lake, wakening up its waters from their sleep of the night. The gay, golden-winged birds that haunt these shores, were, in every direction, skimming along the lake ; while, with a graver consciousness of beauty, the swan and the pelican were seen dressing their white plumage in the mirror of its wave.—pp. 141, 142.

" The swan and the pelican were seen dressing their white plumage in the mirror of its wave." Whether the pelican uses water as a looking-glass to dress itself by, we have never had an opportunity of determining by observation, but we are very certain that the swan does not. The swan never looks into the water for any purpose but to detect food. It trims its plumage with its beak, pretty much as a cat trims its fur with its tongue, and no more uses the water it floats on as a mirror to assist the

MOORE'S EPICUREAN

operation, than the cat uses the carpet or
cushion it sits on for the same purpose.
And even if this were, which it is not, a habit
of the swan, it would have been very inconvenient to practise it on the occasion in
question, on a lake ruffled by a breeze
sufficiently strong to impel a sailing-boat
with considerable speed. This it is to paint
from books and imagination, and not from
nature. Mr. Wordsworth says of a swan and
a lake which he has seen,

> The swan, on still St. Mary's lake,
> Floats double, swan and shadow.

Mr. Moore says of a swan and a lake, which
he has not seen, " The swan dresses its
white plumage in the mirror of the ruffled
waters." In the former passage there are
picturesqueness, simplicity, and truth : in
the latter, a conceit, a misrepresentation,
and an impossibility. We can pardon a
cockney poet who says of a young actress,
more than commonly rosy, that she is as
" white as a cygnet," which all who have
ever seen one know to be brown ; we can
pardon him when he calls the most rigid
of trees the " bending cedar ; " and the
most wiry of foliage the " trembling pine-
leaf ; " we can pardon the magazine-critics
when they extol this, and a great mass of
congenial poetry, for its prodigious truth to

32

nature ; but we cannot allow his and their
impunity to pass into a precedent for a
similar method of dealing with natural objects on the part of an author who quotes
Greek, and has had opportunities of observation beyond the Regent's Park.

The boat has a pavilion in which the
beautiful Egyptian reposes, and in which
Alciphron takes a " reverential " view of
her as she meditates over a small volume,
which afterwards turns out to be the Bible
as appointed to be read in churches in the
third century. An explanation is then given
of the process by which the young Egyptian
priestess had become a Christian. Her
mother, it seems, had been employed as a
scribe by no less a personage than Father
Origen, and had copied for him all the Bible
and all his Commentaries thereon, which
pleasant occupation caused " the divine
truths, so eloquently illustrated, to find
their way by degrees from the page to her
heart." She afterwards married a Pagan,
who left her a widow in Memphis, where
being a lone woman, in want of a situation,
she applied for the first vacancy in the
service of the Sacred College, and was
elected a priestess of Isis. Here she gave
birth to her daughter Alethe.

So here is a pregnant woman elected a
priestess of Isis, and lying-in, as a matter

of course, under the auspices of the Sacred College !

Theora has educated her daughter Alethe secretly as a Christian, and has bequeathed her the sacred volume, and a commission to take the first opportunity of escaping from Memphis to the mountains of the Said, where resides a venerable Father who will take charge of her.

Alciphron conveys her faithfully to her destination, not without reluctance, which he expresses in the following most extraordinary manner :—

Were we left to each other, as on this silent river, in this undisturbed communion of thoughts and feelings, I knew too well, I thought, both her sex's nature and my own, to feel a doubt that love would ultimately triumph. But the severity of the guardianship to which I must resign her,—some monk of the desert, some stern Solitary,—the influence such a monitor would gain over her mind, and the horror with which, ere long, she would be taught to regard the reprobate infidel on whom she now smiled,—in all this prospect I saw nothing but despair. After a few short hours, my happiness would be at an end, and such a dark chasm open between our fates, as must sever them, far as earth is from heaven, asunder.

It was true, she was now wholly in my power. I feared no witnesses but those of earth, and the solitude of the desert was at hand. But though I acknowledged not a heaven, I worshipped her who was, to me, its type and substitute. If, at any

MOORE'S EPICUREAN

moment, a single thought of wrong or deceit,
towards a creature so sacred, arose in my mind,
one look from her innocent eyes averted the
sacrilege. Even passion itself felt a holy fear in
her presence,—like the flame trembling in the
breeze of the sanctuary,—and Love, pure Love,
stood in place of Religion.—pp. 204-206.

The Epicurean, therefore, is a person
altogether without morality ; nothing but
religion, and the acknowledgment of a
heaven, would have prevented him from
ravishing the young lady in the desert ;
and as he had no religion, and no acknowledgment of a heaven, he made both the one
and the other out of the sacredness of his
passion.

This is another new trait in the character
of our Epicurean, that he has no morality ;
and that he is only restrained by a very
curious substitute for religion, of his own
manufacture, from the perpetration of a
flagrant moral wrong.

Before he conducts his fair charge to the
holy man, he dismisses his first boat at a
point of the river above his destination, and
the boatmen, instead of returning home after
their job, accommodate themselves to his
purpose of avoiding observation, by continuing their voyage up the river by themselves, for no purpose of their own that we
can divine, unless that as they had been

well paid by the philosopher, they thought they would give themselves a holiday, and drink out the profits at Thebes : speculating, perhaps, on a back fare from thence to Memphis. If we had hired a " pair of oars " at Westminster, to row us to Windsor, we should be much surprised, after landing at Eton Bridge, to see our badged boatmen pulling away for Maidenhead instead of dropping back to London. Fiction should regard probability even in trifles.

Alciphron now purchases a boat, which he rows himself, and

After a short delay, we were again afloat down the current;—the sun just then sinking, in conscious glory, over his own golden shrines in the Libyan waste.

The evening was more calm and lovely than any that had yet smiled upon our voyage ; and, as we left the bank, there came soothingly over our ears a strain of sweet, rustic melody from the shore. It was the voice of a young Nubian girl, whom we saw kneeling on the bank before an acacia, and singing, while her companions stood round, the wild song of invocation, which, in her country they address to that enchanted tree :—

> Oh ! Abyssinian tree,
> We pray, we pray, to thee ;
> By the glow of thy golden fruit,
> And the violet hue of thy flower,
> And the greeting mute
> Of thy bough's salute
> To the stranger who seeks thy bower.

MOORE'S EPICUREAN

II

Oh ! Abyssinian tree,
How the traveller blesses thee,
When the night no moon allows,
And the sun-set hour is near,
And thou bend'st thy boughs
To kiss his brows,
Saying, " Come rest thee here."
Oh ! Abyssinian tree,
Thus bow thy head to me !

In the burthen of this song the companions of the
young Nubian joined ; and we heard the words,
" Oh ! Abyssinian tree," dying away on the breeze,
long after the whole group had been lost to our
eyes.—pp. 215-217.

We cannot help thinking, that Mr. Moore
had Mr. Coleridge's Abyssinian maid in his
eye :—

A damsel with a dulcimer,
In a vision once I saw ;
It was an Abyssinian maid,
And on her dulcimer she played,
Singing of Mount Abora.

Mr. Moore's is a pleasing picture, and it is
certainly not a copy. Still we cannot help
thinking, that we owe the Nubian girl and
her song, to the Abyssinian damsel and her
dulcimer.

We are the more induced to this opinion,
by the way in which the word Abyssinian is
pressed into the service. The Nubian girl in
Egypt, might, with great propriety, call a
tree of her native land a Nubian tree, but

37

what was Abyssinia more than Egypt to
her ? Why was it to her, more an Abyssinian than an Egyptian tree ? For no
reason we can imagine, but that Mr. Coleridge had seen in a vision an Abyssinian
damsel with a dulcimer, and that the word
Abyssinian had a very pretty effect in Mr.
Coleridge's verses.

At length turning from the Nile up the
remains of an old canal, he lands among
some dreary rocks, and lodges his fair
charge in the hands of Father Melanius,
and being spell-bound by his passion, inti-
mates his desire to remain near the holy
sage and receive ghostly instruction. The
Father gives him an uncomfortable place to
live in, and a comfortable book to read,
and the Epicurean sits down in sober sadness to study the Scriptures.

Impatient, however, to possess myself of the
elements of a faith, on which—whatever it might
promise for hereafter—I felt that my happiness
here depended, I turned over the pages with an
earnestness and avidity, such as never even the
most favourite of my studies had awakened in me.
Though, like all who seek but the surface of learning, I flew desultorily over the leaves, lighting only
on the more prominent and shining points, I
yet found myself, even in this undisciplined career,
arrested, at every page, by the awful, the super-
natural sublimity, the alternate melancholy and
grandeur of the images that crowded upon me.

MOORE'S EPICUREAN

I had, till now, known the Hebrew theology but
through the platonising refinements of Philo ;—
as, in like manner, for my knowledge of the Christian
doctrine I was indebted to my brother Epicureans,
Lucian and Celsus. Little, therefore, was I prepared for the simple majesty, the high tone of
inspiration,—the poetry, in short, of heaven that
breathed throughout these oracles. Could admiration have kindled faith, I should, that night, have
been a believer; so elevated, so awed was my
imagination by that wonderful book,—its warnings
of woe, its announcements of glory, and its un-
rivalled strains of adoration and sorrow.

Hour after hour, with the same eager and
desultory curiosity, did I turn over the leaves ;—
and when, at length, I lay down to rest, my fancy
was still haunted by the impressions it had received.
I went again through the various scenes of which
I had read ; again called up, in sleep, the bright
images that had charmed me, and, when wakened
at day-break by the hymn from the chapel, fancied
myself still listening to the sound of the winds
sighing mournfully through the harps of Israel on
the willows.—pp. 259-261.

The truth of the Christian Religion is too
clearly established amongst us to admit of
dispute. The question is not what we think
of it, but what an Epicurean President was
likely to think of it. The opinions here
expressed, are as un-Epicurean as the language and sentiments are decidedly un-
Attic. The wisdom of St. Paul was " to
the Greeks foolishness." And if Alciphron
had been at all a fair specimen of either an

39

MOORE'S EPICUREAN

Epicurean or an Athenian, Justinian would have spared himself the trouble of suppressing the schools of Athens.

The old hermit visits him every night, and regales him with a sermon in the open air ; and the good Father is so delighted with his exemplary patience under the infliction, that he betroths him to Alethe.

His dreams of happiness are dissipated by a new persecution of the Christians. Melanius is put to death in the forum of Antinöe, and Alethe is destroyed by an artifice of Orcus the high priest of Memphis, who is a very busy agent in the persecution.

Alciphron, who has been wounded in an endeavour to rescue Alethe, is admitted through the friendship of a tribune to the prison, whence she is to be led either to recant or suffer on the morrow.

Even in yielding reluctantly to this brief respite, the inhuman priest would accompany it with some mark of his vengeance. Whether for the pleasure (observed the tribune) of mingling mockery with his cruelty, or as a warning to her of the doom she must ultimately expect, he gave orders that there should be tied round her brow one of those chaplets of coral with which it is the custom of young Christian maidens to array themselves on the day of their martyrdom ;—" and, thus fearfully adorned," said he, " she was led away, amid the gaze of the pitying multitude, to prison."

MOORE'S EPICUREAN

With these details the short interval till night-fall—every minute of which seemed an age—was occupied. As soon as it grew dark, I was placed upon a litter—my wound, though not dangerous, requiring such a conveyance—and conducted, under the guidance of my friend, to the prison. Through his interest with the guard, we were without difficulty admitted, and I was borne into the chamber where the maiden lay immured. Even the veteran guardian of the place seemed touched with compassion for his prisoner, and, supposing her to be asleep, had the litter placed gently near her.

She was half reclining, with her face hid in her hands, upon a couch—at the foot of which stood an idol, over whose hideous features a lamp of naphtha, hanging from the ceiling, shed a wild and ghastly glare. On a table before the image stood a censer, with a small vessel of incense beside it—one grain of which, thrown voluntarily into the flame, would, even now, save that precious life. So strange, so fearful was the whole scene, that I almost doubted its reality. Alethe! my own, happy Alethe! *can* it, I thought, be thou that I look upon?

She now, slowly and with difficulty, raised her head from the couch; on observing which, the kind tribune withdrew, and we were left alone. There was a paleness, as of death, over her features; and those eyes, which when last I saw them, were but too bright, too happy for this world, looked dim and sunken. In raising herself up, she put her hand, as if from pain, to her forehead, whose marble hue but appeared more death-like from those red bands that lay so awfully across it.

MOORE'S EPICUREAN

After wandering vaguely for a minute, her eyes rested upon me,—and, with a shriek, half terror, half joy, she sprung from the couch, and sunk upon her knees by my side. She had believed me dead ; and, even now, scarcely trusted her senses. " My husband ! my love ! " she exclaimed ; " oh, if thou comest to call me from this world, behold I am ready ! " In saying thus, she pointed wildly to that ominous wreath, and then dropped her head down upon my knee, as if an arrow had pierced it.

" Alethe ! "—I cried, terrified to the very soul by that mysterious pang—and the sound of my voice seemed to reanimate her ;—she looked up, with a faint smile, in my face. Her thoughts, which had evidently been wandering, became collected ; and in her joy at my safety, her sorrow at my suffering, she forgot wholly the fate that impended over herself. Love, innocent love, alone occupied all her thoughts ; and the tenderness with which she spoke, —oh, at any other moment, how I would have listened, have lingered upon, have blessed every word !

But the time flew fast—the dreadful morrow was approaching. Already I saw her writhing in the hands of the torturer,—the flames, the racks, the wheels were before my eyes ! Half frantic with the fear that her resolution was fixed, I flung myself from the litter, in an agony of weeping, and supplicated her, by the love she bore me, by the happiness that awaited us, by her own merciful God, who was too good to require such a sacrifice,—by all that the most passionate anxiety could dictate, I implored that she would avert from us the doom that was coming, and—but for once—comply with the vain ceremony demanded of her.

42

Shrinking from me, as I spoke,—but with a look more of sorrow than reproach,—"What, thou, too!" she said mournfully,—" thou, into whose spirit I had fondly hoped the same heavenly truth had descended as into my own! Oh, be not thou leagued with those who would tempt me to ' make shipwreck of my faith ! ' Thou, who couldst alone bind me to life, use not thy power ; but let me die, as He I serve hath commanded,—die for the truth. Remember the holy lessons we heard on those nights, those happy nights, when both the present and future smiled upon us,—when even the gift of eternal life came more welcome to my soul, from the blessed conviction that thou wert to be a sharer in it ;—shall I forfeit now that divine privilege ? shall I deny the true God, whom we then learned to love ?

" No, my own betrothed," she continued,— pointing to the two rings on her finger,—" behold these pledges,—they are both sacred. I should have been as true to thee as I am now to heaven,— nor in that life to which I am hastening shall our love be forgotten. Should the baptism of fire, through which I shall pass to-morrow, make me worthy to be heard before the throne of grace, I will intercede for thy soul—I will pray that it may yet share with mine that ' inheritance, immortal and undefiled,' which Mercy offers, and that thou,— my dear mother,—and I——"

She here dropped her voice ; the momentary animation, with which devotion and affection had inspired her, vanished ;—and a darkness overspread all her features, a livid darkness,—like the coming of death—that made me shudder through every limb. Seizing my hand convulsively, and looking

43

at me with a fearful eagerness, as if anxious to hear some consoling assurance from my own lips,— " Believe me," she continued, " not all the torments they are preparing for me,—not even this deep, burning pain in my brow, which they will hardly equal,—could be half so dreadful to me as the thought that I leave thee——"

Here her voice again failed ; her head sunk upon my arm, and—merciful God, let me forget what I then felt,—I saw that she was dying ! Whether I uttered any cry I know not ;—but the tribune came rushing into the chamber, and looking on the maiden, said, with a face full of horror, " It is but too true ! "

He then told me in a low voice, what he had just learned from the guardian of the prison, that the band round the young Christian's brow was— oh horrible cruelty !—a compound of the most deadly poison,—the hellish invention of Orcus, to satiate his vengeance, and make the fate of his poor victim secure. My first movement was to untie that fatal wreath,—but it would not come away—it would not come away !

Roused by the pain, she again looked in my face ; but, unable to speak, took hastily from her bosom the small silver cross which she had brought with her from my cave. Having prest it to her own lips, she held it anxiously to mine, and seeing me kiss the holy symbol with fervour, looked happy and smiled. The agony of death seemed to have passed away ;—there came suddenly over her features a heavenly light, some share of which I felt descending into my own soul, and in a few minutes more, she expired in my arms.—pp. 299-306.

MOORE'S EPICUREAN

This concluding scene is affectingly drawn. It has, though not altogether free from them, less of affectation and conceit than the greater portion of the volume. It is followed by this supplement.

Here ends the Manuscript; but, on the outer cover there is, in the hand-writing of a much later period, the following Notice, extracted, as it appears, from some Egyptian Martyrology :—

Alciphron,—an Epicurean philosopher, converted to Christianity, A.D. 257, by a young Egyptian maiden, who suffered martyrdom in that year. Immediately upon her death he betook himself to the desert, and lived a life, it is said, of much holiness and penitence. During the persecution under Dioclesian, his sufferings for the faith were most exemplary; and, being at length, at an advanced age, condemned to hard labour, for refusing to comply with an Imperial edict, he died at the brass mines of Palestine, A.D. 297.

As Alciphron held the opinions maintained since by Arius, his memory has not been spared by Athanasian writers, who, among other charges, accuse him of having been addicted to the superstitions of Egypt. For this calumny, however, there appears to be no better foundation than a circumstance, recorded by one of his brother monks, that there was found, after his death, a small metal mirror, like those used in the ceremonies of Isis, suspended round his neck.—pp. 306, 307.

As our philosopher's convictions against Christianity remained unshaken up to the night of his mistress's death, it is left to be concluded, that her death converted him, for she alone has the credit of the conversion. He is converted, therefore, not by reason, but by passion, as a philosopher of Mr. Moore's making ought to be.

In our preceding remarks, we have, for the sake of carrying on the story to its close, glanced briefly at some points which we shall now notice more in detail.

Mr. Moore has misrepresented the Epicurean philosophy, and the character of the later Epicureans. He has drawn an Epicurean according to the vulgar notion entertained of that character by persons who know nothing about the matter.

It is not consistent either with our limits, or with the importance of the subject before us, to give even a general outline of the philosophy of Epicurus. We shall merely give a specimen of it.

Epicurus taught that happiness is the end of life : that there is no happiness without pleasure : that all pleasure is in itself good, and that all pain is in itself evil ; but that present pleasure is to be avoided in the prospect of future pain, and that present pain is to be endured for the sake of future pleasure : that the true and only permanent pleasure of man is peace of body and mind : that the state in which the body is without pain, and the mind without perturbation, is

MOORE'S EPICUREAN

the perfect health of the whole man : that the peace of the body is to be obtained especially by two means—Temperance, or a sober and continent life, to keep off corporeal diseases which arise mostly from the opposite vice, and Fortitude to endure them with a constant mind, and not exasperate them by impatience : that beyond this all that concerns the body belongs to medicine : that Philosophy is the medicine of the mind, that the two capital diseases of the mind are Cupidity and Fear, of which Care is the incessant adjunct, as Pain is of the diseases of the body ; the Cupidity, for instance, of honours and riches, and the Fear of the gods and of death ; and that these diseases being the offspring of ignorance and error, are to be cured by knowledge and reason.

Hunc igitur terrorem animi tenebrasque necesse
    cst
Non radii solis nec lucida tela diei
Discutiant, sed naturæ species, ratioque.—
                                                    Lucr.

He taught that happiness, or the greatest portion of permanent pleasure, is only to be attained by strict obedience to the dictates of right reason ; that strict obedience to those dictates constitutes the virtue called prudence, and that all virtue is either prudence or a derivative from it.

" It is not possible," he says, in the Κυρίαι Δόξαι, " to live pleasurably unless prudently, becomingly, and justly : nor to live prudently, becomingly, and justly, and not at the same time pleasurably : nor to live imprudently, unbecomingly, and unjustly, and not at the same time unpleasurably.

" Natural justice is the symbol of utility, or of that which conduces among men to prevent the inflicting, or suffering, of injury. Τὸ τῆς φύσεως δίκαιον ἐστὶ σύμβολον τοῦ συμφέροντος, εἰς τὸ μὴ βλάπτειν ἀλλήλους, μηδὲ βλάπτεσθαι.

" Universally considered, that which is just, or that which is most useful in the general society of men, is the same to all, but, particularly considered, it results from local circumstances and other causes, that that which is deemed to be just is not the same to all.

" Of those things which are generally held to be just, that which is proved by experience to be useful in the mutual necessities of society has the true character of justice, if it be the same to all. But if any do a thing which is generally held to be just, and yet it result not to the common benefit of society, it has no longer the true character of justice."

Thus Epicurus first taught, that general utility, or as Bentham expresses it, " the greatest happiness of the greatest number," is the legitimate end of philosophy ; and it is curious to see the same class of persons decrying the same doctrine as impracticably dry, when the word utility precedes the word pleasure, and as too practicably voluptuous when the word pleasure precedes the word utility. So much are small minds the slaves of words.

It may be said, however, that the doctrines of the Epicurean philosophy prove nothing for the practice of its disciples ; and that as even the Church of England furnishes an occasional instance of a clergyman, who has no claim but his complexion, to be esteemed the pink of good living, so the school of Epicurus, which was a false light of the gentiles, may have furnished many such instances. But here we must appeal to experience.

Lucian, speaking of Alexander the false prophet, who publicly burned the Κυρίαι Δόξαι of Epicurus, says : " The miscreant did not know of how much good that book is the cause, to those who fall in with it ; how much peace and imperturbability and freedom it works in them, alienating them from fears and phantasies, and portents, and vain hopes, and superfluous desires ; putting into them intellect and truth, and purifying most truly their opinions, not with torch and squill, and such like fooleries, but with

MOORE'S EPICUREAN

right reason, and truth, and free speaking."

"Ἐν γοῦν καὶ γελοιότατον ἐποίησεν ὁ Ἀλέξανδρος·
εὑρὼν γὰρ τὰς Ἐπικούρου κυρίας δόξας, τὸ κάλλιστον,
ὡς οἶσθα, τῶν βιβλίων, καὶ κεφαλαιωδῶς περιέχον,
τῆς τ'ανδρὸς σοφίας τὰ δόγματα, κομίσας ἐς τὴν
ἀγορὰν μέσην, ἔκαυσεν ἐπὶ ξύλων συκίνων, ὡς δῆθεν
αὐτὸν καταφλέγων, καὶ τὴν σποδὸν ἐς θάλασσαν
ἐξέβαλεν, ἔτι καὶ χρησμὸν ἐπιφθεγξάμενος·

Πυρπολέειν κέλομαι δόξας ἀλαοῖο γέροντος·

Οὐκ εἰδὼς ὁ κατάρατος ὅσων ἀγαθῶν τὸ βιβλίον
ἐκεῖνο τοῖς ἐντυχοῦσιν αἴτιον γίγνεται, καὶ ὅσην
αὐτοῖς εἰρήνην καὶ ἀταραξίαν καὶ ἐλευθερίαν ἐνεργά-
ζεται, δειμάτων μὲν καὶ φασμάτων, καὶ τεράτων
ἀπαλλάττον, καὶ ἐλπίδων ματαίων, καὶ περιττῶν
ἐπιθυμιῶν· νοῦν δὲ καὶ ἀλήθειαν ἐντιθὲν, καὶ καθαῖρον,
ὡς ἀληθῶς, τὰς γνώμας, οὐ δᾳδὶ καὶ σκίλλῃ, καὶ ταῖς
τοιαύταις φλυαρίαις, ἀλλὰ λόγῳ ὀρθῷ, καὶ ἀληθείᾳ,
καὶ παῤῥησίᾳ."—Lucian. *in Pseudom.*

This is Lucian's testimony to the practical
effect of the Epicurean philosophy on the
character of its disciples. It would be easy,
by a concise biography of many of the later
Epicureans, from Atticus, Lucretius, Virgil,
and Horace, down to Lucian and his friends,
to show that the picture is true. The very
names we have mentioned, are among the
brightest ornaments of the human race :
and, without entering into any particulars of
their lives, we shall simply say, without
fear of contradiction, that none of them
spoke or acted in any one point like Mr.

50

MOORE'S EPICUREAN

Moore's hero. He has drawn a portrait of every thing that an eminent Epicurean was not, and presents it to us as a fair specimen of what he was. Hamlet's uncle might as fairly have sat for the portrait of Hamlet's father.

It is a crying sin of the work, that it sets at nought the power of education. To the latest hour of the existence of the schools of Athens, the chiefs of the schools were proficients in the philosophy of their masters. We have seen what the Epicurean philosophy was, and what were its effects on the character of its disciples. The language of Mr. Moore's hero shows as little trace of any knowledge of the principles of that philosophy, as his conduct of any practical obedience to its precepts.

There was nothing on which the Epicureans more strongly insisted, than on their favourite dogma of the mortality of the soul. " Death," says Epicurus, " is nothing to us. All good and evil are in sensation, and death is the privation of sensation. The right knowledge of this truth, that death is nothing to us, makes the mortality of life a source of enjoyment ; not adding an uncertain time, but taking away the desire of immortality. For there can be nothing terrible in life to him who clearly perceives that there is nothing terrible in the privation of life. So that he is a fool who says he fears death ; not because it will give him pain when present, but because the anticipation of it is painful. For it is vain to fear the arrival of that which will cause no annoyance when arrived. Therefore, the most fearful of evils, death, is nothing to us, since while we are, death is not present, and when death is present, we are not. Death, accordingly, concerns not either the living or the dead ; since it touches not the living, and the dead have no feeling of its presence.

" But the many shrink from death, both as the greatest of evils, and as the cessation of the things of life. But it is vain to fear the privation of life, when in that privation there is no life to judge, if there be any evil in the privation."

This doctrine his disciples inculcated, never in the language of regret and despondency, but always in that of exultation and triumph. Their philosophy trampled under its feet the fear of death and of Acheron :

—Metus omnes et inexorabile fatum
Subjecit pedibus, strepitumque Acherontis avari !
—Virg.

Nil igitur mors est, ad nos neque pertinet hilum,
Quandoquidem natura animi mortalis habetur, &c.
—Lucr.

Post mortem nihil est, ipsaque mors nihil,
Velocis spatii meta novissima, &c.—*Seneca.* (*Tr.*)

MOORE'S EPICUREAN

They were so little conscious of the error of their way, that they considered the hankerers after immortality as the lowest of the human race, and regarded them with measureless contempt.

Tu verò dubitabis et indignabere obire,
Mortua quoi vita est propè jam vivo atque videnti?
Qui somno partem majorem conteris ævi?
Et vigilans stertis, nec somnia cernere cessas,
Sollicitamque geris cassâ formidine mentem?
                                        —*Lucr.*

The belief in the verity of dreams, they classed with the lowest credulity, with the belief in witchcraft, and raw-head-and-bloody-bones.

Somnia, terrores magicos, miracula, sagas,
Nocturnos lemures, portentaque Thessala rides?
                                        —*Hor.*

In England, we all believe in the immortality of the soul, and some of us believe in the verity of dreams; but, we repeat, the question is not what we think of these matters, but what the Epicureans thought of them; and, knowing what we know of the Epicureans, both in respect of their theories and their practice, we must say, that there never was a more outrageous speculation on the extent of public ignorance, than to send the chief of the sect on such an errand as the quest of immortality, in

53

obedience to such a counsellor as an old man in a dream.

The hero's violent and exclusive passion, which is the mainspring of the entire narrative, is as much out of character as the motives of his visit to Egypt ; and not a whit less so are many of the minor circumstances. He is influenced by omens as well as by dreams. He is scared by a skeleton, and awed by a mummy. He has no more morality than any ordinary " gay deceiver," and makes a substitute for it out of a chivalrous feeling, which scarcely existed before the days of Orlando Innamorato.

We think we could enlighten Mr. Moore with respect, not merely to the Epicurean, but the general Greek notions of love ; but this is not the time and place. We shall not enter into the minor misprisions of character. We shall content ourselves with citing from Diogenes Laertius a few precepts of the Epicurean philosophy, which this precious specimen of a disciple and successor most flagrantly violates.

" Ἐρασθήσεσθαι τὸν σοφὸν οὐ δοκεῖ αὐτοῖς, οὐδὲ θεόπεμπτον εἶναι τὸν Ἔρωτα."—" They consider that the wise man will not fall in love, and that love is not of divine origin." Our hero falls in love like a knight-errant, and talks of the sacredness of his passion like a Petrarch.

MOORE'S EPICUREAN

" Οὐδὲ ῥητορεύσειν καλῶς."—" Not to write in a style made up of figures and flourishes." Our philosopher's style is made up of nothing else.

" Οὐδὲ νυκτερεύσειν ἐν μέθῃ."—" Not to pass the night in getting half-seas-over." Our philosopher, before he falls in love, passes the greater part of his nights in this fashion.

" Τύχῃ τε ἀντιτάξεσθαι."—" To be well prepared against fortune." No man is less so : he is in a fever and a frenzy at every change.

" Ποιήματά τε ἀγνοήσειν, οὐκ ἂν ποιήσειν."— " To abstain from all knowledge of poems, and not to make any." We cannot say that our hero has any knowledge of poems, or that there is not very satisfactory evidence of his abstaining from all knowledge of them, and of every thing else : but he makes a few in the style of sir Hugh Evans's favourite ditty, about fragrant posies and beds of roses, and

> Shallow rivers, to whose falls
> Melodious birds sing madrigals.

If our hero had transgressed this precept to as much purpose as Lucretius, it would be a very different matter.

The author has misrepresented the Egyptian Mysteries almost as much as the Epicurean Philosophy ; and we intended

to have said something on this head, but
we have already exceeded the limits which
we proposed to assign to this work. It
would be easy to show that Mr. Moore has
not provided himself with any portion of
that information respecting the Mysteries
which the classical authors afford, and that
he has contented himself with travestying
a portion of a forgotten French romance ;
but it would be a waste of time to discuss
these matters with an author who elects a
pregnant woman a priestess of Isis ; and
it is a matter more of curiosity than of
importance, to ascertain the precise nature
of the solemn farce, which the priests of
an exploded religion enacted in the bowels
of the earth. It is of much less consequence
to us to set this point in a clear light, than
it will be to our posterity to erue from the
rust of antiquity the genuine representation
of Punch, if that most entertaining personage
should ever be incrusted with that perilous
ærugo. Mr. Moore's picture resembles what
it professes to represent, at least as well as
Macedon does Monmouth : " there are
mummeries in both ; " quite enough, we
hope, to save him from the vengeance of
Isis. But the doctrines and character of
Epicurus and his followers it will always be
important for mankind thoroughly to understand and appreciate, and for all who love

mankind to liberate from that mass of misrepresentation, which the deluders and deluded of all ages have heaped upon them, and not permit them to be made with impunity the playthings of a petty carping at popularity among the most worthless, though, unhappily, not the least influential, portion of the reading public.

The work is evidently that of an author aiming at popularity. Every page, every sentence, is written manifestly *ad captandum*. We always see the actor with his eye on the audience.

For an author recognised by all the Magazines as a " brilliant and sparkling " genius—assumed by himself and his friends to be a most accomplished classic—having written, and in part composed, many scores of tender madrigals, which have been warbled by half the marriageable misses, in half the drawing-rooms of the three kingdoms—having trespassed so far beyond the bounds of every-day opinions, as almost to incur the suspicion of being a whig—for such an author, so learned, so accomplished, and so popular, to offer up such a homage to fashionable truth, as to immolate his Athenian idols on the altar of blue sanctity, it might be expected there would be more rejoicing over him in the cœrulean heaven, than over ninety-nine established sermonisers and regular inditers of tracts : and so we believe it has turned out. The book reads on lightly and pleasantly. It commits no sins on the score of knowledge, which the audience it is made for is likely to detect ; it commits no material offence, except against what was thought good taste in Athens, and against the doctrines and memories of all that. is most illustrious in the Pagan world ; and, if that be an error, it is a pious one, and the author is to be the better loved for it.

The " Quarterly Review " made a very good hit, by demonstrating to the satisfaction of the orthodox, that the character of Socrates was much more correctly drawn by Aristophanes, than by Plato and Xenophon ; that, in short, Aristophanes himself was the great philosopher of Athens, and that Socrates being given to thinking, and other villanies, especially to a most lewd propensity of enlightening the people, was a very fit subject to be twice executed, first, in a farce, and afterwards by the finisher of the law. We believe these articles of the Quarterly have nothing *simile aut secundum* in letters, excepting Jack Cade's judgment on lord Say ; and, as a portion of our morbid anatomy of the periodical press, we may one day exhibit them to the public, stripped of the integuments of cant, sophistry, and false learning, in which they are enveloped.

The notes are chiefly remarkable for a display of reading, the value of which may be judged of by one or two specimens.

Mr. Moore thinks the Egyptians were not negroes, and that they were very handsome people.

De Pauw, the great depreciator of every thing Egyptian, has on the authority of a passage in Ælian, presumed to affix to the countrywomen of Cleopatra, the stigma of complete and unredeemed ugliness. The following line of Euripides, however, is an answer to such charges :—

Νειλου μεν αιδε καλλιπαρθενοι ῥοαι.—p. 310.

In this small space are two great mis-prisions. Cleopatra was a Greek, the daughter of Ptolemy Auletes. The Egyptian women were as much the countrywomen of Cleopatra, as the Hindoo women are the countrywomen of lady Hastings. And with respect to the line of Euripides, which is the first line of Helena, the allusion is so obviously to the nymphs of the stream, that it seems scarcely possible for any reader, even moderately familiar with the Greek poets, to apply it to the mortal maids of the land. If Euripides had been thinking of the latter, he would at least have placed them on the banks, and not in the water.

MOORE'S EPICUREAN

This line signifies, according to Mr. Moore, " These are the streams of the Nile, famous for pretty girls." Certainly a very odd beginning for a tragedy, and entirely unique in the relics of the Greek drama. Euripides had no such stuff in his thoughts. Helen speaks of Nilus not simply in his aquarian, but conjointly therewith in his mythological character : the fair virgins of his streams are his daughters, Memphis, Achirrhöe, &c., some of whom gave their names to the cities of the Nile.

Nothing can be more ludicrous than the ovant air with which Cleopatra and the nymphs of the Nile are brought in to settle a controversy about the beauty of the Egyptian women.

" The Nile, Pliny tells us, was admitted into the Pyramid : " says Mr. Moore, as an illustration of the torrent in which his hero escapes drowning by miracle.

Pliny's words are these :—" In pyramide maxima est intus puteus octoginta sex cubitorum : flumen illo admissum arbitrantur."—Plin. *H. N.* xxxvi. 17.

So because Pliny says that there was a well in the Pyramid to which the Nile was supposed to be admitted, Mr. Moore makes him vouch for a subterranean torrent under it. The Thames is admitted into a cistern in our kitchen, much in the same way as the Nile may have been into the well in the Pyramid ; but it by no means follows from this, that we can bring the power of a waterfall to bear upon our cook, and float her into the area at a moment's notice.

If such a torrent as Mr. Moore describes had been played off under the Pyramids during the inundation of the Nile, what was, or could be, its outlet ? And what relation of level would the outlet bear to the inlet ? A gentleman, who amuses himself with conveying rivers under ground, should understand something of hydraulics.

" Plato speaks of a pure land lying in the pure sky, $\tau\eta\nu$ $\gamma\eta\nu$ $\kappa\alpha\theta\alpha\rho\alpha\nu$ $\epsilon\nu$ $\kappa\alpha\theta\alpha\rho\omega$ $\kappa\epsilon\iota\sigma\theta\alpha\iota$ ουρανω." [p. 318]. (We print Mr. Moore's Greek as he prints it himself). Mr. Moore shows a sublime contempt for the article, for Plato speaks of " *the* pure earth lying in the pure sky, in which the stars are : " $\alpha\dot{v}\tau\dot{\eta}\nu$ $\delta\dot{\epsilon}$ $\tau\dot{\eta}\nu$ $\gamma\dot{\eta}\nu$ $\kappa\alpha\theta\alpha\rho\dot{\alpha}\nu$ $\dot{\epsilon}\nu$ $\kappa\alpha\theta\alpha\rho\hat{\omega}$ $\kappa\epsilon\hat{\iota}\sigma\theta\alpha\iota$ $\tau\hat{\omega}$ $o\dot{v}\rho\alpha\nu\hat{\omega}$, $\dot{\epsilon}\nu$ $\tau\hat{\omega}$ $\pi\epsilon\rho$ $\dot{\epsilon}\sigma\tau\dot{\iota}$ $\tau\dot{\alpha}$ $\ddot{\alpha}\sigma\tau\rho\alpha$: an imaginary elevated portion of our own earth only, and not a detached " luminous world above the shadowless stars," as Mr. Moore seems to suppose.

Mr. Moore, in quoting Greek, always omits the subscribed iota. Is he not aware that it is as much a letter as any in the word ? He is very fond of parading scraps of Greek, and on one occasion treated the public with a Greek ode, which is still an unrepented sin, as we see it figuring in every new edition of his Anacreon. In this ode, measuring, as he manifestly must have done, by accent, and not by quantity, taking the metre of the Battle of Roncesvalles,

Sad and fearful is the story,

for the modulation of that form of the Iambic Anacreontic metre, which begins with an anapæst,*

'Επὶ μυρσίναις τερείναις,

(which is of a class distinct from other forms of Anacreontic metre, even from the Iambic

* Hermann (agreeing in the opinion of Varro, as given by Terentianus Maurus) places this metre in the class of Ionics; because it is permutable with the Ionic à minori acatalectic dimeter; because the numbers are the same with those that terminate the Ionic à majori brachycatalectic tetrameters: because the doctrine of the Scholiast on Hephæstio, of Draco Stratonicensis, Elias Monachus, and others (who speak of a mode of dividing the Anacreontic metre into members of six and two verses each; the six being called οἶκοι and the two κουκούλιον; the οἶκοι consisting each of an anapæst, a diiambus, and an odd syllable; the κουκούλιον of a double series of alternate pyrrhics and spondees in trimeter; of which combination there is, however, not a single clear instance among the Anacreontic relics, although there is one rough specimen of something like it, which Hermann has endeavoured to lick into shape, but which is, after all, nothing but a bundle of fragments), so far favours this opinion, as that, if both the οἶκοι and κουκούλιον must have one denomination, that denomination must be Ionic: and for several other reasons, which are specious, if not convincing.

form, beginning with an Iambus ; and most especially rejects all association with the Trochaic ; the odes for the most part being monostrophic, and bearing, with a few established liberties, very sparingly used, each the same form throughout) he mixed up Iambic catalectic dimeters,

Μεθυων τε και λυριζων,

with Trochiac acatalectic dimeters,

Ουκ εμους νομους διδασκων,

as if they were isochronical, and violated the rules of both metres, by putting long and short syllables promiscuously in every part of the line, adhering solely to the modulation of " Sad and fearful is the story : "—

Επι ροδινοις ταπησι—
Τηϊος ποτ' ο μελιστης—
Η δε θεαων ανασσα—
Αιει γ' ετρυφησας αδων—
'Οτι, θεα, σου γ' ανευ μεν.

He at the same time stuck the poor particles into any part of any sentence, as if their sole use were to eke out a limping verse—

Αμφι αυτον οι δ' Ερωτες—
Σοφε, δ' ως Ανακρεοντα, &c., &c. ;

aberred widely from the true meaning of several very ordinary words ; manifested as splendid a disdain of articles as of particles ; and committed, in short, as many sins against language, syntax, and prosody, as it was almost possible to perpetrate within so small a compass.

We have noticed this ode in this place, because it is of a piece with the Greek pretensions which Mr. Moore is always putting forth : because it is, as we have said, an unrepented sin : and because it is doubly curious as illustrating, at once, the sort of thing that passes with the multitude for scholarship, and the materials of which the great herd of trading critics is made, seeing that none of the gentry who professed to review Mr. Moore's Anacreon took any notice of the matter.

The notes, which are numerous, are mostly of the same character with those we have cited : Herodotus says this, Euripides says that, Plato says the other : small scraps of many authors, raked together, manifestly, not by reading but by dipping, and making a display very nearly equivalent, both in manner and matter, to the series of learned labels on an apothecary's empty boxes : the object of them being, undoubtedly, to establish the author's claim to careful research and minute accuracy, which would be all very well if it were well-founded, and made subservient to good purposes : but here, as it seems to us, it is not well

founded, and is subservient to a purpose
very far from good—that of establishing the
fidelity of the author's picture of a chief
of the Epicurean School of Philosophy :
for, if the author had been so scrupulously
correct in his minutest details, it would have
seemed to follow, that he had been most
especially so in the main point of his book
—the character of his hero : whereas, he is
as inaccurate in the smaller matters as he
is altogether wide of the mark in the greater.

Aut prodesse volunt aut delectare poetæ.
The *prodesse* Mr. Moore probably does not
value ; he confines his aim to the *delectare*.
But he could have found abundance of playthings for the grown children of society
without dressing up in false apparel the
chief of an Athenian School of Philosophy
to play the fool and coxcomb for their
entertainment. If he had wished to amuse
the public with *ces Egyptiens si fameux par
des monceaux de pierres*, and had left the
Athenians alone, it would, at any rate,
have been as innocent amusement as his
previous florilegia in Ireland, Persia, and
Paradise. But when he steps out of his
way into the garden of Epicurus, and commits havoc among the roses planted by that
illustrious philosopher,

Qui genus humanum ingenio superavit, et omneis
Præstinxit, stellas exortus uti ætherius sol,

he must be treated like a mischievous boy in a flower-garden, and turned back into the fields where he has been accustomed to pick nosegays with impunity. And, with respect to this nosegay-making operation : a man who, in a course of serious study, picks flowers in his way, and a man who takes up books which might be materials of serious study, for no purpose but to pick flowers out of them, will each produce a fasciculus, which, though they may be somewhat similar in show, will carry with them indisputable evidence of the *modus operandi* of their respective collectors. The first cannot fail to afford evidence that he has a thorough knowledge of the entire field of his operation, nor the latter that he is a mere here-there-and-away visitor, whose whole acquaintance with the matter is confined to what he has carried off for exhibition. Nothing really valuable can result from such a process : nothing permanently agreeable : nothing even temporarily so, except to the ignorant. He who aims (we will not say at utility—Mr. Moore despises the word—but) at reputation beyond the hour, will take a very different course. He will go really through the preliminary labour of accumulating all that is essential to his object, instead of making a vain parade of scraps and fragments, which will be found, on due examination, to be not the relics of a rich table, but the contents of a beggar's wallet. *Multum enim præstat, etiam magni laboris exiguum fructum reportare, quàm non explorato fundamento superstruere, quæ levi impulsu ruitura prævideas.**

Even if the work had merits of any kind, poetical, descriptive, narrative, or dramatic, much higher than any which it, in our judgment, possesses, they would scarcely reconcile us to the total absence of any moral purpose in a work of so much pretension. Still less, of course, can we consider its merits, such as they are, in these respective kinds, and we have given very fair specimens of them all, as affording any compensation for the heavy delinquency of misrepresenting the Athenians, traducing the noblest philosophy of antiquity, and setting forth the impotence of philosophical education in the formation of moral character.

* Hermann. in Præf. ad Eurip. *Herc. Fur.* P. xxiv.

LETTERS AND JOURNALS OF LORD BYRON

MOORE'S LETTERS AND JOURNALS OF LORD BYRON *

THIS first volume takes us at some disadvantage. *Respice finem* is especially
applicable to biography. Much of the pleasure, as well as of the utility, arising from
works of this description, consists in the
study of character : and in this point of
view, the last act of the drama of life often
throws light on the first. Few men are so
ingenuous as to enable their most intimate
friends to discriminate very accurately the
artificial from the real in their characters :
we mean by the artificial, the assumed
semblance, which, on an adequate occasion,
would be thrown aside as easily as a mask
and domino, as easily as the character of
priest was thrown aside in the French
Revolution by many of the dignified persons
to whom it ceased to bring revenue. Extreme cases of this artificial character are

* *Letters and Journals of Lord Byron, with Notices of
his Life.* By Thomas Moore. 2 vols. 4to. Vol. I.
London. 1830. Murray.

to be found in the stolidity of the elder
Brutus, in the madness of Edgar, and the
folly of Leon. In a minor degree, this assumption of an unreal exterior exists more
or less in all men : few have been so fortu-
nate in this world's transactions, as never
to see an old friend with a new face : it
is time alone, (ὁ παντέλεγχος χρόνος, as
Sophocles most happily says,) that shews
whether the young popularity-carping sena-
tor, is a true Patriot, or a Whig, acting
patriotism ; whether the young soldier of
a republic is, at heart, a Napoleon or a
Washington. By the real in character, we
mean those qualities, moral and intellectual,
which remain unchanged through the entire
course of " man's maturer years ; " and
which the collision of events, however ad-
verse, only serves to develope and confirm.
For examples of these qualities in their
worst and best forms, we need look no
further than, on the one hand, to the love
of excitement in gamblers and drunkards,
whom it conducts to ruin and the grave :
and on the other, to the love of country and
mankind in the characters of Washington,
Jefferson, Franklin, and their principal coadjutors in the North American Revolution.

Solon bade Crœsus look to the end of life,
before he could pronounce on individual
happiness : it is not less necessary to do

so before pronouncing a final judgment on individual character. The principal attraction of this work is the light which it has been expected to throw on the character of Lord Byron. So far, it has, to us at least, thrown little new light upon it, and much of that little by no means calculated to render any essential service to his memory.

Lord Byron was always "himself the great sublime he drew." Whatever figures filled up the middle and back ground of his pictures, the fore-ground was invariably consecrated to his own. As somebody, on a different occasion, said of Mr. Coleridge, " he made the public his confidant : " but his confidences were only half-confidences, more calculated to stimulate than to satisfy curiosity. He gave full vent to his feelings : but he hinted, rather than communicated, the circumstances of their origin : and he mixed up in his hints shadowy self-accusations of imaginary crimes, on which, of course, the liberal public put the worst possible construction. Indeed, both in his writings and conversation he dealt, in his latter years especially, very largely in *mystification;* and said many things which have brought his faithful reminiscents into scrapes, by making them report, what others, knowing he could not have believed, think he never could have asserted : which are very different matters. His confidences to Captain Medwin and Mr. Leigh Hunt, were many of them of this mystificatory class. They were of that sort of confidences which are usually reposed in the butt of an Italian *opera buffa;* where the words "*In confidenza*" invariably signify, that there is not a word of truth in any thing the party is going to say. Lord Byron was early distinguished by a scrupulous regard to truth : but the attrition of the world blunts the fine edge of veracity, even in the most ingenuous dispositions : and making the most liberal allowance for misapprehension and misrepresentation, we still think it impossible to read Medwin's and Hunt's reminiscences, without perceiving that those two worthy gentlemen had been very egregiously *mystified*. Lord Byron talked to them in the same spirit in which he wrote much of his *badinage* in Don Juan : such for instance as the passage :—

> I've bribed my grandmother's review, the British.
> I sent it in a letter to the editor,
> Who thanked me duly by return of post :
> I'm for a handsome article his creditor, &c.

The editor took this as a serious charge, and most pathetically implored Lord Byron, as a gentleman and a man of honour, to disavow it. He was handsomely laughed at for his pains : for nobody believed the charge, or regarded it as having been seriously made.

Mr. Moore bears testimony to Lord Byron's disposition in this way. He says of a letter to Mr. Dallas :—

In addition to the temptation, never easily resisted by him, of displaying his wit at the expense of his character, he was here addressing a person who, though, no doubt, well-meaning, was evidently one of those officious, self-satisfied advisers, whom it was the delight of Lord Byron at all times to astonish and *mystify*. The tricks which, when a boy, he played upon the Nottingham quack, Lavender, were but the first of a long series with which, through life, he amused himself, at the expense of all the numerous quacks, whom his celebrity and sociability drew around him.—p. 135.

It must be evident that a person, who would write in this vein, would also talk in it, especially to persons whom he did not much respect. We shall not enter into the casuistry of the question, nor endeavour to decide how far this same weapon of mystification may be justifiably employed, either for the purpose of playing with self-conceited credulity, or for that of parrying or misleading impertinent curiosity. Great men have used it, and great men have justified it :—

Quantunque il simular sia le più volte
Ripreso, e dia di mala mente indici,

LETTERS AND JOURNALS

Si trova pur' in molte cose e molte
Aver fatti evidenti benefici,
E danni, e biasmi, e morti aver già tolte,
Che non conversiam sempre con gli amici,
In questa, assai più oscura, che serena,
Vita mortal, tutta d'invidia piena.*

For ourselves, we hope we shall never adopt, we certainly shall not justify, the practice. We are for the maxim of the old British bards : " The Truth against the World." But if there be any one case of human life, in which this practice is justifiable, it is in the case of an individual living out of society, and much talked of in it, and haunted in his retirement by varieties of the small Boswell or eavesdropping genus, who, as a very little penetration must shew him, would take the first opportunity of selling his confidences to the public, if he should happen to drop any thing for which the prurient appetite of the reading rabble would present a profitable market. Some light will be thrown on this point by Mr. Hunt's naïve observation, that the " natural Byron " was never seen but when he was half-tipsy, and that the said Byron was particularly careful not to get tipsy in Mr. Hunt's company. The " artificial Byron " was all mockery and despair ; and allowed himself to be regularly set

* Ariosto : Canto IV.

76

down, half a dozen times a day, by the
repartees of Mr. Hunt, and Mrs. Hunt,
and all the little Master Hunts. In short,

> Man but a rush against Othello's breast,
> And he retired.*

* The following extracts from Mr. Hunt's publication
will substantiate what we have said in the text.

" Lord Byron, who was as acute as a woman in those
respects, very speedily discerned that he did not stand
very high in her [Mrs. Hunt's] good graces ; and accordingly he set her down to a very humble rank in his own.
As I oftener went to his part of the house, than he came
to mine, he seldom saw her ; and when he did, the
conversation was awkward on his side, and provokingly
self-possessed on her's. He said to her one day, ' What
do you think, Mrs. Hunt ? Trelawney has been speaking
against my morals ! What do you think of that ? '
—' It is the first time,' said Mrs. Hunt, ' I ever heard
of them.' This, which would have set a man of address
upon his wit, completely dashed and reduced him to
silence. But her greatest offence was in some thing
which I had occasion to tell him. He was very bitter
one day upon some friends of mine, criticising even their
personal appearance, and that in no good taste. At the
same time, he was affecting to be very pleasant and
good-humoured, and without any ' offence in the world.'
All this provoked me to mortify him, and I asked if he
knew what Mrs. Hunt had said one day to the Shelleys,
of his picture by Harlowe ? (It is the fastidious, scornful
portrait of him, affectedly looking down.) He said he
did not, and was curious to know. An engraving of it,
I told him, was shown her, and her opinion asked ; upon
which she observed, that ' it resembled a great school-
boy, who had a plain bun given him, instead of a plum-
one.' I did not add, that our friends shook with laughter
at this idea of the noble original, because it was ' so like
him.' He looked as black as possible, and never again
criticised the personal appearance of those whom I
regarded. It was on accounts like these, that he talked
of Mrs. Hunt as being ' no great things.' Myself, because
I did not take all his worldly common-places for granted,

77

We did not review Mr. Hunt's publication. The Quarterly Review did it ample justice ; and though that Review left unsaid some things which we should have said, and said some things which we certainly should not

nor enter into the merits of his bad jokes on women, he represented as a 'proser;' and the children, than whom I will venture to say it was impossible to have quieter or more respectable in the house, or any that came less in his way, he pronounced to be 'impracticable.' But that was the reason. I very soon found that it was desirable to keep them out of his way ; and although this was done in the easiest and most natural manner, and was altogether such a measure as a person of less jealousy might have regarded as a consideration for his quiet, he resented it, and could not help venting his spleen in talking of them. The worst of it was, that when they did come in his way, they were nothing daunted. They had lived in a natural, not an artificial state of inter-course, and were equally sprightly, respectful, and self-possessed. My eldest boy surprised him with his address, never losing his singleness of manner, nor exhibiting pretensions of which he was too young to know any thing, yet giving him his title at due intervals, and appearing, in fact, as if he had always lived in the world instead of out of it. This put him out of his reckoning. To the second, who was more struck with his reputation, and had a vivacity of temperament that rendered such lessons dangerous, he said, one day, that he must take care how he got notions in his head about truth and sincerity, for they would hinder him getting on in the world. This, doubtless, was rather intended to vent a spleen of his own, than to modify the opinions of the child ; but the peril was not the less, and I had warning given me that he could say worse things when I was not present. Thus the children became 'impracticable;' and, luckily, they remained so."—pp. 27, 28.

" It is a credit to my noble acquaintance, that he was by far the pleasantest when he had got wine in his head. The only time I invited myself to dine with him, I told him I did it on that account, and that I meant to push

OF LORD BYRON

have said, it would have been *actum agere*
to go again over the same ground. We
are not solicitous about the motives which
influenced the Quarterly Reviewers. They
had an old political enemy at a manifest

the bottle so, that he should intoxicate me with his good
company. He said he would have a set-to ; but he
never did it. I believe he was afraid. It was a little
before he left Italy ; and there was a point in contest
between us (not regarding myself) which he thought
perhaps I should persuade him to give up.

"When in his cups, which was not often, nor im-
moderately, he was inclined to be tender ; but not weakly
so, nor lachrymose. I know not how it might have been
with every body, but he paid me the compliment of being
excited to his very best feelings ; and when I rose late
to go away, he would hold me down, and say with a look
of entreaty, 'Not yet.'

"Then it was that I seemed to talk with the proper
natural Byron, as he ought to have been ; and there was
not a sacrifice I could not have made to keep him in
that temper, and see his friends love him, as much as
the world admired. Next morning it was all gone. His
intimacy with the worst part of mankind, had got him
again in its chilling crust ; and nothing remained, but
to despair and joke."—p. 68.

"With men I have seen him hold the most childish
contests for superiority ; so childish, that had it been
possible for him to divest himself of a sense of his pretensions and public character, they would have exhibited
something of the conciliating simplicity of Goldsmith.
He would then lay imaginary wagers ; and in a style
which you would not have looked for in high life, thrust
out his chin, and give knowing, self-estimating nods of
the head, half-nod and half-shake, such as boys playing
at chuck-farthing give when they say, 'Come, I tell you
what now.' A fat dandy who came upon us at Genoa,
and pretended to be younger than he was, and to wear
his own hair, discomposed him for the day. He declaimed
against him in so deploring a tone, and uttered the word
'wig' so often, that my two eldest boys, who were in

moral disadvantage. The querulous ego-
tisms, the scaturient vanity bubbling up in
every page like the hundred fountains
of the river Hoangho, the readiness to
violate all the confidences of private life,
the intrinsic nothingness of what the
writer had it in his power to tell,
the shallow mockeries of philosophical
thinking, the quaint and silly figures of
speech, the out-of-the-way notions of morals
and manners, the eternal reference of every
thing to self, the manifest labour and effort
to inflate a mass of insignificancies into the
bulk of a quarto, for the sake of the liberal
bookseller, who wanted to append a given

the next room, were obliged to stifle their laughter."—
p. 77.
"The love of money, the pleasure of receiving it,
even the gratitude he evinced when it was saved him,
had not taught him the only virtue upon which lovers of
money usually found their claims to a good construction :
he did not like paying a debt, and would undergo pestering
and pursuit to avoid it. 'But what,' cries the reader,
'becomes then of the stories of his making presents of
money and manuscripts, and his not caring for the profits
of his writings, and his giving 10,000l. to the Greeks!'
He did care for the profits of what he wrote, and he
reaped a great deal : but as I have observed before, he
cared for celebrity still more ; and his presents, such as
they were, were judiciously made to that end. 'Good
heavens!' said a fair friend to me the other day, who
knew him well, 'if he had but foreseen that you would
have given the world an account of him! What would
he not have done to cut a figure in your eyes!'"—pp. 80,
81.—From *Lord Byron and some of his Contemporaries*,
by Leigh Hunt. Colburn. 1828.

number of pages to the name of Lord Byron, the constantly recurring " Io Triumphe " over the excellent hits and clinches of the author and his family, and the obvious *malus animus* of the entire work ; presented so many inviting prominences to the hand of castigation, that the Quarterly could for once come forth on fair ground, and flagellate an opponent without having recourse to its old art of wilful misrepresentation.

Many traces of that spirit of *badinage* which says things not meant or expected to be believed, and which literal interpretation would turn into something never dreamed of by the writer, occur throughout the letters in this volume. For example, Lord Byron writing from Constantinople, says to his mother :—

H. who will deliver this is bound straight for England : and as he is bursting with his travels, I shall not anticipate his narratives, but merely beg you not to believe one word he says, but reserve your ear for me, if you have any desire to be acquainted with the truth.

No one, who reads this volume, will suppose this to be anything but jest ; but we can easily conceive his reminiscents reporting it thus :—" He had a very bad opinion of Mr. Hobhouse's veracity, and emphatically cautioned me against believing a word he said."

LETTERS AND JOURNALS

We shall not multiply instances. The volume abounds with them. We believe that Captain Medwin and Mr. Leigh Hunt were both gentlemen to take every thing literally. Lord Byron did not, in truth, admit either of them into his confidence, more than one step further, if even that, than he did the public in general : and their imperfect and flippant communications answered scarcely any purpose but to disappoint expectation.

Curiosity was never more strongly excited, nor disappointment more strongly experienced, than by the memoirs which Lord Byron left of himself, and which Mr. Moore committed to the flames. Mr. Moore calls them " the memoirs or rather memoranda, which it was thought expedient, for various reasons, to sacrifice." [p. 655.]—These being gone beyond recovery, Mr. Moore remained, with the reputation of being the best-informed person in the kingdom on the subject of the noble poet, of having access to the most ample materials for his biography, and of being the best qualified person to put those materials together.

It turns out, however, most unluckily, that all that is best worth telling is not fit to be told. In the points about which the public were most curious, what was before mystery, is still mystery. It remains, like Bottom's dream, in the repositories of the incommunicable.

Bottom. The eye of man hath not heard ; the ear of man hath not seen ; man's hand is not able to taste, his tongue to conceive, nor his heart to report, what my dream was.

Masters, I am to discourse wonders : but ask me not what; for if I tell you, I am no true Athenian. I will tell you every thing, right as it fell out.

Quince. Let us hear, sweet Bottom.

Bottom. Not a word of me. All that I will tell you is, that the duke hath dined.

And of matter about as important as the duke's dinner, is at least one half of this goodly volume composed.

We shall now give an account of this first volume, making such remarks as suggest themselves, and reserving our general observations till the conclusion of the second.

The work begins with an account of Lord Byron's ancestry.

" In the character of the noble poet," says Mr. Moore, " the pride of ancestry was undoubtedly one of the most decided features." His descent is cursorily traced from " Ralph de Burun, whose name ranks high in Dooms-day book, among the tenants of land in Nottinghamshire," [page 1.]

through Sir John Byron the Little, with the Great Beard [page 3.] who, " at the dissolution of the monasteries, obtained, by a royal grant, the church and priory of Newstead, with the lands adjoining : " Sir John Byron, who, in the year 1643, was created by Charles the 1st " Baron Byron of Rochdale in the county of Lancaster," and is described as having been to the last a most faithful, persevering, and disinterested follower of the king : down to the grandfather, grand uncle and father of the poet : the first Mr., afterwards Admiral Byron, whose shipwreck and sufferings, about the year 1750, awakened, in no small degree, the attention and sympathy of the public : the second, the Lord Byron, who, in the year 1765, stood his trial before the House of Peers for killing in a duel, or rather scuffle, his relation and neighbour, Mr. Chaworth : and the third, Captain Byron, a worthless profligate, who married, first, the divorced wife of Lord Carmarthen, whom he had previously carried off from her husband ; and afterwards, on her death, Miss Catharine Gordon, only child and heiress of George Gordon, esq. of Gight. The only offspring of the first marriage was the honourable Augusta Byron, now the wife of Colonel Leigh : the only offspring of the second was the subject of this memoir, who was born

in Holles Street, London, on the 22nd of
January 1788 : by which time his mother,
who had been married in 1785, was reduced
from competence to a pittance of 150*l.* per
annum ; her husband having squandered the
whole of her fortune. The lady was no
exception to Master Silence's axiom, that
" women are shrews, both short and tall : "
on the contrary, she was a virago of the
first magnitude. This hopeful pair separated in 1790 ; and the husband died in
1791. Little Byron was left with his mother,
who taught him to rage and storm ; and
his nurse, who taught him to repeat the
psalms, and sang him to sleep with stories
and legends. He read the Bible through
and through, before he was eight years old.
The Old Testament he read as a pleasure,
the New as a task.

The malformation of his foot, occasioned
by an accident at his birth, was a subject
of pain, inconvenience, and mortification to
him, from his earliest years.

He began his scholastic education at a
cheap day-school in Aberdeen, where he
made little progress. In 1796 he was removed by his mother, for the change of air,
into the Highlands, where he acquired his
first enthusiasm for mountain scenery: and
fell in love at eight years old with a " Highland
Mary " of his own. On these two points,

mountain scenery and precocious love, Mr. Moore philosophizes.

In 1798, by the death of his grand uncle, he succeeded to the title and estates, the latter being much involved, and the former, consequently, a great calamity. He was now placed in the hands of a quack, at Nottingham, named Lavender, who tortured him grievously under pretence of curing his foot, and, during this infliction, he received lessons in Latin from a respectable school-master, Mr. Rogers.

In 1799, he was removed to London, and placed under the medical care of Dr. Baillie, and in the scholastic establishment of Dr. Glennie at Dulwich, where, having been carefully untaught the little he had learned in Scotland, he started afresh and began to make way : but was much impeded by his mother having him too much at home.

In 1800, he had a second boyish passion for his young cousin Miss Parker.

In 1801, he went to Harrow, " as little prepared," says Dr. Glennie, " as it is natural to suppose from two years of ele-mentary instruction, thwarted by every art that could estrange the mind of youth from preceptor, from school, and from all serious study."

At Harrow, however, he distinguished himself as an athlete, neglecting his school-

OF LORD BYRON

books, and picked up some general knowledge by reading history, philosophy, and
so forth, contrary to the good order and
discipline of our public establishments for
eradicating the love of letters. He fought
his way into the respect of his school-
fellows. A vast deal of childish matter is
here narrated, very inficete and unprofitable to peruse.

In 1803, he fell in love with his cousin,
Miss Chaworth. As much is supposed to
hang upon this unsuccessful attachment,
and as the narration will serve as a favourable specimen of the matter and manner of
the work, we shall extract the entire passage,
in which this event is related :—

We come now to an event in his life which,
according to his own deliberate persuasion, exercised
a lasting and paramount influence over the whole
of his subsequent character and career.

It was in the year 1803 that his heart, already
twice, as we have seen, possessed with the childish
notion that it loved, conceived an attachment
which,—young as he was even then for such a
feeling,—sunk so deep into his mind as to give a
colour to all his future life.

That unsuccessful loves are generally the most
lasting, is a truth, however sad, which unluckily
did not require this instance to confirm it. To
the same cause, I fear, must be traced the perfect
innocence and romance which distinguish this very
early attachment to Miss Chaworth from the many
others that succeeded, without effacing, it in his

87

heart ;—making it the only one whose details can be entered into with safety, or whose results, however darkening their influence on himself, can be dwelt upon with a pleasurable interest by others.

On leaving Bath, Mrs. Byron took up her abode in lodgings, at Nottingham,—Newstead Abbey being at that time let to Lord Grey de Ruthven,—and during the Harrow vacation of this year she was joined there by her son. So attached was he to Newstead, that even to be in its neighbourhood was a delight to him ; and before he became acquainted with Lord Grey, he used sometimes to sleep for a night at the small house near the gate which is still known by the name of " the Hut." * An intimacy, however, soon sprang up between him and his noble tenant, and an apartment in the Abbey was from thenceforth always at his service. To the family of Miss Chaworth, who resided at Annesley, in the immediate neighbourhood of Newstead, he had been made known, some time before, in London, and now renewed his acquaintance with them. The young heiress herself combined with the many worldly advantages that encircled her, much personal beauty, and a disposition the most amiable and attaching. Though already fully alive to her charms, it was at the period of which we are speaking, that the young poet, who was then in his sixteenth year, while the object of his adoration was about two years older, seems to have drank deepest of that fascination whose effects were to be so lasting ;—six short summer weeks which he now passed in her

---

* I find this circumstance, of his having occasionally slept at the Hut, though asserted by one of the old servants, much doubted by others.

company being sufficient to lay the foundation of a feeling for all life.

He used, at first, though offered a bed at Annesley, to return every night to Newstead to sleep ; alleging as a reason, that he was afraid of the family pictures of the Chaworths,—that he fancied " they had taken a grudge to him on account of the duel, and would come down from their frames at night to haunt him." * At length, one evening, he said gravely to Miss Chaworth and her cousin, "in going home last night I saw a bogle ; " which Scotch term being wholly unintelligible to the young ladies, he explained that he had seen a ghost, and would not therefore return to Newstead that evening. From this time, he always slept at Annesley during the remainder of his visit, which was interrupted only by a short excursion to Matlock and Castleton, in which he had the happiness of accompanying Miss Chaworth and her party, and of which the following interesting notice appears in one of his memorandum-books :—

" When I was fifteen years of age, it happened that, in a cavern in Derbyshire, I had to cross in a boat (in which two people only could lie down), a stream which flows under a rock, with the rock so close upon the water as to admit the boat only to be pushed on by a ferry-man (a sort of Charon),

* It may possibly have been the recollection of these pictures that suggested to him the following lines in the Siege of Corinth :—

Like the figures on arras that gloomily glare,
Stirr'd by the breath of the wintery air,
So seen by the dying lamp's fitful light,
Lifeless, but life-like and awful to sight ;
As they seem, through the dimness, about to come down
From the shadowy wall where their images frown.

who wades at the stern, stooping all the time. The companion of my transit was M. A. C., with whom I had been long in love, and never told it, though she had discovered it without.

"I recollect my sensations, but cannot describe them, and it is as well. We were a party, a Mr. W. two Miss W.'s, Mr. and Mrs. Cl—ke, Miss R., and my M. A. C. Alas! Why do I say My? Our union would have healed feuds in which blood had been shed by our fathers, it would have joined lands broad and rich, it would have joined at least one heart, and two persons not ill matched in years (she is two years my elder), and—and—and—what has been the result?"

In the dances of the evening at Matlock, Miss Chaworth, of course, joined, while her lover sat looking on, solitary and mortified. It is not impossible, indeed, that the dislike that he always expressed for this amusement may have originated in some bitter pang, felt in his youth, on seeing "the lady of his love" led out by others to the gay dance from which he was himself excluded. On the present occasion, the young heiress of Annesley having had for her partner (as often happens at Matlock) some person with whom she was wholly unacquainted; on her resuming her seat, Byron said to her pettishly, "I hope you like your friend." The words were scarcely out of his lips, when he was accosted by an ungainly-looking Scotch lady, who rather boisterously claimed him as "cousin," and was putting his pride to the torture with her vulgarity, when he heard the voice of his fair companion retorting archly in his ear, "I hope you like your friend."

His time at Annesley was mostly passed in

riding with Miss Chaworth and her cousin—sitting
in idle reverie, as was his custom, pulling at his
handkerchief, or in firing at a door which opens
upon the terrace, and which still, I believe, bears
the marks of his shots. But his chief delight was
in sitting to hear Miss Chaworth play ; and the
pretty Welsh air, " Mary Anne," was (partly, of
course, on account of the name) his especial
favourite. During all this time he had the pain
of knowing that the heart of her he loved was
occupied by another ; that as he himself expressed
it,

> Her sighs were not for him, to her he was
> Even as a brother—but no more.

Neither is it, indeed, probable, had even her
affections been disengaged, that lord Byron would,
at this time, have been selected as the object of
them. A seniority of two years gives to a girl,
" on the eve of womanhood," an advance into life,
with which the boy keeps no proportionate pace.
Miss Chaworth looked upon Byron as a mere school-
boy. He was in his manners, too, at that period,
rough and odd, and (as I have heard from more
than one quarter) by no means popular among girls
of his own age. If at any moment, however, he
had flattered himself with the hope of being loved
by her, a circumstance mentioned in his " Memoranda," as one of the most painful of those humilia-
tions to which the defect in his foot had exposed
him, must have let the truth in with dreadful
certainty upon his heart. He either was told of,
or over-heard, Miss Chaworth saying to her maid,
" Do you think I could care any thing for that
lame boy ? "

This speech, as he himself described it, was

like a shot through his heart. Though late at
night when he heard it, he instantly darted out of
the house, and scarcely knowing whither he ran,
never stopped till he found himself at Newstead.

The picture which he has drawn of this youthful
love, in one of the most interesting of his poems,
" The Dream," shows how genius and feeling can
elevate the realities of life, and give to the com-
monest events and objects an undying lustre. The
old hall at Annesley, under the name of " the
antique oratory," will long call up to fancy, the
" maiden and the youth " who once stood in it ;
while the image of the lover's steed, though suggested
by the unromantic race-ground of Nottingham,
will not the less conduce to the general charm of
the scene, and shed a portion of that light which
only genius could shed over it.

He appears already at this boyish age to have
been so far a proficient in gallantry as to know the
use that may be made of the trophies of former
triumphs in achieving new ones ; for he used to
boast, with much pride, to Miss Chaworth, of a
locket which some fair favourite had given him,
and which, probably, may have been a present
from that pretty cousin, of whom he speaks with
such warmth in one of the notices already quoted.
He was also, it appears, not a little aware of his
own beauty, which, notwithstanding the tendency
to corpulence derived from his mother, gave
promise at this time, of that peculiar expression
into which his features refined and kindled afterwards.

With the summer holidays ended this dream of
his youth. He saw Miss Chaworth once more in
the succeeding year, and took his last farewell of

OF LORD BYRON

her (as he himself used to relate) on that hill near Annesley,* which, in his poem of "The Dream," he describes so happily as "crowned with a peculiar diadem." No one, he declared, could have told how much he felt, for his countenance was calm, and his feelings restrained. "The next time I see you," said he, in parting with her, "I suppose you will be Mrs. Chaworth," †—and her answer was, "I hope so." It was before this interview that he wrote, with a pencil, in a volume of "Madame de Maintenon's Letters" belonging to her, the following verses, which have never, I believe, before been published :—

> Oh Memory, torture me no more,
>   The present's all o'ercast ;
> My hopes of future bliss are o'er,
>   In mercy veil the past.
> Why bring those images to view,
>   I henceforth must resign ?
> Ah ! why those happy hours renew,
>   That never can be mine ?
> Past pleasure doubles present pain,
>   To sorrow adds regret,
> Regret and hope are both in vain,
>   I ask but to—forget.

* Among the unpublished verses of his in my possession, I find the following fragment written not long after this period :—

> Hills of Annesley, bleak and barren,
>   Where my thoughtless childhood stray'd,
> How the northern tempests warring,
>   Howl above thy tufted shade !
> Now no more, the hours beguiling,
>   Former favourite haunts I see ;
> Now no more my Mary smiling,
>   Makes ye seem a Heaven to me.

† The lady's husband, for some time, took her family name.

LETTERS AND JOURNALS

In the following year, 1805, Miss Chaworth was married to his successful rival, Mr. John Musters ; and a person who was present when the first intelligence of the event was communicated to him, thus describes the manner in which he received it. —" I was present when he first heard of the marriage. His mother said, ' Byron, I have some news for you.'—' Well, what is it ? '—' Take out your handkerchief first, for you will want it.'— ' Nonsense ! '—' Take out your handkerchief, I say.' He did so, to humour her. ' Miss Chaworth is married.' An expression, very peculiar, impossible to describe, passed over his pale face, and he hurried his handkerchief into his pocket, saying, with an affected air of coldness and nonchalance, ' Is that all ? ' ' Why, I expected you would have been plunged into grief ! '—He made no reply, and soon began to talk about something else."— pp. 53-58.

Now that this affair gave a colour to all his future life, we do not in the slightest degree believe. It was his own mind that gave the colour to the affair. It was his disposition to aim always at unattainable things. If he had married this idol, he would very soon have drawn the same conclusion respecting her, which he drew respecting all the objects of his more successful pursuit :—

'Tis an old lesson ; Time approves it true,
And they who know it best deplore it most ;
When all is won that all desire to woo,
The paltry prize is hardly worth the cost.
Childe Harold : Canto I., St. 35.

94

Through life he aimed at what he could not compass. He took the best substitutes which circumstances placed in his way, and consoled himself with a handmaid for the loss of a Helen : the latter being still longed for because she was inaccessible. As a Greek poet says,

"Α γ' ὖς τὰν βάλανον τὰν μὲν ἔχει, τὰν δ' ἔραται λαβεῖν,

Κᾀγὼ παῖδα καλὴν τὰν μὲν ἔχω, τὰν δ' ἔραμαι λαβεῖν.

There is nothing singular in this state of mind, nor even in a man's deluding himself into the belief, that a single disappoint-ment of this sort has coloured his life. The singularity is, finding another man to believe it.

Apropos of Lord Byron's reading at Harrow, Mr. Moore has a side cut or two at classical literature [pp. 59, 60], which, when we remember his Epicurean, and certain observations thereon,* makes us think of the fox and the grapes.

In 1805, Lord Byron was removed to Trinity College, Cambridge. In 1806, being on a visit to his mother at Southwell, the lady's temper exploded on some occasion, and she converted the poker and tongs into the thunderbolts of her wrath. From this

* *Westminster Review*, No. XVI.

Juno Tonans and her missiles he fled to London, and made it his chief care to keep himself out of her reach.

In 1807, he printed a small volume of poems, for private distribution among his friends. This being a very interesting subject, and very safe to dilate upon, occupies a large share of the biographer's attention. There is a good deal also about his enjoyment of athletic exercises, his ignorance of horses, his fondness for dogs and fire-arms, his belief in second-sight, *fetches*, and so forth ; his horror of growing fat, his sensitiveness on the score of his foot, his multifarious reading, and the delight with which he seasoned his academical studies by a copy of Mother Goose's Tales, which he bought of a hawker. *Res memoranda novis annalibus.*

A long list is given of the books which he had read up to that time, November 1807. It is very copious, especially in history. Few young men at College, Mr. Moore thinks, had read so much : we think so too : we may make large deductions from it, and still think so. There is, however, a way of scouting through books, which some people call reading, and we are afraid much of the reading here set down was of that description. " Greek and Latin poets, without number." We are sceptical on this point at any rate. If he had read and understood —we include understanding in our idea of reading—if he had read and understood as many Greek poets as he could count on his fingers, he never could have fallen into the preposterous blunder which he committed in Don Juan :—

The European with the Asian shore
Sprinkled with palaces : the *ocean stream*
Here and there studded with a seventy four, &c.

Canto V., St. 3.

He says in a note on " *the ocean stream :* "—

This expression of Homer has been much criticised. It hardly answers to our Atlantic ideas of the ocean, but is sufficiently applicable to the Hellespont and the Bosphorus, with the Ægean intersected with islands.

Who were the parties that had criticised Homer out of his obvious meaning, we know not : but could it have been necessary to tell a man who had " read Greek poets without number," that, according to the ideas of the ancients, the Ocean River flowed entirely round the earth, and that the seas were inlets from it ? The Shield of Achilles alone would have set this point at rest, without looking to any more recondite sources. The River Ocean surrounded the work immediately within the edge of the

LETTERS AND JOURNALS

shield ; and the earth, which it enclosed, was imaged in the interior.]

Ἐν δὲ τίθει ποταμοῖο μέγα σθένος Ὠκεανοῖο,
Ἄντυγα πὰρ πυμάτην σάκεος πύκα ποιητοῖο.

"Hic utique manifestum fit," says Heyne, "auctorem voluisse orbem terrarum in clypeo esse adumbratum."

" Much criticised," indeed ! It is impossible that the expression could ever have been criticised at all, except by mere English readers, puzzling themselves over Pope's translation, or Milton's passage about Leviathan. But let those who wish to see the matter in broad daylight, read the beginning of the Periegesis of Dionysius.

Ex pede Herculem. A man who could speculate in this strain, after reading Greek and Latin poets without number (unhappily they are too easily numerable) must have read to little good purpose. " The utility of reading," says Horne Tooke, " depends not on the swallow, but on the digestion."

Lord Byron had read enough to produce a general effect with a multitude of inaccurate recollections. This is the best sort of reading for those who aim merely at amusing the public: and for the space of his life before us, he aimed at nothing higher.

OF LORD BYRON

" I see," he says (October 1810), "the Lady of the Lake advertised. Of course, it is in his old ballad style, and pretty. ⹀After all, Scott is the best of them. The end of all scribblement is to amuse, and he certainly succeeds there."—p. 241.

And in the same spirit, Captain Medwin reports him to have said : " The great object is effect, no matter how produced." His reading, and that of his friend and biographer, are much of a piece in this respect, and remind us of a French treatise on music, which we saw advertised the other day, as containing *tout ce qui est nécessaire pour en parler sans l'avoir étudié.*

His life, at college, was not different from that of most young gentlemen there.

" Since my last," he says (writing from Trinity College, Cambridge, July 5, 1807) " I have determined to reside another year at Granta, as my rooms, &c., &c. are finished in great style, several old friends come up again, and many new acquaintances made, consequently my inclination leads me forward ; and I shall return to college in October, if still alive. My life here has been one continued routine of dissipation—out at different places every day, engaged to more dinners, &c., &c. than my *stay* would permit me to fulfil. At this moment, I write with a bottle of claret in my *head*, and *tears* in my *eyes*, for I have just parted with my Cornelian, who spent the evening with me."—p. 113.

Farther on, he says more seriously (Jan. 21, 1808) :—

I am a member of the University of Cambridge, where I shall take my degree of A.M. this term : but were reasoning, eloquence, or virtue, the objects of my search, Granta is not their metropolis, nor is the place of her situation an El Dorado, far less an Utopia. The intellects of her children are as stagnant as her Cam, and their pursuits limited to the church, not of Christ, but of the nearest benefice. —p. 134.

Mr. Moore philosophizes on this passage, and is of opinion that the hatred and contempt which Milton and Gray entertained for Cambridge, and Gibbon and Locke for Oxford, " may well be thought to have had their origin in that antipathy to the trammels of discipline which is not unusually observable among the characteristics of genius ; " and goes on discussing " the tendency of genius and taste to rebel against discipline,"

In proper terms, such as men smatter,
When they throw out, and miss the matter :

And here Mr. Moore misses the matter most completely, as, in all cases in which a grain of philosophy is requisite, he makes a point of doing. If the Universities can make nothing of genius, their discipline, if it were good for anything, might make something of mediocrity or of dulness : but

OF LORD BYRON

their discipline is mere pretence, and is
limited to the non-essentials of education :
they settle down mediocrity into a quiet
hatred of literature, and confirm a question-
able dunce into a hopeless, incurable, and
self-satisfied blockhead. Milton, Locke,
Gibbon, and Gray (and Lord Byron himself),
all professedly learned a great deal in spite
of all the efforts of their respective universities to prevent them, and when our most
illustrious names in poetry, philosophy, and
history, are arrayed against the universities,
it is, forsooth, according to Mr. Moore, the
dislike of genius to discipline, and not the
antipathy of intellect, knowledge, reason and
truth, to ignorance, avarice, and political
servility, in the false assumption of learning
and science.

We shall not, however, leave this question
to inference. We shall show in their own
words, *why* Milton, Gibbon, and Gray hated
and despised their respective universities.

Milton says :—[*Animadversions upon the
Remonstrant's defence against Smectymnuus*]

It had been happy for this land if your priests had
been but only wooden. All England knows they
have been to this island not wood, but wormwood,
that have infected the third part of our waters, like
that apostate star in the Revelation, that many
souls have died of their bitterness ; and if you mean
by wooden, illiterate or contemptible, there was
no want of that sort among you ; and their number

increasing daily, as their laziness, their tavern-hunting, their neglect of all sound literature, and their liking of doltish and monastical schoolmen, daily increased. What, should I tell you how the universities, that men look should be fountains of learning and knowledge, have been poisoned and choaked under your governance? And if to be wooden be to be base, where could there be found among all the reformed churches, nay in the church of Rome itself, a baser brood of flattering and time-serving priests? according as God pronounces by Isaiah: the prophet that teacheth lies, he is the tail. As for your young scholars, that petition for bishoprics and deaneries to encourage them in their studies, and that many gentlemen else will not put their sons to learning, away with such young mercenary striplings, and their simoniacal fathers; God has no need of such, they have no part or lot in his vineyard: they may as well sue for nunneries, that they may have some convenient stowage for their withered daughters, because they cannot give them portions answerable to the pride and vanity they have bred them in. This is the root of all our mischief: that which they allege for the encouragement of their studies should be cut away forthwith as the very bait of pride and ambition, the very garbage that draws together all the fowls of prey and ravin in the land, to come and gorge upon the church.

Gibbon says, in his Memoirs :—

To the university of Oxford *I* acknowledge no obligation, and she will as cheerfully renounce me for a son, as I am willing to disclaim her for a mother. I spent fourteen months at Magdalen

College : they proved the fourteen months the most idle and unprofitable of my whole life : the reader will pronounce between the school and the scholar : but I cannot affect to believe that nature had disqualified me for all literary pursuits. The specious and ready excuse of my tender age, imperfect preparation, and hasty departure, may doubtless be alleged ; nor do I wish to defraud such excuses of their proper weight. Yet, in my six-teenth year, I was not devoid of capacity or applica-tion ; even my childish reading had displayed an early, though blind propensity for books, and the shallow flood might have been taught to flow in a deep and a clear stream. In the discipline of a well constituted academy, under the guidance of skilful and vigilant professors, I should gradually have risen from translations to originals, from the Latin to the Greek classics, from dead languages to living science : my hours would have been occupied by useful and agreeable studies, the wanderings of fancy would have been restrained, and I should have escaped the temptations of idle-ness, which finally precipitated my departure from Oxford.

Perhaps, in a separate annotation, I may coolly examine the fabulous and real antiquities of our sister universities, a question which has kindled such fierce and foolish disputes among their fanatic sons. In the mean while, it will be acknowledged, that these venerable bodies are sufficiently old to partake of all the prejudices and infirmities of age. The schools of Oxford and Cambridge were founded in a dark age of false and barbarous science ; and they are still tainted with the vices of their origin. Their primitive discipline was adapted to the education of priests and monks ; and the government still remains in the hands of the clergy, an order of men whose manners are remote from the present world, and whose eyes are dazzled by the light of philosophy.

Gray says, in a letter to Mr. West :—

You must know that I do not take degrees, and, after this term, shall have nothing more of college impertinence to undergo, which I trust will be some pleasure to you as it is a great one to me. I have endured lectures daily and hourly since I came last, supported by the hopes of being shortly at full liberty to give myself up to my friends and classical companions, who, poor souls ! though I see them fallen into great contempt with most people here, yet I cannot help sticking to them, and out of a spirit of obstinacy (I think) love them the better for it ; and, indeed, what can I do else ? Must I plunge into metaphysics ? Alas ! I cannot see in the dark ; nature has not furnished me with the optics of a cat. Must I pore upon mathematics ? Alas ! I cannot see in too much light ; I am no eagle. It is very possible that two and two make four, but I would not give four farthings to demonstrate this ever so clearly ; and if these be the profits of life, give me the amusements of it. The people I behold all around me, it seems, know all this and more, and yet I do not know one of them who inspires me with any ambition of being like him. Surely it was of this place, now Cambridge, but formerly known by the name of Babylon, that the prophet spoke when he said, " the wild beasts of the desart shall dwell there, and their houses shall be full of doleful creatures, and owls shall

build there, and satyrs shall dance there; their
forts and towers shall be a den for ever, a joy of
wild asses; there shall the great owl make her
nest, and lay, and hatch, and gather under her
shadow; it shall be a court of dragons; the screech
owl also shall rest there, and find for herself a
place of rest." You see here is a pretty collection
of desolate animals, which is verified in this town
to a tittle; and perhaps it may also allude to
your habitation, for you know all types may be
taken by abundance of handles; however, I defy
your owls to match mine.

Again, to Dr. Wharton :—

The spirit of laziness (the spirit of the place)
begins to possess even me, who have so long
declaimed against it; yet has it not so prevailed,
but that I feel that discontent with myself, that
ennui, that ever accompanies it in its beginnings.
Time will settle my conscience, time will reconcile
me to this languid companion : we shall smoke,
we shall tipple, we shall doze together : we shall
have our little jokes like other people, and we shall
have our old stories : brandy will finish what port
began : and a month after the time you will see in
some corner of a London Evening Post :—" Yesterday died the Rev. John Gray, senior fellow of Clare
Hall, a facetious companion, and well respected
by all that knew him. His death is supposed to
have been occasioned by a fit of apoplexy, being
found fallen out of bed with his head in the chamber-
pot.

Again, to Dr. Clarke :—

I would wish to continue here till Michaelmas;
but I fear I must come to town much sooner.

LETTERS AND JOURNALS

Cambridge is a delight of a place, now there is nobody in it. I do believe you would like it, if you knew what it was without inhabitants. It is they, I assure you, that get it an ill name and spoil all. Our friend Dr. —— (one of its nuisances) is not expected here in a hurry. He is gone to his grave with five fine mackerel (large and full of roe) in his belly. He eat them all at one dinner; but his fate was a turbot on Trinity Sunday, of which he left little for the company besides bones. He had not been hearty all the week; but after this sixth fish he never held up his head more, and a violent looseness carried him off. They say he made a very good end.

These are only specimens. We could easily multiply them : but they are sufficient for the purpose. With respect to Locke, we cannot at present cite any thing in point in his own words, and must content ourselves with a passage from his life by Lord King ; which, however, is quite enough to refute Mr. Moore's proposition :—

Locke was sent to Westminster School, and from thence to Christ Church, Oxford, in 1651. His friend, Mr. Tyrrell, the grandson of the celebrated Usher, Archbishop of Armagh, relates that Locke, in the earliest period of his residence at Oxford, was distinguished for his talents and learning amongst his fellow-students. That he lost much time at Oxford, is however certain, from his own confession ; and if he derived little advantage from the place of his education, it cannot be ascribed to the inaptitude of his mind to make useful

106

acquirements : the fault is to be found in his instructors and in their system. It appears that he would have thought the method of Des Cartes preferable (though no admirer of his philosophy) to that of the established practice, either because the study of that writer gave him the first taste for philosophy, or because he admired the distinctness of this method ; or, perhaps, he might consider any alteration to be an improvement, and any change a change for the better.

Although he acquired this early reputation at the university, yet he was often heard to express his regret that his father had ever sent him to Oxford ; aware, from his own experience, that the method of instruction then pursued was ill calculated to open the understanding or prepare the way for any useful knowledge.

It is really something *un peu fort*, even for Mr. Moore, to pretend that these learned and laborious men, all of whom subjected their minds to the severest discipline, disliked their universities only because discipline is distasteful to genius. But the universities are influential, and Mr. Moore must stand well with the influential in all its forms. This will be more and more apparent as we proceed.

In 1807, Lord Byron published his "Hours of Idleness," and in 1808, the Edinburgh Review attacked it in the spirit of its usual dealings with all authors, young authors especially, who were not within the corrupt

circle of its political and literary favouritism.
Mr. Moore had been similarly dealt with not
long previously : but both Mr. Moore and
Lord Byron successively forced themselves
into the enchanted circle : the first having
introduced himself by proposing to shoot
his critic, which proved that he was not only
a gentleman but a great poet : the second
by laying about him, with the figurative
horse-whip of satire, indiscriminately on his
reviewer, and on all he had ever praised,
which, as the public sided with the young
satirist, set his pretensions to genius in an
entirely new light. The review having been
written without principle, and merely as a
piece of catering for idle malignity, " the
most gifted of critics " pocketed the invec-
tive which consigned him to the Tolbooth,
and the three " gifted " parties, of whom one
had challenged two, and two had, in critical
phraseology, cut up two, (Moore having
challenged Jeffrey and Byron, Jeffrey having
cut up Moore and Byron, and Byron
having cut up Jeffrey and Moore), became
three of the best friends in this literary
world, ·to the great advantage of their respective reputations with the enlightened
and discerning public. As Mr. Moore is
both poet and musician, we recommend
this to him as a matchless subject for a
catch.

OF LORD BYRON

Mr. Moore apologizes, in a very lame and irresolute way, for his friend the critic's original treatment of his friend the poet. " The knave, sir, is mine honest friend," says Davy to Justice Shallow, pleading for Vizor of Wincot. We shall pass over this point for the present, because we shall have a better opportunity of noticing the system which the Edinburgh Review adopted in its literary criticisms.

Much information is given respecting the progress of the Satire through the press. Lord Byron's sole standard of judgment of persons was in his own personal feelings of favour and resentment. Mr. Moore euphonises this into " the susceptibility of new impressions and influences which rendered both his judgment and feelings so variable." It is amusing to see how Lord Carlisle was turned from a Roscommon into a blockhead ; Professor Smith, the English Lyrist, from one who discredited even the University, to one who almost redeemed his name : Sir William Gell, from coxcomb to classic, by a single stroke of the pen, because, in his chrysalis state between coxcomb and classic, Lord Byron accidentally became acquainted with him ; and so forth. This was pretty much the way in which he formed his opinions through life.

In 1809, he came of age, and took his

seat in the House of Lords. There was some delay opposed to him by the necessity of obtaining from Carhais, in Cornwall, the affidavit required in proof of the marriage of Admiral Byron with Miss Trevanion.

The affidavits which he here mentions, as expected from Cornwall, were those required in proof of the marriage of Admiral Byron with Miss Trevanion, the solemnization of which having taken place, as it appears, in a private chapel at Carhais, no regular certificate of the ceremony could be produced. The delay in procuring other evidence, coupled with the rather ungracious refusal of Lord Carlisle to afford any explanations respecting his family, interposed those difficulties which he alludes to in the way of his taking his seat. At length, all the necessary proofs having been obtained, he on the 13th of March, presented himself in the House of Lords in a state more lone and unfriendly, perhaps, than any youth of his high station had ever before been reduced to on such an occasion, not having a single individual of his own class either to introduce him as friend or receive him as acquaintance. To chance alone was he even indebted for being accompanied as far as the bar of the House by a very distant relative, who had been, little more than a year before, an utter stranger to him. This relative was Mr. Dallas, and the account which he has given of the whole scene is too striking in all its details, to be related in any other words than his own :

" The Satire was published about the middle of March, previous to which he took his seat in the House of Lords, on the 13th of the same month.

OF LORD BYRON

On that day, passing down St. James's-street, but with no intention of calling, I saw his chariot at his door, and went in. His countenance, paler than usual, showed that his mind was agitated, and that he was thinking of the nobleman to whom he had once looked for a hand and countenance in his introduction to the House. He said to me—I am glad you happened to come in, I am going to take my seat, perhaps you will go with me.

" I expressed my readiness to attend him ; while at the time I concealed the shock I felt, on thinking that this young man, who by birth, fortune, and talent, stood high in life, should have lived so un-connected and neglected by persons of his own rank, that there was not a single member of the senate to which he belonged to whom he could or would apply to introduce him in a manner becoming his birth. I saw that he felt the situation, and I fully partook his indignation. * * * *

" After some talk about the Satire, the last sheets of which were in the press, I accompanied Lord Byron to the House. He was received in one of the ante-chambers by some of the officers in attend-ance, with whom he settled respecting the fees he had to pay. One of them went to apprize the Lord Chancellor of his being there, and soon returned for him. There were very few persons in the House. Lord Eldon was going through some ordinary business. When Lord Byron entered, I thought he looked still paler than before ; and he certainly wore a countenance in which mortification was mingled with, but subdued by, indignation. He passed the woolsack without looking round, and advanced to the table where the proper officer was attending to administer the oaths. When he had gone through them, the Chancellor quitted his seat, and went towards him with a smile, putting out his hand warmly to welcome him ; and though I did not catch his words, I saw that he paid him some compliment. This was all thrown away upon Lord Byron, who made a stiff bow, and put the tips of his fingers into the Chancellor's hand.

* * * * * * * *

" The Chancellor did not press a welcome so received, but resumed his seat ; while Lord Byron carelessly seated himself for a few minutes on one of the empty benches to the left of the throne, usually occupied by the Lords in opposition. When, on his joining me, I expressed what I had felt, he said : ' if I had shaken hands heartily, he would have set me down for one of his party, but I will have nothing to do with any of them, on either side ; I have taken my seat, and now I will go abroad.' We returned to St. James's-street, but he did not recover his spirits."

To this account of a ceremonial so trying to the proud spirit engaged in it, and so little likely to abate the bitter feeling of misanthropy now growing upon him, I am enabled to add, from his own report in one of his note-books, the particulars of the short conversation which he held with the Lord Chancellor on the occasion.

"When I came of age, some delays, on account of some birth and marriage certificates from Cornwall, occasioned me not to take my seat for several weeks. When these were over and I had taken the oaths, the Chancellor apologized to me for the delay, observing that these forms were a part of his duty. I begged him to make no apology, and added (as he certainly had shown no violent

hurry), your lordship was exactly like Tom Thumb
(which was then being acted) you did your duty,
and you did no more."—pp. 163-165.

We have extracted this passage because
we anticipate occasion to refer to it hereafter.

Shortly after this event, and the publication of his Satire, Lord Byron left England
for the Levant. Some of his letters from
the East are interesting. Though his judgments of individual men are not worth a
rush, his general observations, and especially his local descriptions, are often valuable, and always amusing. His exploit of
swimming across the Hellespont is com-
memorated in many of his letters, and seems
to have been, of all his achievements, that
which he most rejoiced in.

A gentleman, who is called Mr. Hanson
when remittances are received, and Mr.
H** when they are not (from which we
are left to infer that Mr. Hanson was an
exemplary agent, and Mr. H** a very so
so one), not having sent remittances in
proper time and amount, Lord Byron returned home in 1811. In this year he lost
his mother and his two friends, Wingfield
and Charles Skinner Matthews. Mr. Moore
gives some account of this latter gentleman,
who, it seems, like his noble friend, had
" lost his way in the mazes of scepticism."
This infection, labyrinth, canker, blastment,

light that leads astray, cloud, eclipse, &c.,
&c., &c. so bewilders Mr. Moore with its
mere imagination, that he loses his own
way irretrievably in a labyrinth of figures.
We cannot help him out of it : but requesting
him, as Falstaff did Pistol, to deliver himself
like a man of this world, we will make a
remark or two on the subject that has
made "chaos come again" amongst his
metaphors.

We find, in the letters of Lord Byron to
Mr. Dallas, Mr. Hodgson, and Mr. Gifford,
replies to expostulations and arguments
which those gentlemen had addressed to
him on the subject of his infidelity. Now,
if any of these gentlemen, after his death,
had lamented his infidelity in writing of
him to the public, it would have been
consistent with their conduct towards him
during his life. But in his letters to Mr.
Moore, and in all Mr. Moore's account of
their intercourse, there is not a vestige of
any expostulation or argument on the
subject addressed to him by Mr. Moore.
He therefore comes forward now with a
very ill grace, saying that of Lord Byron,
after his death, which there is no evidence
to shew, and not the least reason to believe,
he ever said to him during his life. We
think it quite of a piece with Mr. Moore's
general system of acquiescence with the

influential in all its forms, to conclude, that having first courted the favour of Lord Byron by silence, at least, on the one hand, he now courts that of the public by talk on the other.

" The staple commodity of the present age in England," says Lord Byron himself somewhere, " is cant : cant moral, cant religious, cant political ; but always cant." How much of this staple commodity there may be in Mr. Moore's lamentations, we shall leave our readers to judge.

Lord Byron's letters to Mr. Moore contain not a syllable of replication to any shadow of an expressed solicitude on the subject of his infidelity. It was assuredly very unkind in Mr. Moore not even to offer his hand to extricate him from " the labyrinth in which he was bewildered ; " " the eclipse in which he was labouring : " more especially as, from the confidence with which Mr. Moore ascribes error to Lord Byron, he must be himself in the possession of something very nearly approaching the infallibility of the Catholic church. A man cannot say unhesitatingly, that another is grossly wrong, unless in the confidence that he himself is perfectly right. We think it, therefore, a very unfriendly measure on his part to have withheld his " short and easy method " from his deistical friend, while he was yet living and able to profit by it ; and now to come forward, shaking his head over him, and pelting his infidel memory with a hailstorm of metaphors, by way of making a good orthodox presentment of himself in the eyes of the religious community. But we do not think that any direct-dealing man, be his religious opinions what they may, can admire the figure which Mr. Moore makes on this occasion.

In all his remarks on this subject, it is most manifest to us that he has no other aim than to say fine and palatable things. To the latter quality let those who relish them speak. To the former we will say a word or two.

" The canker showed itself in the morn and dew of youth." What is a canker in the morn, or a canker in the dew ? He means, we presume, a canker on the rosebud while the morning dew is upon it. Does the canker-worm begin its operations by showing itself ? Does it come with the morning dew ? Neither. There is a false metaphor to start with. " The canker showed itself in the morn and dew of youth," when the effect of such " blastments ; "— here the canker-worm is turned into a " blastment," a blastment coming with morning dew : let Mr. Moore watch his garden twelve months round, and if he find blight or blastment of any description coming with morning dew, let him publish the particulars of what will really be a great phytological and meteorological discovery. Thus is the false metaphor doubly falsified. " When the effect of such blastments is for every reason most fatal, and, in addition to the real misfortune of being an unbeliever at any age, he exhibited the rare and melancholy spectacle of an unbelieving school-boy. The same prematurity of developement, which brought his passions and genius so early into action, enabled him also to anticipate this worst, dreariest result of reason." We have suddenly lost sight of the canker-worm, and now we find that, according to Mr. Moore, error is a result of reason. This is a discovery in logic, worthy of his preceding discoveries in physics.

A little after this we find that " Lord Byron had begun to bewilder himself in the mazes of scepticism," that is, in other words, had set about leading himself astray : a somewhat Irish process : " his mind disported itself most wantonly on the brink of all that is most solemn and awful ; " here he is out of the labyrinth and on the edge of a precipice : but " he never was at any time of his life a confirmed unbeliever." Why, then, what was he ? Mr. Moore does not know. If he was not a confirmed unbeliever, he was to a certain extent a believer; and then the question arises, to what extent? and whether among all the sects into which the Christian world is divided, there was not one which would have received him within its pale?

"Infidelity," says a wiser man than Mr. Moore [Richard Payne Knight, in the preface to the *Progress of Civil Society*, p. xvii], "is a vague term of general accusation, which every hypocrite or fanatic applies to those who appear to be less hypocritical or fanatical than himself. I shall, therefore, take no further notice of it than merely to say, that I have never printed or written any opinion on the subject of Christianity, which I cannot prove to be consistent with the duties of a good subject, a good citizen, and a good man: I might perhaps add, of a good Christian, did I understand the meaning of the term, or know the duties which it implies; but having found, by some little reading and observation, that it has not only had a different signification in every age and country, but in the mouth of almost every individual who has ever used it, I will not pretend to it, till its meaning is so far determined, that I may know whether I can justly pretend to it or not. What is established by law, I respect and obey; but still, as it appears to me to be in many respects extremely different from what was inculcated by the Founder of Christianity and his immediate successors, I am not certain that I can thereby claim the title of a good Christian."

Mr. Moore wishes to persuade the public that he denies the right of private judgment in respect of religious belief. He seems to think that belief can be enforced, and treats disbelief as an offence. He talks of infidelity as " a dangerous state of freedom from moral responsibility." We will cite for his instruction, a passage from the writings of one of the most sober-minded, calm-judging men, and one of the greatest benefactors of his species, that the modern world had produced : a religious man too himself : THOMAS JEFFERSON.

On the subject of religion, Jefferson writes to his young friend Peter Carr :—

Your reason is now mature enough to examine this object. In the first place, divest yourself of all bias in favour of novelty and singularity of opinion. Indulge them in any other subject rather than that of religion. It is too important, and the consequences of error may be too serious. On the other hand, shake off all the fears and servile prejudices, under which weak minds are servilely crouched. Fix reason firmly in her seat, and call to her tribunal every fact, every opinion. Question with boldness even the existence of a God ; because if there be one, he must more approve the homage of reason, than of blindfolded fear. You will naturally examine, first, the religion of your own country.

* * * * * * * *

Do not be frightened from this inquiry by any fear of its consequences. If it ends in a belief that there is no God, you will find incitements to virtue in the comfort and pleasantness you feel in its exercise, and the love of others which it will procure you. If you find reason to believe there is a God, a consciousness that you are acting under his eye, and that he approves you, will be a vast additional incitement; if that there be a future state, the hope of a happy existence in that, increases the appetite to deserve it : if that Jesus was also a God, you will be comforted by a belief of his aid and love. In fine, I repeat, you must lay aside all prejudice on both sides, and neither believe nor reject any thing, because any other person or description of persons, have rejected or believed it. *Your own reason is the only oracle given you by heaven, and you are answerable not for the rightness, but uprightness of the decision.*—*Jefferson's Memoirs*, vol. ii. pp. 216-218.

In another place, Jefferson writes to Dr. Rush :—

I am averse to the communication of my religious tenets to the public ; because it would countenance the presumption of those who have endeavoured to draw them before that tribunal, and to seduce public opinion to erect itself into that inquisition over the rights of conscience, which the laws have so justly proscribed. *It behoves every man who values liberty of conscience for himself, to resist invasions of it in the case of others ;* or their case may, by change of circumstances, become his own. It behoves him too, in his own case, to give no example of concession, *betraying the common right of independent opinion*, by answering questions of faith, which the laws have left between God and himself.—*Jefferson's Memoirs*, vol. iii. p. 515.

Mr. Moore makes his friend " answerable

for the *rightness* of the decision " and as far as in him lies, " invades the liberty of conscience in others," and "betrays the common right of independent opinion."

Of Matthews, Mr. Moore writes thus :—

Of this remarkable young man, Charles Skinner Matthews, I have already had occasion to speak, but the high station which he held in Lord Byron's affection and admiration, may justify a somewhat ampler tribute to his memory.   There have seldom, perhaps, started together in life, so many youths of high promise and hope, as were to be found among the society of which Lord Byron formed a part at Cambridge.   Of some of these, the names have since eminently distinguished themselves in the world, as the mere mention of Mr. Hobhouse, and Mr. William Bankes, is sufficient to testify ; while in the instance of another of this lively circle, Mr. Scrope Davies, the only regret of his friends is, that the social wit of which he is such a master, should, in the memories of his hearers alone, be likely to leave any record of its brilliancy.   Among all these young men of learning and talent (including Byron himself, whose genius was, however, as yet, "an undiscovered world,") the superiority, in almost every department of intellect, seems to have been, by the ready consent of all, awarded to Matthews ; a concurrence of homage, which considering the persons from whom it came, gives such a high notion of the powers of his mind at that period, as renders the thought of what he might have been, if spared, a matter of interesting, though vain and mournful speculation.   To mere mental preeminence, unaccompanied by the kindlier qualities of the heart, such a tribute, however deserved, might not perhaps have been so uncontestedly paid. But young Matthews appears, in spite of some little asperities of temper and manner, which he was already beginning to soften down when snatched away,—to have been one of those rare individuals who, while they command deference, can, at the same time, win regard, and who, as it were, relieve the intense feeling of admiration which they excite, by blending it with love.

To his religious opinions, and their unfortunate coincidence with those of Lord Byron, I have before adverted. Like his noble friend, ardent in the pursuit of truth, he, like him, had unluckily lost his way in seeking her, " the light that led astray " being by both friends mistaken for hers. That in his scepticism he proceeded any further than Lord Byron, or ever suffered his doubting, but still ingenuous, mind to persuade itself into the " incredible creed" of atheism, is I find, (notwithstanding an assertion in a letter of the noble poet to this effect) disproved by the testimony of those among his relations and friends, who are the most ready to admit, and of course lament, his other heresies ; nor should I have felt that I had any right to allude thus to the religious opinions of one, who had never, by promulgating his heterodoxy, brought himself within the jurisdiction of the public, had not the wrong impression, as it appears, given of those opinions, on the authority of Lord Byron, rendered it an act of justice to both friends to remove the imputation.—pp. 277-279.

This passage contains several points worthy of remark : 1st, the highest possible

OF LORD BYRON

panegyric on the moral and intellectual excellence of an individual, whose religious opinions were unfortunately like lord Byron's, though what lord Byron's opinions were, as we have just seen, Mr. Moore does not know. 2nd, that Mr. Moore himself can most clearly distinguish the light of truth from the light that leads astray, though he had the unkindness never to shew his friend a glimpse of the former, basking as he does in its meridian blaze. 3rd, that it is an act of justice to both friends to prove that one had grossly misrepresented the other. 4th, that the friends of Mr. Matthews, *of course*, lament his heresies ; they lament them as a matter of course.—Why, of course ? There is nothing stated respecting them but that they were his friends. They might have agreed or disagreed with him. " Of course," says Mr. Moore, they disagreed with him. Why *of course?* we repeat. There can be but one answer : because it is of course that Mr. Moore should say of those he wishes to flatter just what he thinks the majority of his readers would wish to have said.

We next come to the following fantastical speculation about the poems to Thyrza :—

It was about the time when he was bitterly feeling, and expressing, the blight, which his heart had suffered from a real object of affection,

123

that his poems on the death of an imaginary one, "Thyrza," were written ; nor is it any wonder, when we consider the peculiar circumstances under which these beautiful effusions flowed from his fancy, that of all his strains of pathos, they should be the most touching and most pure. They were, indeed, the essence, the abstract spirit, as it were, of many griefs ;—a confluence of sad thoughts from many sources of sorrow, refined and warmed in their passage through his fancy, and forming thus one deep reservoir of mournful feeling. In retracing the happy hours he had known with the friends now lost, all the ardent tenderness of his youth came back upon him.

His school-sports with the favourites of his boyhood, Wingfield and Tattersall—his summer days with Long, and those evenings of music and romance, which he had dreamed away in the society of his adopted brother, Eddlestone—all these recollections of the young and dead now came to mingle themselves in his mind with the image of her who, though living, was, for him, as much lost as they, and diffused that general feeling of sadness through his soul, which found a vent in these poems. No friendship, however warm, could have inspired sorrow so passionate, as no love, however pure, could have kept passion so chastened. It was the blending of the two affections in his memory and imagination, that thus gave birth to an ideal object combining the best features of both, and drew from him these saddest and tenderest of love-poems, in which we find all the depth and intensity of real feeling touched over with such a light as no reality ever wore.—pp. 302, 303.

This passage presents a curious instance

of confusion of imagery :—A blight is felt :
a blight is expressed : the heart suffers a
blight from an object of affection : the
effusions that flow from the fancy become
touching and pure strains : these again
become an essence, an abstract spirit :
these are changed into a confluence of
streams from many sources : and these,
being refined and warmed, form a reservoir. Effusions, strains, essences, confluent
streams, are all different and discrepant
things ; and though streams may fill a
reservoir, they cannot form one. And, after
all, depth and intensity are touched over
with light. No doubt this is all very pretty,
and sweetly sentimental.

A little further on in the volume is the
following still more fantastical passage :—

In all such speculations and conjectures as to
what might have been, under more favourable
circumstances, his character, it is invariably to be
borne in mind, that his very defects were among
the elements of his greatness, and that it was out
of the struggle between the good and evil principles
of his nature that his mighty genius drew its
strength. A more genial and fostering introduction
into life, while it would doubtless have softened
and disciplined his mind, might have impaired its
vigour ; and the same influence that would have
diffused smoothness and happiness over his life,
might have been fatal to its glory. In a short
poem of his,* which appears to have been produced

* Written beneath the picture of ———.

at Athens (as I find it written on a leaf of the
original MS. of Childe Harold, and dated "Athens,
1811 ") there are two lines which, though hardly
intelligible as connected with the rest of the poem,
may, taken separately, be interpreted as implying
a sort of prophetic consciousness that it was out
of the wreck and ruin of all his hopes the immortality of his name was to arise :—

> Dear object of defeated care,
>   Though now of love and thee bereft,
> To reconcile me with despair,
>   Thine image and my tears are left.
> 'Tis said with sorrow Time can cope,
>   But this I feel can ne'er be true ;
> *For, by the death-blow of my hope,*
>   *My memory immortal grew !*—p. 323.

This is really curious. Here is a gentleman dabbling all his life in poetry and
criticism, and still incapable of seizing a
meaning so obvious, that it is most marvellous how any one could miss it. *By the
death-blow of my hope—the blow that deprived
me of the original of this picture—my memory
grew immortal :—my remembrance of her
became so strong that it shews not the slightest
symptom of decay ; now, when after a lapse
of time I look at her picture, the painful
feelings of memory are as vivid as on the day
I lost her. This proves that " Time cannot
cope with sorrow."* Mr. Moore, however,
expounds the passage thus :—

By the death-blow of my hope in the loss

of this object, I laid the foundation of an immortal memory for myself: of my being immortally remembered. This proves that " Time cannot cope with sorrow." A most contorted interpretation, and a most exemplary *non sequitur.*

This specimen of Mr. Moore's method of understanding his friend's poetry speaks very ill for the sort of selection he has been likely to make from his remains.

The publication of Childe Harold—the non-publication of Hints from Horace, an imitation of the Art of Poetry—the manner in which Mr. Moore *scraped acquaintance* with Lord Byron (a phrase which we use designedly, because we find it so felicitously illustrated in this very curious procedure)— the history of Lord Byron's life at Newstead and in London—the publication of the Giaour, Bride of Abydos, and Corsair—his marriage with Miss Milbanke, the daughter of Sir Ralph Noel Milbanke, on the 2nd of January, 1815—his share in the management of Drury Lane Theatre—his separation from his wife in January, 1816—and his final departure from England on the 25th of April, 1816, are the principal events recorded in the remainder of this volume. No new light, as we have said, is thrown upon anything about which the public curiosity had been strongly excited : but there is a great deal of detail about minute corrections of the press, about alterations and re-alterations in that very important theatrical state-paper, the Address for the opening of Drury Lane Theatre ; a great deal of gossip about all sorts of people, much that should not have been published, and more that is not worth publishing ; some peeps behind the curtain of the Edinburgh Review, for which the parties principally implicated in that shallow and dishonest publication will scarcely thank the exhibitor ; a few things said, and many hinted, about Lord Byron's amours ; a few touches on the politics of Lord Byron and his biographer ; and a speculation by Mr. Moore about the usual unhappiness of intellectual persons in marriage.

The gossip about individuals is given with one or two peculiarities worthy of note. An initial is given in one page which sets the reader guessing ; a name is given in another which saves him the trouble ; or circumstances are so detailed as to point to the name unerringly. In one page we find " Bold W." going to be thrown out of a window ; in another we find a friendly mention of " Bold Webster." A gentleman who sometimes neglects to send remittances is always Mr. H. : a gentleman who sometimes sends them is always Mr. Hanson.

OF LORD BYRON

In one place lord Byron sees S***'s mistress and her mother in an opposite box at the theatre; and who S***'s mistress was is indicated a dozen lines lower :—

Went to my box at Covent-Garden to-night; and my delicacy felt a little shocked at seeing S***'s mistress (who, to my certain knowledge, was actually educated from her birth for her profession) sitting with her mother, " a three-piled b——d, b——d-major to the army," in a private box opposite. I felt rather indignant; but, casting my eyes round the house, in the next box to me, and the next, and the next, were the most distinguished old and young Babylonians of quality—so I burst out a laughing. It was really odd; lady ** divorced—lady **, and her daughter, lady **, both divorceable—Mrs. **, in the next, the like, and still nearer ******! What an assemblage to me, who know all their histories. It was as if the house had been divided between your public and your understood courtesans; but the intriguantes much outnumbered the regular mercenaries. On the other side were only Pauline and her mother, and, next box to her, three of inferior note. Now, where lay the difference between her and her mamma, and lady ** and daughter? except that the two last may enter Carleton and any other house, and the two first are limited to the opera and b—— house. How I do delight in observing life as it really is!—and myself, after all, the worst of any. But, no matter —I must avoid egotism, which, just now, would be no vanity.—p. 470.

Now as there were only one mother and

daughter opposite, and as they were Pauline
and her mother, S***'s mistress was Pauline. Who S *** was, is therefore as clear as
if his name had been printed. The volume
abounds with these mockeries of reserve.

In other cases, and there is an instance
in the last-cited passage, asterisks only are
given, which communicate nothing. The
following is another instance :—

To-morrow there is a party of purple at the
" blue " Miss * * *'s. Shall I go ? Um !—I don't
much affect your blue-bottles ; but one ought to
be civil. There will be (" I guess now," as the
Americans say), the Staëls and Mackintoshes—
good—the * * *s and * * *s—not so good—the
* * *s, &c., &c.—good for nothing. Perhaps that
blue-winged Kashmirian butterfly of book-learn-
ing, lady * * *, will be there. I hope so ; it is a
pleasure to look upon that most beautiful of
faces.—p. 458.

What can be the possible use of printing
such passages ? Sometimes we have things
in this way :

P.S. Oh ! the anecdote ! * * * * * * * * * * * *
* * * *.—p. 558.

The extreme folly of such a specimen of
publication is really sufficiently ludicrous
to amount to an excellent jest. Oh ! the
anecdote, indeed ! This should stand at
the head of anecdotes of book-making, if
ever Sholto and Reuben Percy take them
in hand.

OF LORD BYRON

We shall cite two passages which throw a little light on the politics of Lord Byron, and still more on those of his biographer :—

It was at this time that Lord Byron became acquainted (and, I regret to have to add, partly through my means) with Mr. Leigh Hunt, the editor of the well-known weekly journal, the Examiner. This gentleman I had myself formed an acquaintance with in the year 1811, and, in common with a large portion of the public, entertained a sincere admiration of his talents and courage as a journalist. The interest I took in him personally had been recently much increased by the manly spirit which he had displayed throughout a prosecution instituted against himself and his brother, for a libel that had appeared in their paper on the Prince Regent, and in consequence of which they were both sentenced to imprisonment for two years. It will be recollected that there existed among the Whig party, at this period, a strong feeling of indignation at the late defection from themselves and their principles of the illustrious personage, who had been so long looked up to as the friend and patron of both. Being myself, at the time, warmly,—perhaps, intemperately,—under the influence of this feeling, I regarded the fate of Mr. Hunt with more than common interest, and, immediately on my arrival in town, paid him a visit in his prison. On mentioning the circumstance, soon after, to Lord Byron, and describing my surprise at the sort of luxurious comforts with which I had found the wit in the dungeon surrounded,—his trellised flower-garden without, and his books, busts, pictures, and piano-forte within,—the noble poet, whose political views of the case coincided entirely with my own, expressed a strong wish to pay a similar tribute of respect to Mr. Hunt, and accordingly, a day or two after, we proceeded for that purpose to the prison. The introduction which then took place was soon followed by a request from Mr. Hunt that we would dine with him, and the noble poet having good-naturedly accepted the invitation, the Cold Bath Fields prison had, in the month of June, 1813, the honour of receiving Lord Byron, as a guest, within its walls.—pp. 400, 401.

It was, we believe, in Horsemonger-Lane gaol, and not in that of Cold-Bath-Fields, that Mr. Leigh Hunt was imprisoned. Mr. Moore is too genteel to know one gaol from another. But it appears that Mr. Moore's patriotic sympathy was aroused on this occasion, not by the specific case of oppression, but by its coincidence with the Prince Regent's defection from the Whigs. If the Whigs had been in place, Mr. Hunt, as a part of the arrangement, might have been very properly in gaol. If Mr. Moore should say, the Whigs would not have sent him there, let our present Whig attorney-general answer him for us. It is always, *quo, non quomodo*, with Mr. Moore. His movement to the state prison was not a patriotic, nor a philosophic, nor a philanthropic, movement. It was a Whig movement. He has thought proper to apologise for it, and we have translated his apology into plain English.

The second passage is this :—

On the second of June, in presenting a petition to the House of Lords, he made his third and last appearance as an orator, in that assembly. In his way home from the House that day, he called, I remember, at my lodgings, and found me dressing in a very great hurry for dinner. He was, I recollect, in a state of most humourous exaltation after his display, and, while I hastily went on with my task in the dressing-room, continued to walk up and down the adjoining chamber, spouting forth for me, in a sort of mock-heroic voice, detached sentences of the speech he had just been delivering. "I told them," he said, "that it was a most flagrant violation of the constitution—that, if such things were permitted, there was an end of English freedom, and that—" "But what is this dreadful grievance?" I asked, interrupting him in his eloquence. "The grievance?" he repeated, pausing as if to consider—"Oh, that I forget." * It is impossible, of course, to convey an idea of the dramatic humour with which he gave effect to these words, but his look and manner on such occasions were irresistibly comic, and it was, indeed, rather in such turns of fun and oddity than in any more elaborate exhibition of wit that the pleasantry of his conversation existed.—p. 402.

A man in earnest would not have spoken in parliament about a grievance, without believing that the thing spoken of was a

* This speech was on presenting a Petition from Major Cartwright.

grievance. A man in earnest would not, having spoken of a public grievance in parliament, have afterwards professed to forget what the grievance was. A man, whether in earnest or not himself, would not, in speaking to a man whom he believed to be in earnest, have treated his own advocacy of public grievances as a jest. Lord Byron would not have spoken in this strain to Mr. Shelley. And a man, whose own political opinions were anything but a farce, would not record an anecdote, so discreditable to both parties, as a mere piece of pleasantry, and nothing more.

The only political affairs about which Lord Byron seems to have felt any real and earnest interest, within the period here recorded, were those of Napoleon. He concluded a journal which he had kept for some time, and from which Mr. Moore has given ample extracts, in these words :—

April 19*th*, 1814.—There is ice at both poles, north and south—all extremes are the same—misery belongs to the highest and the lowest only, —to the emperor and the beggar, when unsixpenced and unthroned. There is, to be sure, a damned insipid medium—an equinoctial line—no one knows where, except upon maps and measurement.

> And all our yesterdays have lighted fools
> The way to dusty death.

I will keep no further journal of that same

hesternal torch-light ; and, to prevent me from returning, like a dog, to the vomit of memory, I tear out the remaining leaves of this volume, and write in Ipecacuanha,—that the Bourbons are restored ! ! ! Hang up philosophy. To be sure, I have long despised myself and man, but I never spat in the face of my species before—" O fool ! I shall go mad."—pp. 513, 514.

Lord Byron wished to serve Mr. Coleridge. He persuaded Mr. Murray to publish Christabel. He tried, through Mr. Moore, to persuade Mr. Jeffrey to review it favorably in the Edinburgh Review. But Mr. Jeffrey knew better than to compromise the character of his publication, by giving a true and just account of any literary work, even to please his new friend Lord Byron. This most beautiful little poem was therefore consigned to the hands of that one of Mr. Jeffrey's coadjutors, who combined the most profound ignorance, and the grossest obtuseness of intellect, with the most rancorous malignity, and the most unblushing literary dishonesty. The Edinburgh Review has furnished many specimens of all these qualities : but in this article on Coleridge's Christabel, they were all combined in the most striking degree. Every thing was garbled, falsified, distorted, misrepresented. The Review has not destroyed Mr. Coleridge's poetical fame : that was, and is, beyond its reach : but it destroyed his chance of popularity by extinguishing curiosity towards his poem at the time of its publication, at a time especially, when to have assisted him to that share of public attention which he has always merited as a poet, would, though nothing more than an act of justice, have had the effect of an act of generosity. Of course, neither was to be expected from the Edinburgh Review.

We must say a word or two more about Mr. Moore's figures. The following is a curious specimen :—

There is a healthfulness in the moral feeling so unaffectedly expressed in this letter, which seems to answer for a heart sound at the core, however passion might have scorched it.—pp. 231, 232.

What is the relation between scorching and a sound core ? Half the metaphor is from a rotten apple, and half from a roasted one.

Mr. Moore never produces a figure that will stand the test of analysis. His figures are all made up of disparates and non-existences. We do not know in all his writings, a single exception to this rule. The more his images are examined, the more unreal and incoherent they appear. Throughout the present work, he seems often to aim at simplicity : a good aim, but not easily attainable by one who has so long indulged in the rhetoric of false sentiment. He writes figures in spite of himself, and the only result of his endeavour at a simple and natural style is, that, by not fixing his attention on any predominant image, he makes his figurative language more than ever chaotic and caleidoscopical. We will give one example taken at random.

When we look back to the *unbridled career*, of which his marriage was meant to be the *goal*,—to the *rapid and restless course* in which his life had *run along*, like a *burning train*, through a *series* of wanderings, adventures, successes, and passions, the *fever* of all which was still upon him, when, with the same *headlong* recklessness, he *rushed* into this marriage—it can but little surprise us, that in the space of one short year, he should not have been able to recover all at once from his *bewilderment*, or to *settle down* into that tame *level* of conduct which the officious spies of his privacy required. As well might it be expected that a *steed* like his own Mazeppa's, should stand still, when reined, without *chafing* or *champing the bit.*—pp. 649, 650.

What a chaos with horses, goals, fire-trains, fevers, levels, and bewilderments ! And this is about the ordinary style of the work.

The volume contains many allusions to persons who have never obtruded themselves on public notice, and whose names and circumstances ought not to have been dragged before the world. It is, on the whole, a production little instructive to the reader, little creditable to the author, little honorable to its subject : a speculation, perhaps a profitable one, on the public appetite for gossip, backed by a systematical deference to every widely-diffused prejudice, and to every doctrine and opinion which the influential classes of readers desire to be popular. And amongst these classes, the influential in the press are by no means forgotten. The " great talents " of Mr. Thomas Barnes, of the Times ; the " ingenious and remarkable " Mr. Hogg, of Blackwood's Magazine ; the " most gifted of critics," Mr. Jeffrey, and so forth, receive, and of course repay, the meed of just and discriminating praise.

> Discedo Alcæus puncto illius.   Ille meo quis ?
> Quis, nisi Callimachus ?

We shall, for the reasons assigned in the commencement of this article, postpone our observations on the personal character of Lord Byron, and on some other matters, till we have gone through the second volume. Amongst the other matters, we include the whole of his amours, and the illustrations of the morality of the higher classes in this country, which his adventures and correspondence afford.

We have given very fair specimens of the

matter and manner of the volume before us, and an outline of its contents, with such remarks as were imperiously demanded from us by our sense of the moral duty of exhibiting to our readers the real scope and purpose of a series of shallow sophisms and false assumptions, wrapped up in bundles of metaphors, put forth with a specious semblance of reason and liberality, and directed to the single end of upholding all abuses and delusions by which the aristocracy profit. In the second volume, Mr. Moore will be on more perilous ground. To do justice to his friends who are gone, and to please those among the living, whose favor he most studiously courts in his writings, must be, in the treatment of that period which his second volume will embrace, impossible. He will endeavour to do both, after his fashion : and we think we can pretty accurately anticipate the result.

MEMOIRS OF THOMAS JEFFERSON

JEFFERSON'S MEMOIRS *

THIS is one of the most important publi-
cations ever presented to the world.   In the
catalogue of the benefactors of mankind,
few deserve so high a station as Thomas
Jefferson.   As the author of the Declaration
of Independence, and as one of the principal
movers of the North American Revolution,
his claims on the gratitude and admiration
of posterity are divided with Washington,
Franklin, and others, so excellent in their
respective spheres, that it might be difficult,
and would certainly be invidious, to say
which was the most wise, the most disinterested, the most persevering in the perilous,
and, at times, almost hopeless path, of
arduous and self-devoting duty.   But American liberty was destined to a second,
scarcely less perilous, though less conspicuous struggle ; a struggle in which

* *Memoirs, Correspondence, and Private Papers of
Thomas Jefferson, late President of the United States.*
Now first published from the original Manuscripts.
Edited by Thomas Jefferson Randolph.   4 vols.   1829.
Colburn and Bentley.

143

there were no wounds, and guns, and drums, to fix the attention of Europe ; but one in which the best energies of feeling and thought were necessary to save the United States from the effects of the vague terrors, with which many of their well-meaning citizens were inspired by the excesses of the French Revolution ; and which, being worked on with all the arts of persuasion, by a large and influential party, in possession, for a time, of the government, who saw, or professed to see, no safety or permanence for political institutions, but in a government of corrupt influence, had very nearly thrown the young republic into the arms of something very like our own happy aristocratical constitution. The good sense of the bulk of the people preserved them from this blessing ; but the main glory of the signal victory over the domestic enemy belongs, on this occasion, undividedly to Jefferson.

The doctrines of anarchy and confusion, as they were called here ; the doctrines against which, under the watchword of " social order " and shouts " for God and the King," we fired away in thirty years nearly three thousand millions of money in gunpowder, including the cost of the machinery, animate and inanimate, by which the said gunpowder was borne over land

and sea for the final purposes of ignition, rarefaction, expansion, and explosion ; the doctrines of the right of the possessors of life and property to choose for themselves the legislators who dispose of that life and property ; of the right of the governed to discuss fully and freely, in censure as in praise, the public measures of their rulers, and the principles of their political and religious institutions ; these doctrines were brought at once and efficiently into action on the accession of Jefferson to the Presidency, and " the dissolution of social order," which our fire-and-sword logicians so long and confidently preached as the infallible consequence of the establishment of such maxims of government, consisted in the total abolition of internal taxes, in the rapid extinction of national debt, in the preservation of peace with all the world, in the bloodless acquisition of the important territory of Louisiana, and the complete possession of the Mississippi, in the efficient protection and ample reward of domestic industry, and in the establishment, beyond the reach of injury from the combined despotisms of the earth, of an asylum for the oppressed and unfortunate of all nations.

Mr. Randolph, the editor of these volumes, has done little more than publish Jefferson's papers as he found them ; not supplying any connecting link, nor even the date of Jefferson's death. We do not much object to this, because to impose on an executor the necessity of being an author, might be the cause of depriving the world of many valuable remains. All that can fairly be required from any one, to whom the papers of another are consigned in trust for the public, is an early and ungarbled publication of all that do not in any way trespass on the privacy of the living. To require more would be to require what must be sometimes difficult, sometimes impossible, and always a source of delay. The publication before us carries with it intrinsic evidence of being an honest and complete publication of all papers of public interest. The sanctity of private life is respected throughout. It abounds with materials of knowledge and reflection to the historian, the philosopher, the patriot, the philanthropist; with examples of high encouragement to all who make it their study to ameliorate the condition of their fellow-men ; examples of the noblest objects of public good, pursued through good and evil fortune, through good and evil report, with undeviating and inflexible rectitude.

The first paper in the collection is a memoir of himself, which Jefferson began in 1821, at the age of seventy-seven, but which he did not bring down later than the 21st of March, 1790. The first settler of the family appears to have been from the vicinity of Snowdon, a fact which may be recorded to the honour of Wales, though Jefferson is not a Cymric name. This must have been at a very early period of the American settlements. Jefferson's father was the first of the family who occupied the lands which Jefferson inherited, called Shadwell, in Virginia.

Jefferson himself was born in 1743 or 1744 : he always concealed his birth-day, that it might not be publicly celebrated. He saw in such celebrations a germ of aristocratical distinctions ; and discouraged them, to the extent of his power, both by precept and example. He received a tolerably good education, which he finished at William and Mary College in 1762. He then became a student of law, and in 1767 was inducted to the bar, at which he continued till the Revolution.

In 1769, he became a member of the Virginia Legislature. In 1772, he married Mrs. Bathurst Skelton, a widow of twenty-three. In 1774, when the bill had passed in the English Parliament for shutting up the Port of Boston on the 1st of June, he was one of the young members of the Virginia Legislature, who (as always happens in great emergencies) took the lead out of the hands of the old ones, and who carried a Resolution for fixing on the 1st of June as "a day of fasting, humiliation, and prayer, to implore Heaven to avert from us the evils of civil war, to inspire us with firmness in support of our rights, and to turn the hearts of the King and Parliament to moderation and justice." The effect of this measure on the minds of the people appears to have been very great. Jefferson was one of the first delegates to the Convention, which was then elected for choosing delegates to a general Congress of the Colonies, which met for the first time, at Philadelphia, on the 5th of September, 1774. He was himself one of the delegates to the second Congress, in which he took his seat on the 21st of June, 1775.

On the 7th of June, 1776, the delegates from Virginia (Jefferson being one), in obedience to instructions from their constituents, proposed to Congress to declare the Colonies independent of Great Britain. The proposal was adopted. Jefferson drew up the Declaration, which, after three days of discussion, was carried with some alterations, and signed by every member present, except one. It affords a remarkable proof of the general good sense and judgment of the members of this Congress, that every change which was sanctioned in this most important of documents was a change for the better.

On the 1st of June, 1779, Jefferson, was appointed governor of the Commonwealth of Virginia. At the end of the second year he resigned his administration, from a persuasion that under the pressure of invasion the civil and military power should be united in a military commander : General Nelson was appointed to succeed him. About this time he appears to have been marked out as an especial object of vengeance by Lord Cornwallis.

Lord Cornwallis then proceeded to the Point of Fork, and encamped his army from thence all along the main James River, to a seat of mine, called Elk-hill, opposite to Elk Island, and a little below the mouth of the Byrd Creek. [You will see all these places exactly laid down in the map annexed to my notes on Virginia, printed by Stockdale.] He remained in this position ten days, his own head-quarters being in my house at that place. I had time to remove most of the effects out of the house. He destroyed all my growing crops of corn and tobacco ; he burnt all my barns, containing the same articles of the last year, having first taken what corn he wanted ; he used, as was to be expected, all my stock of cattle, sheep, and hogs, for the sustenance of his army, and carried off all the horses capable of service ; of those too young for service he cut the throats ; and he burned all the fences on the plantation, so as to

leave it an absolute waste. He carried off also
about thirty slaves. Had this been to give them
freedom he would have done right; but it was to
consign them to inevitable death, from the small
pox and putrid fever then raging in his camp.
This I knew afterwards to be the fate of twenty-
seven of them : I never had news of the remaining
three, but presumed they shared the same fate.
When I say that Lord Cornwallis did all this, I do
not mean that he carried about the torch in his
own hands, but that it was all done under his
eye ; the situation of the house in which he
was, commanding a view of every part of the
plantation, so that he must have seen every fire.
I relate these things on my own knowledge, in a
great degree ; as I was on the ground soon after
he left it. He treated the rest of the neighbourhood
somewhat in the same style, but not with that
spirit of total extermination with which he seemed
to rage over my possessions. Wherever he went
the dwelling-houses were plundered of every thing
which could be carried off. Lord Cornwallis's
character in England would forbid the belief that
he shared in the plunder ; but that his table was
served with the plate thus pillaged from private
houses can be proved by many hundred eye-
witnesses.—Vol. ii. p. 336.

On the 6th of June, 1783, he was appointed by the Legislature of Virginia a
delegate to Congress, which was then
sitting at Annapolis ; and was one of the
delegates who ratified the definitive treaty of
peace which was signed at Paris on the 3rd
of September, 1783, and ratified in Congress,

without a dissenting voice, on the 14th of
January, 1784.

On the 7th of May following, he was
appointed a minister plenipotentiary, in
addition to Mr. Adams and Dr. Franklin,
for negociating treaties of commerce with
foreign nations. He arrived at Paris in
August, accompanied by Dr. Franklin from
Passy, and being shortly afterwards joined
by Mr. Adams from the Hague. He remained in Europe till October, 1789, and
witnessed the origin of the French Revolution, respecting which his correspondence
gives much interesting and authentic detail,
and much valuable opinion ; and his observations are recapitulated in his unfinished
Memoir. In this Memoir, begun, be it
remembered, in 1821, he winds up this
portion of his subject thus :—

Here I discontinue my relation of the French
Revolution. The minuteness with which I have
so far given its details, is disproportioned to the
general scale of my narrative. But I have thought
it justified, by the interest which the whole world
must take in this Revolution. As yet we are but
in the first chapter of its history. The appeal to
the rights of man, which had been made in the
United States, was taken up by France, first of the
European nations. From her the spirit has spread
over those of the South. The tyrants of the North
have allied indeed against it, but it is irresistible.
Their opposition will only multiply its millions of

human victims ; their own satellites will catch it, and the condition of man through the civilized world, will be finally and greatly ameliorated. This is a wonderful instance of great events from small causes. So inscrutable is the arrangement of causes and consequences in this world, that a two-penny duty on tea, unjustly imposed, in a sequestered part of it, changes the condition of all its inhabitants.—Vol. i. p. 90.

Jefferson returned to America at the end of 1789, on a temporary leave of absence ; but he had scarcely landed in America, when he received from General Washington (then President) the appointment of Secretary of State, which prevented his intended return to Paris. Much as the cessation of his invaluable testimony to the progressive events of the French Revolution is to be lamented, it is still evident that his proper sphere of action was in America. His residence in Europe had served, by the contrasts which were continually before his eyes in the condition of the people, to confirm him in the love of the young institutions of his own country ; and his presence in America was essential to the existence of those institutions. Hamilton, the Secretary of the Treasury, a staunch federalist, carried through many measures which Jefferson cordially disapproved ; amongst others a tax on home-distilled spirits, which laid the foundation of an Excise, produced dissatisfaction and open resistance, and had nearly broken up the Union. Hamilton's object was, to strengthen the hands of the general government, to give it sufficient strength to do right in spite of the people.

At a cabinet dinner in April, 1791, Adams having said of the British Constitution, " Purge that Constitution of its corruption, and give to its popular branch equality of representation, and it would be the most perfect Constitution ever devised by the wit of man ; " Hamilton paused, and said, " Purge it of its corruption, and give to its popular branch equality of representation, and it would become an impracticable government : as it stands at present, with all its supposed defects, it is the most perfect government which ever existed." " And this," says Jefferson, " was assuredly the exact line which separated the political creed of these two gentlemen. Adams was for two hereditary branches and an honest elective one ; Hamilton for an hereditary king, with a House of Lords and Commons corrupted to his will, and standing between him and the people."—Vol. iv. p. 461.

Certainly of all the men that ever set about establishing a " firm of Corrupter-General and Company " on the other side of the Atlantic, Hamilton was one of the most zealous and efficient. Proceeding on the principle, that man could be governed by one of two motives only, force or sinister interest, and that force in the United States was out of the question, he adapted his financial schemes to the securing of a majority in Congress. The act for paying off at par the certificates of debt given in the latter part of the Revolution, was one of these schemes. Many of these certificates had been sold by the original holders at two shillings in the pound. As soon as the passing of the act was foreseen by Hamilton and his friends, expresses were sent all over the Union to purchase up the certificates, before the holders, in the more distant places especially, could possibly know that Congress had provided for their redemption at par. " Immense sums were thus filched from the poor and ignorant, and fortunes accumulated by those who had themselves been poor enough before. Men thus enriched by the dexterity of a leader, would follow of course the chief who was leading them to fortune, and become the zealous instruments of his enterprises."

Another of Hamilton's fiscal manœuvres was the Assumption. The debts contracted, and the money expended, by the separate States during the war, was pretended to have been for general purposes; the amount, not being ascertainable, was guessed to be twenty millions; the fair distribution of these twenty millions among the several States was the subject of another guess; and those who, in the midst of all this guessing, guessed that the partisans of the Treasury got the largest share of the spoil, were not the least correct guessers on the occasion.

Hamilton did not, and could not, corrupt a majority of the Congress ; but his purchased partizans turned the balance which the honest men of both parties had held nearly in equipose. His next scheme was the Bank of the United States at Philadelphia, which, till the seat of government was removed to Washington, gave the Treasury great and permanent influence in the appointment and re-appointment of members of both Houses as Directors.

General Washington did not understand these devices, and Jefferson, to whom they were abhorrent, determined to withdraw from all political connection with their authors and supporters. He would allow of no compromise with the first steps of despotism ; he would give the General Government no power which the State Government could exercise ; he would have the General Government strong to execute the national will, and impotent to coerce it ; he would furnish it with no means of corruption, or of intimidation, or of delusion. He was less dismayed by the temporary excesses of the French Revolution, than fixed in his abhorrence of the inflictions of

unrestrained power which had preceded and
caused it.   Washington vainly endeavoured
to reconcile Jefferson and Hamilton, to induce them to draw together for the advance-
ment of public business.   It was impossible;
their principles were wide as the poles
asunder.   Jefferson resigned his office on
the 31st of December, 1793.

" This gentleman," says the biographer of
General Washington, " withdrew from his
political station at a moment when he stood
particularly high in the esteem of his
countrymen.   His fixed opposition to the
financial schemes which had been proposed
by the Secretary of the Treasury, and
approved by the legislative and executive
departments of the government ; his ardent
and undisguised attachment to the revolu-
tionary party in France ; the dispositions
which he was declared to possess in regard
to Great Britain, and the popularity of his
opinions respecting the constitution of the
United States, had devoted to him that
immense party, whose sentiments were
supposed to comport with his, on most or
all of these interesting subjects.

" To the opposite party he had of course
become particularly unacceptable ; but the
publication of his correspondence with M.
Genet, dissipated much of the prejudice
which had been excited against him.   He

had in that correspondence maintained, with great ability, the opinions embraced by the federalists on those points of difference which had arisen between the two republics, and which, having become universally the subjects of discussion, had in some measure displaced those topics on which parties had previously divided. The partiality for France that was conspicuous through the whole of it, detracted nothing from its merit in the opinion of the friends of the administration, because, however decided might be their determination to support their own government in a controversy with any nation whatever, they felt all the partialities for that republic which the correspondence expressed. The hostility of his enemies therefore was, for a time, considerably lessened, without a corresponding diminution of the attachment of his friends. In office it would have been impracticable long to preserve these dispositions ; and it would have been difficult to maintain that ascendancy which he held over the minds of those who had supported, and probably would continue to support, every pretension of the French republic, without departing from principles and measures which he had openly and ably defended."—See Marshall's *Life of Washington*, Vol. v. p. 406.

Jefferson resided in retirement at his seat, Monticello, on his paternal estate in Virginia, from the beginning of 1794, till the Spring of 1797, when John Adams was elected President and Jefferson Vice-President, for four years, from the 4th of March. We may remind our readers incidentally, that the first President and Vice-President of the United States were General Washington and John Adams, who were elected for four years, from the 4th of March, 1789, and re-elected for four years, from the 4th of March, 1793.

The office of Vice-President did not impose much public duty on its holder, and consequently did not much interrupt the domestic retirement of Jefferson, who, differing decidedly from the President, on almost all essential points of politics, abstained as much as possible from interference in the business of government.

The federalists (as the advocates for a strong General Government were called), made great strides towards Anglicising the American constitution during the Presidency of Adams. Amongst other blessings, they established a Libel-law, making all printed matter that did not please them, seditious and blasphemous. They were for a strong hand over every thing, the press included. It is futile to say of them, as some of their advocates do, that they were as true republicans as their opponents, and had no intention to introduce either monarchy or aristocracy. It is sufficient for us to be convinced that the tendency of their measures was to introduce one or both of them. If they had brought about such a result, it would have been no satisfaction to the friends of liberty to be assured, that the authors of the mischief were men of honesty and honour, who had gone further than they intended. Hell is paved with good intentions ; but heaven forbid that any portion of the pavement should be made of the liberties of America.

Now came the Presidential elections of 1800. The republicans, throughout the States, felt the necessity of arousing themselves to restore and preserve the purity of their constitution. The federalists, on the other hand, redoubled their exertions to maintain the ground they had gained, and the excesses committed by the French people on breaking the chains of centuries, had terrified many well-meaning persons into the federal ranks. The comparative strength of the parties was doubtful ; and had not the high moral and political character of Jefferson presented itself as a rallying point for the republicans, the triumph of the federalists would have been secure. It is impossible to read the events and opinions of that time, without perceiving that never were the best interests of mankind in more imminent danger. This election was not like one of ours, a mere contest of nick-names : it was really and truly a contest for civil and religious liberty, against the principles of despotism.

The federal candidates for the Presidency and Vice-Presidency were Adams and Pinckney ; the republican candidates were Jefferson and Burr.

At that time (for the law has since been altered) the State electors did not vote for President and Vice-President distinctly, but the highest number of votes determined the President, and the next highest number the Vice-President. The intention of the republicans was to have Jefferson President, and Burr Vice-President ; but the votes for them were equal : the numbers being, Jefferson 73 ; Burr 73 ; Adams 65 ; Pinckney 64. The choice between the two highest candidates devolved on Congress, and it became the object of the federalists to defeat the intention of the republicans, by making Burr President. The law required that the successful candidate should have, not merely a majority in Congress, but a majority of all the States. There were then sixteen States in the Union. Two of these neutralised their votes by

taking opposite sides. Eight voted for
Jefferson, six for Burr. Nine votes were
required for a majority of the States. The
Congress voted thirty-five times on this
question. At length some of the less
factious of the federalists became alarmed,
and the first votes were ten for Jefferson,
and four for Burr.

If the original opposition had been perse-
vered in, there would have been no election,
and the federalists had it in contemplation
to nominate a President of the Senate *pro
tempore* by what, they said, would be only
a stretch of the constitution. The republican party met this menace by declaring
their intention, in the event of the constitution being so stretched, to call a convention
for re-organising and amending the government. This was and is the constitutional
remedy for abuses of power in the American
Legislature.

"If they could have been permitted," says
Jefferson to Monroe, "to pass a law for putting the
government into the hands of an officer, they would
certainly have prevented an election. But we
thought it best to declare, openly and firmly, one
and all, that the day such an act passed, the middle
States would arm, and that no such usurpation,
even for a single day, should be submitted to.

"This first shook them, and they were completely
alarmed at the resource for which we declared ; to
wit, a convention to re-organise the government,

and to amend it. The very word convention gives them the horrors, as in the present democratical spirit of America, they fear they should lose some of the favourite morsels of the constitution. Many attempts have been made to obtain terms and promises from me. I have declared to them unequivocally, that I would not receive the government on capitulation—that I would not go into it with my hands tied."—Vol. iii. p. 460.

In another place Jefferson says :—

When the election between Burr and myself was kept in suspense by the federalists, and they were meditating to place the President of the Senate at the head of the government, I called on Mr. Adams, with a view to have this desperate measure prevented by his negative. He grew warm in an instant, and said, with a vehemence he had not used towards me before, " Sir, the event of the election is within your own power. You have only to say you will do justice to the public creditors, maintain the navy, and not disturb those holding offices, and the government will instantly be put into your hands. We know it is the wish of the people it should be so." " Mr. Adams," said I, " I know not what part of my conduct in either public or private life, can have authorised a doubt of my fidelity to the public engagements. I say, however, I will not come into the government by capitulation ; I will not enter on it but in perfect freedom to follow the dictates of my own judgment."—Vol. iv. p. 161.

When the election was determined in Jefferson's favour he expressed himself as follows, to John Dickinson :—

THOMAS JEFFERSON

The storm through which we have passed has been tremendous indeed. The tough sides of our argosie have been thoroughly tried : her strength has stood the waves into which she was steered, with a view to sink her. We shall put her on her republican tack, and she will now shew, by the beauty of her motion, the skill of her builders. Figure to yourself apart, our fellow citizens have been led hood-winked from their principles, by a most extraordinary combination of circumstances. But the band is removed, and they now see for themselves. I hope to see shortly a perfect consolidation, to effect which, nothing shall be spared on my part, short of the abandonment of the principles of our revolution. A just and solid republican government maintained here, will be a standing monument and example for the aim and imitation of the people of other countries ; and I join with you in the hope and belief that they will see, from our example, that a free government is of all others the most energetic ; that the inquiry which has been excited among the mass of mankind by our revolution, and its consequences, will ameliorate the condition of man over a great portion of the globe. What a satisfaction have we in the contemplation of the benevolent effects of our efforts, compared with those of the leaders on the other side, who have discountenanced all advances in science as dangerous innovations, have endeavoured to render philosophy and republicanism terms of reproach, to persuade us that man cannot be governed but by the rod, &c. I shall have the happiness of living and dying in the contrary hope. —Vol. iii. p. 462.

Jefferson, in one of his subsequent letters,

calls the result of this first contest the Revolution of 1800 :—

It was as real a revolution in the principles of our government as that of 1776 was in its form ; not effected, indeed, by the sword, as that, but by the rational and peaceable instrument of reform— the suffrages of the people. The nation declared its will by dismissing functionaries of one principle and electing those of another, in the two branches, executive and legislative, submitted to their election.—Vol. iv. p. 324.

The principles then established have been the governing principles from that time to the present. At Jefferson's second election in 1804, he received 162 votes against 14 ; and it is a most remarkable circumstance, and one which speaks volumes in favour of the elective system and the manner of conducting it in America, that the two men who appear in the whole course of his previous correspondence to have been most after his own heart—Madison and Monroe—were those who succeeded him for eight years each in the Presidency, accomplishing " twenty-four years of administration in republican forms and principles," which (changing, as we confidently may do, the language of Jefferson from the future to the past) have " so consecrated them in the eyes of the people as to secure them against

the danger of change." * The election of
General Jackson, after the younger Adams
had served four years only, strongly con-
firms this opinion.

The administration of Jefferson was, as
has been observed by Waden,† " perhaps
the first instance in the history of parties,
of a body of men raised to power abiding
faithfully by the principles they had professed during their exclusion, and with self-
denying honesty labouring to diminish the
amount of influence and patronage they
received from their predecessors." This
administration was distinguished by many
important events :—The entire abolition of
internal taxes—the repeal of the alien law—
the extinction of the seditious libel law—
the effective diminution of the national
debt—the reduction of the annual expenditure—the discarding of all forms of state—
the extinction of the native right to a hundred million acres of the national domain—
the purchase of Louisiana—and " the preservation of peace with the civilized world

* Nor is the election of Monroe an inefficient circumstance in our felicities. Four-and-twenty years, which
he will accomplish, of administration in republican
forms and principles, will so consecrate them in the eyes
of the people as to secure them against the danger of
change.—*Jefferson to La Fayette*, May 14, 1817.—Vol. iv.
p. 312.

† Statistical, Political, and Historical Account of the
United States, vol. iii. p. 489.

through a season of uncommon difficulty and trial." *

To this catalogue of inestimable benefits to his country and the world, it would be idle to look for anything *simile aut secundum* in the longest reigns which history calls glorious. Of contrasts there is a miserable superabundance ; and will be, till men shall be wise enough, throughout the world, to give more honour to their benefactors than to their destroyers.

Jefferson established the inviolate liberty of the press, and maintained it inviolate in spite of the strongest personal temptations to the contrary ; for never were mendacity, calumny, and scurrility carried to a more unblushing extent, than in the attacks on his character in the federal papers during his administration. We speak from our most distinct recollection of the American newspapers of that time. His forbearance only stimulated further outrages ; but he opposed to them, in calmness and silence, the shield of his own undeviating rectitude ; and wisely did he so, as the immense majority by which he was re-elected, and the testimonials of public approbation which accompanied him into retirement, abundantly testify.

* Address of the General Assembly of Virginia, vol. iv. p. 449.

THOMAS JEFFERSON

He had very early expressed an opinion, that it would be " better to have newspapers without a government, than a government without newspapers." When at a time long subsequent to this he expressed his conviction of " the melancholy truth, that a complete suppression of the press could not more effectually deprive the nation of its benefits than was done by its abandoned prostitution to falsehood," and by " the demoralising practice of feeding the public mind habitually on slander, and the depravity of taste which this nauseous aliment induces," he still never thought for a moment of repressing or circumscribing public discussion by positive law. He placed the strongest reliance on the good sense of the people to counteract the misleadings of the press ; and at a still later period (Nov. 1823) he repeated his original and unaltered opinion :—" The only security for honest and unoppressive government is in a free press. The agitation it produces must be submitted to. It is necessary to keep the waters pure."

After his retirement from the presidency he was elected a visitor and rector of the University which was founded within a few miles of his seat, Monticello ; and he divided his time between the superintendence of this institution, the business of his farm, and reading ; carrying on at the same time a very extensive correspondence, much of it against his will ; but he seems, though free from most superstitions, to have been not free from that of thinking it necessary to answer letters ; and as he received one thousand two hundred and sixty-seven in a single year, we may see to what an extent he was a victim to his urbanity. He says he had rather be a cabbage than have to write so many letters ; this, too, with a crippled wrist. The majority of these were " letters of inquiry, always of good will— sometimes from friends—oftener from persons unknown, but written kindly and civilly, and to which, therefore, civility required answers."

Barring this dreadful infliction, his submission to which is wonderful, his life in retirement seems to have been a happy one, though latterly embittered by pecuniary difficulties. He had necessarily neglected his patrimonial estate during the course of his public life. He had gained nothing in the public service, and had retired from office " with hands as clean as they were empty." He had to pay 1200 dollars on account of some guarantee for a friend, and he felt this very severely on the depreciation of land and produce, which was consequent on one of the periodical ex-

plosions in the wretched paper-currency of
America. He applied to Congress for permission to dispose of his estate by lottery.
The application was rejected ; wisely, we
think, on general principles : though, if an
exception were ever to be admitted, this
was undoubtedly the case. There is much
to be said on both sides, and we have not
space for the discussion.

The friendship between Jefferson and
Adams, which had existed for years, when
it was interrupted by the circumstances
which placed them in opposition to each
other as the heads of the federal and republican parties, was renewed after Jefferson's
retirement, and appears to have continued
uninterrupted till their deaths. Jefferson
and Adams, by a singular coincidence,
died both on the same day, the 4th of July,
1826, the fiftieth anniversary of the Declaration of Independence : Jefferson being
then eighty-two, and Adams nearly ninety.

The last letter in these volumes is from
Jefferson to Mr. Weightman, dated ten days
before his death, June 24th, 1826, expressing
his sorrow at being unable to be present at
the celebration of this fiftieth anniversary
in Washington. The calm judgment of his
age adhered with undiminished earnestness
to the deliberately-adopted principles of his
earliest political life, and the repetition of

his principles and his hopes, in these his last recorded words, will be read with double interest, from the occasion on which they were written, and because they may be justly regarded as the *divini hominis cycnea vox et oratio*.

Monticello, June 24, 1826.

The kind invitation I received from you, on the part of the citizens of the City of Washington, to be present with them at their celebration of the fiftieth anniversary of American Independence, as one of the surviving signers of an instrument pregnant with our own, and the fate of the world, is most flattering to myself, and heightened by the honourable accompaniment proposed for the comfort of such a journey. It adds sensibly to the suffering of sickness to be deprived by it of a personal participation in the rejoicings of that day, but acquiescence is a duty under circumstances not placed among those we are permitted to control. I should, indeed, with peculiar delight, have met and exchanged these congratulations personally with the small band, the remnant of that host of worthies who joined with us on that day in the bold and doubtful election we were to make for our country, between submission or the sword, and to have enjoyed with them the consolatory fact, that our fellow-citizens, after half a century of experience and prosperity, continue to approve the choice we made. May it be to the world, what I believe it will be (to some parts sooner, to others later, but finally to all), the signal of arousing men to burst the chains under which monkish ignorance and superstition had persuaded them to bind themselves, and to assume the blessings and security of self-government. That form which we have substituted restores the free right to the unbounded exercise of reason and freedom of opinion. All eyes are opened, or opening to the rights of man. The general spread of the light of science has already laid open to every view the palpable truth, that the mass of mankind has not been born with saddles on their backs, nor a favoured few booted and spurred, ready to ride them legitimately by the grace of God. These are grounds of hope for others. For ourselves let the annual return of this day for ever refresh our recollections of these rights, and an undiminished devotion to them.

I will ask permission here to express the pleasure with which I should have met my ancient neighbours of the City of Washington and its vicinities, with whom I passed so many years of a pleasing social intercourse—an intercourse which so much relieved the anxieties of the public cares, and left impressions so deeply engraved in my affections as never to be forgotten. With my regret that ill health forbids me the gratification of an acceptance, be pleased to receive for yourself, and those for whom you write, the assurance of my highest respect and friendly attachments.—THOMAS JEFFERSON.—Vol. iv. p. 451.

We know nothing more beautiful in the records of the retirement of illustrious men, than the manner in which these veteran statesmen renewed and continued their correspondence. Their opposition had been one of real and most important principle.

It was ardent in proportion to its sincerity. It is obvious, however, that in respect to their private intercourse, Adams had fallen off from Jefferson, not Jefferson from Adams. But in 1811 (two years after Jefferson's retirement from the Presidency) Adams, in conversation with a mutual friend, adverted to the unprincipled licentiousness of the press against Jefferson, and added, " I always loved Jefferson, and still love him." This was communicated to Jefferson, who had always lamented the interruption of their private friendship, and in another month we find their correspondence renewed.

The opinions of Jefferson on all the most important questions in morals, politics, and religion :—On the true principles of good Government : [1]—On the characters of

1. FEDERALISTS AND REPUBLICANS.—" Both of our political parties, at least the honest part of them, agree conscientiously in the same object—the public good ; but they differ essentially in what they deem the means of promoting that good. One side believes it best done by one composition of the governing powers ; the other by a different one. One fears most the ignorance of the people ; the other the selfishness of rulers independent of them. Which is right, time and experience will prove. We think that one side of this experiment has been long enough tried, and proved not to promote the good of the many ; and that the other has not been fairly and sufficiently tried.

" Our opponents think the reverse. With whichever opinion the body of the nation concurs, that must prevail. My anxieties on the subject will never carry me beyond

THOMAS JEFFERSON

European Governments in practice, both
from distant views of their great proceed-
ings, and from close observations, during his
residence in Europe, of their minor details,
of the subdivisions of their machinery, of
their influence on the well-being of the
unprivileged producers, who compose the
bulk of the people, and of their consecration
to the exclusive interests of the privileged
non-producers, who compose the ruling and
sub-ruling few :—On their kings,[2] their
aristocracy,[3] and their rabble, as contrasted

the use of fair and honourable means, of truth and
reason ; nor have they ever lessened my esteem for moral
worth, nor alienated my affections for a single friend,
who did not first withdraw himself. Whenever this has
happened, I confess I have not been insensible to it :
yet have ever kept myself open to a return of their
justice. I conclude with sincere prayers for your health
and happiness, that yourself, and Mr. Adams may long
enjoy the tranquillity you desire and merit, and see, in
the prosperity of your family, what is the consummation
of the last and warmest of human wishes."—1804. Vol.
iv. p. 28.

2. KINGS.—" So much for the blessings of having kings,
and magistrates who would be kings. From these events
our young republics may learn useful lessons—never to
call on foreign powers to settle their differences ; to
guard against hereditary magistrates ; to prevent their
citizens from becoming so established in wealth and
power as to be thought worthy of alliance by marriage
with the nieces, sisters, &c. of kings."—Paris, 1787.
Vol. ii. p. 224.

3. ARISTOCRACY.—" Though the day may be at some
distance, beyond the reach of our lives perhaps, yet it
will certainly come, when a single fibre left of this
institution (the order of the Cincinnati) will produce an

173

with anything that can properly be called a
people : [4]—On the practical excellencies of
the government of the United States ; on
the actual defects in it, and on the means
of amending them : [5]—On the foreign policy

hereditary aristocracy, which will change the form of
our government from the best to the worst in the world.
To know the mass of evil which flows from this fatal
source, a person must be in France ; he must see the
finest soil, the finest climate, the most compact State,
the most benevolent character of people, and every
earthly advantage combined, insufficient to prevent this
scourge from rendering existence a curse to twenty-four
out of twenty-five parts of the inhabitants of this
country."—*Jefferson to Washington*, 1786.   Vol. ii. p. 62.

4. RABBLE OF EUROPEAN CITIES.—" But even in
Europe a change has sensibly taken place in the mind
of man.   Science had liberated the ideas of those who
read and reflect, and the American example had kindled
feelings of right in the people.   An insurrection has consequently begun, of science, talents, and courage, against
rank and birth which have fallen into contempt.   It has·
failed in its first effort, because the mobs of the cities,
the instruments used for its accomplishment, debased by
ignorance, poverty, and vice, could not be restrained
to rational action.   But the world will recover from the
panic of this first catastrophe.   Science is progressive,
and talents and enterprise on the alert.   Resort may be
had to the people of the country, a more governable
power from their principles and subordination ; and rank
and birth and tinsel-aristocracy will finally shrink into
insignificance, even there.   This, however, we have no
right to meddle with.   It suffices for us, if the moral
and physical condition of our own citizens qualifies
them to select the able and good for the direction of
their government, with a recurrence of elections at such
short periods as will enable them to displace an un-
faithful servant before the mischief he meditates be
irremediable."—1813.   Vol. iv. p. 236.

5. IMPROVEMENTS DESIRED.—" The sum of these
amendments is—1. General suffrage.   2. Equal repre-

THOMAS JEFFERSON

of the United States, which he frequently embodies in the comprehensive words, " *Free commerce with all nations, alliance with none;* " to which he added, in substance, " Quarrels with none but where our vital interests force them upon us," as in the question of English impressment of American seamen, which America must always resist, even at the price of eternal war : [6]—On the formation of an efficient pro-

sentation in the legislature. 3. An executive chosen by the people. 4. Judges elective or amovable. 5. Justices, jurors, and sheriffs elective. 6. Ward divisions. And 7. Periodical amendments of the constitution."—1816. Vol. iv. p. 297.

6. ENGLISH IMPRESSMENT.—" Entering our ships, I say, under a pretext of searching for, and taking out their seamen, they took ours, native as well as naturalized, knowing them to be ours, merely because they wanted them, insomuch that no American could safely cross the ocean, or venture to pass by sea from one to another of our own ports. It is not long since they impressed at sea two nephews of general Washington, returning from Europe, and then put them, as common seamen, under the ordinary discipline of their ships-of-war. There are certainly other wrongs to be settled between England and us, but of a minor character, and such as a proper spirit of conciliation on both sides would not permit to continue them at war. The sword, however, can never again be sheathed until the personal safety of an American on the ocean, among the most important and most vital of the rights we possess, is completely provided for."—1813. Vol. iv. p. 193.

(2). ENGLISH IMPRESSMENT.—P.S. *February* 26.—" My letter had not yet been sealed, when I received news of our peace. I am glad of it, and especially that we closed the war with the éclat of the action at New Orleans. But I consider it as an armistice only, because no security

MEMOIRS OF

tecting navy :—On their true interests in respect of acquisition of territory, especially in the two great practical cases, now settled, of Louisiana and the Floridas, and in those which remain to be settled, of Mexico and Cuba : of their domestic policy in respect of taxes, paper currency,[7] domestic

is provided against the impressment of our seamen. While this is unsettled, we are in hostility of mind with England, although actual deeds of arms may be suspended by a truce. If she thinks the exercise of this outrage is worth eternal war, eternal war it must be, or extermination of the one or the other party. The first act of impressment she commits on an American will be answered by reprisal, or by a declaration of war here ; and the interval must be merely a state of preparation for it. In this we have much to do, in further fortifying our sea-port-towns, providing military stores, classing and disciplining our militia, arranging our financial system, and above all, promoting our domestic manufactures, which have taken such roots as never again can be shaken."—1815. Vol. iv. pp. 258, 259.

7. PAPER-CURRENCY AND BANKS.—" We seem equally incorrigible in our financial course. Although a century of British experience has proved to what a wonderful extent the funding on specific redeeming taxes enables a nation to anticipate in war the resources of peace, and although the other nations of Europe have tried and trodden every path of force or folly in fruitless quest of the same object, yet we still expect to find in juggling tricks and banking dreams, that money can be made out of nothing, and in sufficient quantity to meet the expenses of a heavy war by sea and land. It is said, indeed, that money cannot be borrowed from our merchants, as from those of England : but it can be borrowed from our people. They will give you all the necessaries of war they produce, if, instead of the bankrupt trash they are now obliged to receive for want of any other, you will give them a paper promise, founded on a specific pledge, and of a size for common circulation. But you say the

176

manufactures,[8] defensive military force,
merchants will not take this paper. What the people
take the merchants must take, or sell nothing. All these
doubts and fears prove only the extent of all the dominion
which the banking institutions have obtained over the
minds of our citizens, and especially of those inhabiting
cities or other banking places ; and this dominion must
be broken, or it will break us. But here, as in the other
case, we must make up our mind to suffer yet longer,
before we can get right. The misfortune is, that in the
meantime we shall plunge ourselves into inextinguishable
debt, and entail on our posterity an inheritance of eternal
taxes, which will bring our government and people into
the condition of those of England, a nation of pikes and
gudgeons, the latter bred merely as food for the former."
—Vol. iv. p. 251.

8. DOMESTIC MANUFACTURES.—" Of company establishments we have none. We use little machinery.
The spinning-jenny, and loom, with the flying shuttle
can be managed in a family ; but nothing more complicated. The economy and thriftiness resulting from
our household manufactures are such that they will never
again be laid aside ; and nothing more salutary for us
has ever happened than the British obstructions to our
demands for their manufactures. Restore free intercourse when they will, their commerce with us will have
totally changed its form, and the articles we shall in
future want from them will not exceed their own con-
sumption of our produce."—1812. Vol. iv. p. 172.

" I have now thirty-five spindles going, a hand-carding
machine, and looms with the flying shuttle, for the
supply of my own farms, which will never be relinquished
in my time. The continuance of the war will fix the
habit generally, and out of the evils of Impressment,
and of the Orders of Council a great blessing for us
will grow. I have not formerly been an advocate for
great manufactories. I doubted whether our labour,
employed in agriculture, and aided by the spontaneous
energies of the earth, would not procure us more than
we could make ourselves of other necessaries. But other
considerations entering into the question have settled
my doubts."—1813. Vol. iv. pp. 186, 187.

education,[9] freedom of the press,[10] religious

9. FREEDOM OF OPINION.—" If all the sovereigns of Europe were to set themselves to work to emancipate the minds of their subjects from their present ignorance and prejudices, and that as zealously as they now endeavour the contrary, a thousand years would not place them on that high ground on which our common people are now setting out. Ours could not have been so fairly placed under the control of the common sense of the people, had they not been separated from their parent stock and kept from contamination, either from them or the other people of the old world, by the intervention of so wide an ocean. To know the worth of this, one must see the want of it here : I think by far the most important bill in our own code is that for the diffusion of knowledge among the people. No other sure foundation can be devised for the preservation of freedom and happiness. If any body thinks that kings and nobles, or priests, are good conservators of the public happiness, send him here. It is the best school in the universe to cure him of that folly. He will see here, with his own eyes, that these descriptions of men are an abandoned confederacy against the happiness of the mass of the people. The omnipotence of their effect cannot be better proved than in this country, particularly where, notwithstanding the finest soil upon earth, the finest climate under heaven, and a people of the most benevolent, the most gay and amiable character of which the human form is susceptible ; where such a people, I say, surrounded by so many blessings from nature, are loaded with misery, by kings, nobles and priests, and by them alone. Preach, my dear Sir, a Crusade against ignorance ; establish and improve the law for educating the common people : let our countrymen know that the people alone can protect us against these evils, and that the tax which will be paid for this purpose is not more than the thousandth part of what will be paid to kings, priests, and nobles, who will rise up among us if we leave the people in ignorance."—1786, Paris. Vol. ii. p. 45.

10. FREEDOM OF OPINION—POLITICAL.—" The tumults in America I expected would have produced in Europe an unfavourable opinion of our political state ; but it

has not. On the contrary, the small effect of these tumults seems to have given more confidence in the firmness of our governments. The interposition of the people themselves on the side of government has had a great effect on the opinion here [Paris, 1787]. I am persuaded myself, that the good sense of the people will always be found to be the best army. They may be led astray for a moment, but will soon correct themselves. The people are the only censors of their governors ; and even their errors will tend to keep these to the true principles of their institution. To punish these errors too severely would be to suppress the only safeguard of the public liberty. The way to prevent these irregular interpositions of the people, is to give them full information of their affairs through the channel of the public papers, and to contrive that those papers should penetrate the whole mass of the people. The basis of our government being the opinion of the people, the very first object should be to keep that right ; and were it left to me to decide whether we should have a government without newspapers, or newspapers without a government, I should not hesitate a moment to prefer the latter. But I should mean that every man should receive those papers, and be capable of reading them. I am convinced that those societies (as the Indians) which live without government, enjoy in their general mass an infinitely greater degree of happiness than those who live under the European governments. Among the former, public opinion is in the place of law, and restrains morals as powerfully as laws ever did anywhere. Among the latter, under pretence of governing, they have divided their nations into classes—wolves and sheep. I do not exaggerate. This is a true picture of Europe. Cherish, therefore, the spirit of our people, and keep alive their attention. Do not be too severe upon their errors, but reclaim them by enlightening them. If once they become inattentive to public affairs, you, and I, and congress, and assemblies, judges, and governors, shall all become wolves. It seems to be the law of our general nature, in spite of individual exceptions ; and experience declares that man is the only animal which devours his own kind ; for I can apply no milder term to the governments of Europe, and to the general prey of the rich on the poor."
—1787. Vol. ii. p. 84.

liberty,[11] laws of entail and primogeniture,[12]

11. RELIGION.—" The result of your fifty or sixty years
of religious reading in the four words, ' be just and good,'
is that in which all our inquiries must end ; as the riddles
of all the priesthoods end in four more—' *ubi panis, ibi
deus.*' What all agree in, is probably right. What no
two agree in, most probably wrong. One of our fan-
colouring biographers, who paints small men as very
great, inquired of me lately, with real affection too,
whether he might consider as authentic the change in
my religion, much spoken of in some circles. Now this
supposed that they knew what had been my religion
before, taking for it the word of their priests, whom I
certainly never made the confidents of my creed. My
answer was, ' say nothing of my religion. It is known
to God and myself alone. Its evidence before the world
is to be sought in my life ; if that has been honest and
dutiful to society, the religion which has regulated it
cannot be a bad one.' "—1817. Vol. iv. p. 308.

12. IMPROVEMENTS REALISED AND DESIRED.—" At the
first session of our legislature after the declaration of
independence, we passed a law, abolishing entails. And
this was followed by one abolishing the privilege of
primogeniture, and dividing the lands of intestates
equally among all their children or other representatives.
These laws, drawn by myself, laid the axe to the root
of pseudo-aristocracy. And had another which I prepared been adopted by the legislature, our work would
have been complete. It was a bill for the more general
diffusion of learning. This proposed to divide every
county into wards of five or six miles square, like your
townships ; to establish in each ward a free school for
reading, writing, and common arithmetic ; to provide
for the annual selection of the best subjects from these
schools, who might receive, at the public expense, a
higher degree of education at a district school, and from
these district schools to select a certain number of the
most promising subjects, to be completed at a University,
where all the useful sciences should be taught. Worth
and genius would thus have been sought out from every
condition of life, and completely prepared, by education,
for defeating the competition of wealth and birth for

(which were, chiefly by his instrumentality, abolished), the state and probable consequences of negro slavery,[13] and the Missouri question, which arose out of this fearful subject :—On the prospects of the United

public trusts. My proposition had, for a further object, to impart to these wards those portions of self-government for which they are best qualified, by confiding to them the care of their poor, their roads, police, elections, the nomination of jurors, administration of justice in small cases, elementary exercises of militia ; in short, to have made them little republics, with a warden at the head of each, for all those concerns which, being under their eye, they would better manage than the larger republics of the county or state. A general call of ward-meetings by their wardens on the same day through the State, would at any time produce the genuine sense of the people on any required point, and would enable the State to act in mass, as your people have so often done, and with so much effect, by their own meetings. The law for religious freedom, which made a part of this system, having put down the aristocracy of the clergy, and restored to the citizens the freedom of the mind, and those of entails and descents maintaining an equality of condition among them, their own education would have raised the mass of the people to the high ground of moral respectability necessary to their own safety, and to orderly government ; and would have completed the great object of qualifying them to select the veritable *aristoi* for the trusts of government, to the exclusion of the pseudalists : and the same Theognis who has furnished the epigraphs of your two letters assures us, that Οὐδεμιαν πω Κύρν', ἀγαθοὶ πόλιν ὤλεσαν ἄνδρες."—1813.Vol. iv. p. 234.

13. SLAVES.—" There is, I think, a way in which the deportation of Slaves may be effected : that is, by emancipating the after-born, leaving them, on due compensation, with their mothers until their services are worth their maintenance, and then putting them to industrious occupations, until a proper age for deportation. This was the result of my reflections on the subject

MEMOIRS OF

States;[14] on the probabilities of their future power among the nations of the world; of the permanence of the Union ;[15] of the continued ascendancy of republican principles ; of the comparative progress among them of fanaticism on the one hand, and of free opinions in religion on the other: [16]—On the influence and interests of priests :—On the administration of justice :—On agricul-

five and forty years ago, and I have never yet been able to conceive any other practicable plan.

* * * * * *

A million and a half are within our control ; but six millions (which a majority of those now living will see them attain), and one million of these fighting men, will say, ' we will not go.' "—1824. Vol. iv. pp. 398, 399.

14. PROSPECTS OF THE UNITED STATES.—" For my part, I wish that all nations may recover and retain their independence ; that those which are overgrown may not advance beyond safe measures of power, that a salutary balance may be ever maintained among nations, and that our peace, commerce, and friendship, may be sought and cultivated by all. It is our business to manufacture for ourselves whatever we can, and to keep all markets open for what we can spare or want ; and the less we have to do with the amities or enmities of Europe, the better. Not in our day, but at no distant one, we may shake a rod over the heads of all, which may make the stoutest of them tremble. But I hope our wisdom will grow with our power, and teach us that the less we use our power the greater it will be."—1815. Vol. iv. pp. 271, 272.

15. PERMANENCE OF THE UNION.—" The cement of this Union is in the heart-blood of every American. I do not believe there is on earth a government established on so immovable a basis."—1815. Vol. iv. p. 257.

16. RELIGION.—" The atmosphere of our country is unquestionably charged with a threatening cloud of

ture and the introduction of new plants :—
On literature and science :—On the wisdom
of ancestry :[17] his notices of the great events

fanaticism, lighter in some parts, denser in others, but
too heavy in all.

      *   *   *   *   *

" The diffusion of instruction, to which there is now
so growing an attention, will be the remote remedy to
this fever of fanaticism, while the more proximate one
will be the progress of Unitarianism. That this will,
ere long, be the religion of the majority, from North
to South, I have no doubt."—1822. Vol. iv. pp. 366, 367.

17. WISDOM OF ANCESTRY.—" Laws and institutions
must go hand in hand with the progress of the human
mind. As that becomes more developed, more enlightened, as new discoveries are made, new truths disclosed,
and manners and opinions change with the change of
circumstances, institutions must advance also, and keep
pace with the times. We might as well require a man
to wear still the coat which fitted him when a boy, as
civilized society to remain ever under the regimen of
their barbarous ancestors. It is this preposterous idea
which has lately deluged Europe in blood. Their
monarchs, instead of wisely yielding to the gradual
changes of circumstances—of favouring progressive
accommodation to progressive improvement, have clung
to old abuses, entrenched themselves behind steady
habits, and obliged their subjects to seek, through blood
and violence, rash and ruinous innovations, which, had
they been referred to the peaceful deliberations and
collected wisdom of the nation, would have been put
into acceptable and salutary forms. Let us follow no
such examples, nor weakly believe that one generation
is not as capable as another of taking care of itself, and
of ordering its own affairs."—Vol. iv. p. 298.

GOVERNMENTS OF EUROPE AND AMERICA.—" Buonaparte and the Allies have now changed sides. They are
parcelling out among themselves, Poland, Belgium,
Saxony, Italy, dictating a ruler and government to
France, and looking askance too at *our republic, the
splendid libel on their governments,* and he is fighting for

MEMOIRS OF

in which he was either a mover or a close
observer; those of the American Revolution;
those of the early part of the French Revolution; those of his own presidency; of
Burr's conspiracy :—his views of the more
recent events of importance, on which he
looked from a distance in his later years;
the quarrels of Europe; and the last
British war with America, not forgetting
the burning of Washington :—his sketches
or judgments of the characters of eminent
persons; of Louis XVI. and his queen;
of George the Third; of George the Fourth,
when Prince of Wales; and of the Duke
of York; of Washington, of Franklin, of
Hamilton, of Adams, of Madison, of Monroe;
of Napoleon, in his glory and in his exile;
of Lord Castlereagh and his colleagues; of
many others who have been in the last
half century conspicuous for good or for
ill:—present such a body of good sense,
of careful and comprehensive investigation,
of sound and dispassionate decision, of
kindly feeling, of enlarged philanthropy, of

the principles of national independence, of which his
whole life hitherto has been a continued violation."—
1815. Vol. iv. p. 276.

BANKS.—" I sincerely believe, with you, that banking
establishments are more dangerous than standing
armies; and that the principle of spending money to
be paid by posterity, under the name of funding, is
but swindling futurity on a large scale."—1816. Vol. iv.
p. 288.

184

THOMAS JEFFERSON

spotless integrity ; such a rare combination of an enthusiasm almost chivalrous for the liberty and happiness of mankind, with a calm philosophical judgment, restraining its pursuits within the limits of the attainable ; such a picture of political sincerity, presenting always the same character in appearance as in reality, in public as in private life, as will not easily find a parallel (at least on this side the Atlantic) in the records of any individual who has had so large a share in the government of nations.

Our limits do not admit of our doing justice, in the form of extracts, to the invaluable contents of these volumes, of which we have given an imperfect enumeration. We have under some of the heads of that enumeration subjoined some brief specimens: but we most earnestly commend the volumes themselves to all our readers who have not yet perused them, as containing numerous and rich materials of authentic history ; as presenting, on almost all truly important questions, views sometimes new, most frequently just, and always worthy of patient consideration ; as abounding with incitements to moral courage and political honesty ; as confirming rational hopes of the progress of knowledge and liberty ; as elevating our opinion of human nature ; and in all these points counteracting the soul-withering influence of our own frivolous and sycophantic literature.

America is deeply indebted to Jefferson. He had the sagacity to see her true interests in the beginning of his career, the honesty to sacrifice all other considerations to them, and the moral courage to pursue them inflexibly to the end. And the interests of America being peace and liberty, were and still are the interests of mankind. He was a great instrument in the foundation of her liberties in 1776 ; the main instrument in their restoration in 1800. He lived to see the community of which he was a member, proceed from infancy to maturity : he lived to see it rise from a struggle in which it with difficulty maintained its existence, to grow strongly and rapidly into one of the most noble and important communities of the world ; and he left it in a fair train for becoming the very greatest of the nations. For how much of this progress it was indebted to him, will be most clearly manifest to those who dwell most on the history of his times, especially on the portion of them which intervened between that scarecrow of well-meaning simplicity, the French Reign of Terror, and his first election to the Presidency. The first steps of his administration dissipated for ever the phantoms of fear and delusion, with which artifice and cowardice had surrounded the image of liberty ; and established principles of government, which remain to this day, not only unshaken, but apparently taking deeper and deeper hold of the affections of the American people. He was undoubtedly the greatest public benefactor that has yet appeared in the nineteenth century ; whatever may be his station in the eighteenth, in which it is difficult to say that he was second, even to Washington.

LONDON BRIDGE

LONDON BRIDGE *

HERE will have been, by the time this job is done with, an expenditure of some THREE MILLIONS of public money. Let us see for what good end.

A bridge, like every other work of art, is either useful or ornamental, or both, or neither. The bridge between Hyde Park and Kensington Gardens, over the penned-up water which used to trickle through two or three holes in the wall, has been built for ornament only ; it was clearly not wanted for utility. The old wooden bridge at Putney has long been useful : nobody will call it ornamental. The Suspension-bridge at Hammersmith is both useful and orna-

* *Chronicles of London Bridge.* By an Antiquary Smith, Elder, and Co. 1827.
Reports from the Select Committee of the House Commons on the State of London Bridge, and Minutes of Evidence taken before the Committee. 1820, 1821.
Minutes of Evidence taken before the Lords Committees, on the Approaches to London Bridge : and Appendix to the Minutes. 1829.

mental : useful as shortening the distance from London to Richmond and Hampton ; ornamental in the highest degree, as a beautiful work of art. A bridge that is neither useful nor ornamental, is a Chinese bridge over a royal fish-pond, interdicted to all but royalty, which never sets foot on it. The new London Bridge will be more ornamental than the old one in the eyes of all but antiquaries and lovers of the picturesque. It will be in some respects as useful to those who pass over it, though far less convenient to many, without being more so to any. The increased utility, if any, will be in the enlarged waterway. We shall inquire whether, on this ground, a sufficient case has been made out for demolishing the old structure, with its nineteen irregular arches, and setting up the new one, with its " five beautiful elliptical arches, constructed on the most scientific principles of any arches in Europe : " to borrow the words of a paragraph, which we may suppose somebody paid for very handsomely, as it appeared simultaneously in all the newspapers of one morning. If it should turn out that we have got nothing by it but a pretty toy, it will be worth while to see how much it is to cost, who is to pay for it, and how the whole concern has been schemed and executed.

LONDON BRIDGE

The old London Bridge * was begun in 1176, and finished in 1209. It was built on such unscientific principles, that it ought to have been carried away before it was finished, when it was finished, and at any given time subsequently ; but partly by the awkward contrivances of barbarous men, partly by its own obstinacy, it has stood six centuries and a quarter, amidst the perpetual prophecies of disinterested engineers that it could not stand any longer : while one bridge after another, on different parts of the same river, in which no son of science had espied a flaw, has wilfully tumbled to pieces, by the sinking of the piers, or the yielding of the abutments, in despite of the most mathematical demonstrations of the absurdity and impropriety of such a proceeding.†

* Previously to this stone bridge there was a wooden bridge, which had existed, as some suppose, from 994 : having of course required and received great and frequent repairs.

† The bridge over the Thames at Staines is a notable instance of this perversity in brute matter. About thirty years ago there was, at this place, a wooden bridge, which was condemned, and a stone bridge of three arches was built just below it. This was scarcely finished, when the piers sunk, and the arches cracked ; luckily in time to stop the removal of the condemned wooden bridge, which, it was discovered, might be trusted till another new bridge was completed. It was now taken for granted that the bed of the river could not support piers, and an iron bridge of one arch, with comely stone abutments, spanned the Thames with infinite grace.

LONDON BRIDGE

During the six centuries and a quarter of its existence, London Bridge has undergone many changes, and projectors have always been busy in proposing more. The waterway has been contracted for the benefit of the water-works, which wanted a head of water for a fall to turn the wheels ; widened for the benefit of the navigation, which wanted a broad and safe passage through the bridge ; contracted again for the benefit of the navigation, which wanted a head of water to give a sufficient depth during the latter half of the ebb. These two last wants of the navigation, being incompatible, have oscillated in petitions and counter-petitions, for keeping up the head of water, or for making a clear waterway. Committee after Committee of the Corporation of London and of the Parliament, have had before them persons, statements, and plans, exhausting all modes, anticipating all consequences, and computing all expenses of change. This accumulated wisdom of evidence, having

But this again had scarcely been opened, when, under the pressure of a herd of cattle, the arch stove-in the Middlesex abutment, and again, luckily, in time to stop the removal of the wooden bridge, which, it was again found would serve till the completion of a third new edifice. This was a wooden bridge with an iron railing ; of which the piles rotted with a celerity quite edifying : and now, after repeated repairs, this is condemned in its turn, and another stone bridge is in progress, and nearly completed, which will of course last till Doomsday.

been digested by the Collective Wisdom of the nation in 1821, the New Bridge is the result.

The waterworks are gone : the starlings will go : there will be a clear waterway : no more lives and property will be lost in shooting the bridge : and the new structure will have been completed in a manner that will make it an egregious impertinence to doubt of its eternal duration. Nothing but an earthquake can disturb it.

The first advantage gained is the clear waterway, and the consequent saving of life and property in the passage under the bridge.

First, of life. There is a return, in the Appendix to the Report of 1821, of Coroner's Inquests on persons drowned in passing, or attempting to pass, through London Bridge, from 1800 to 1820 inclusive. The number is eighteen for twenty-one years ; not one per annum. It would have been well to have called at the same time for a return of the inquests on persons drowned in passing, or attempting to pass, through Chelsea Reach. We take it the result would have been as formidable. We should like also to see, by-and-by, a return of the number of lives lost during, and in consequence of, the building of the new bridge and the removing of the old one   We should expect

195

that the comparison would shew anything but an economy of life.

Amongst the papers in the same Appendix,* we find the evidence of some lightermen on the loss of life and property at London Bridge. One of these gentry estimated the loss of lives at twenty, another at thirty, annually ; one estimated the annual loss of property at 20,000*l*., another at 40,000*l*. Rectifying their opinions on loss of life by the coroner's returns (after making allowance for bodies not found) and by all the specific facts we can discover in the evidence, and applying the same principles to their opinions on loss of property, we conclude, that in setting down the loss of life at two, and the loss of property at 3,000*l*. per annum, we greatly over-estimate both.

We will cite from the evidence a specimen of accidents in both classes : and first, of loss of life.

Thomas Robinson and another man were rowing their master and his son from Vauxhall to Deptford, at midnight.

We came, says Robinson, past St. Mary Overy's Church, and I heard St. Mary Overy's clock strike a quarter after twelve. I told him we had better stop, for the bridge roared, it was not safe to go through. He said, "we will lie by for a while ;"

* *Commons*, 1821, p. 99.

and we pulled to the Old Swan, and made fast to a craft below the stairs : we waited there about half an hour. My master says to me, " it is flood." "No," says I, "it is not flood." He says, "it was flood to-day at Deptford at a quarter after ten." I said, " No, it was not, for I was on the Causeway a quarter before eleven, and there was no flood had made." The answer he made was, " You know best then ; I know it is flood." As such I shoved the boat off, and we rowed out into the stream. Being dark, he looked at the middle lights of the centre arch to shoot it : it was so dark we could not see any other arch. I was shooting it ; the boat went down that declivity ; she took in so much water that she filled the lower side with the surf. The boat upset and turned over ; my master and his son and the mate were drowned.—*Minutes of Evidence, Commons,* 1820, p. 18.

Is it possible to preserve such desperate rashness as this from accidents ? London Bridge can be passed with safety downwards, on the flood tide, only on what is literally the nick of time—the few minutes during which the water is level, or nearly so, and not flowing forcibly upwards. This point of time it is difficult to ascertain from above bridge even in the day, and the attempt to hit it in a night totally dark, without knowledge even of the computed time of flood, could not be expected to have any other result. Most of the accidents detailed in the evidence are of this description, and are such as common prudence might have avoided.

Next, of loss of property. The following is a memorandum of Mr. Samuel Pegge :—

1814 : January 15. Saturday evening, about half-past six o'clock, put J. Bencroft, our lighter-man, in the Martha barge, laden with fourteen chaldrons of coals, then lying off the Tower, to take home to Old Barge House Wharf (I came up in this barge, thinking it would be safer than coming up in the skiff). While driving up a little below London Bridge, with several other barges, heard a confused noise of men, upon and under the bridge, of " keep your barge to the southward ;" others said, " keep to the northward." The lighter-man put the barge's head to shoot the great arch, but was prevented from going through by Messrs. Johnson's barge and a quantity of ice, and she sunk with several others.—*Commons*, 1820, p. 7.

Here was total darkness and the river covered with floating ice. A few days after this date there was a fair on the Thames. There is scarcely a bridge between London and Oxford under which barges have not been sunk in floods and frosts. The only conclusion we should draw from the accidents we have cited (and the majority of the accidents in the evidence may be classed with them) would be, that there can be very little danger in daylight and ordinary circumstances, where, in darkness and extraordinary circumstances, danger is so readily risked by men who have been familiar with the navigation for years. This conclusion is borne out by some pretty old practitioners ; one or two of whom we shall cite.

Mr. James Grant—

How many craft are you master of ?—Twenty-one or twenty-two.

How long have you been in the habit of navigating the river through London Bridge ?—About twenty-six years.

Has your practice of going through been frequent or casual ?—Frequent, both during the night and day. At all times of tide, and at all times of night and day.

During this period of years have you met with any serious accidents ?—No.

Have you seen accidents happen to other craft ?

* * * * * * *

I have seen accidents very often happen at the bridge through carelessness. I believe most of the accidents happen through carelessness.—*Commons,* 1821, pp. 19, 20.

Mr. William Waller, the next witness,

Had passed through the bridge for twenty years, four or five times a week, and sometimes two or three times a day, and had never met with an accident.—p. 24.

Mr. J. W. Goss, wharfinger, was addressed with this question :—

Have you yourself received any damage from the bridge in its present unfortunate state ?—I believe,

about three-and-thirty years ago, my lighterman,
or a man who stowed a cask in a skiff fore and aft,
instead of athwart, did not secure it sufficiently ;
and going through at the tail of a lug-boat, the
boat got a cant and turned the cask out.

And that was owing to the bad stowage of the
cask in your skiff ?—Entirely : it was the only
accident I ever had that I paid for.

How many years is that ago ?—Thirty-three
years ago ; and I have been at the wharf where I
now am three-and-forty years, and do not believe
I have paid 5*l.* of damage for forty years ; and I
think I sent as many craft through as Mr. Sills.

How many craft a day ?—Two or three on an
ebb tide, and two or three on a flood tide, every
day and every night.—*Commons*, 1821, p. 70.

James Kelly, lighterman, [p. 17] had lost
a cask in a somewhat similar manner,
and this was his only accident in forty
years.

All sorts of persons most familiar with
the bridge and the river, for twenty, thirty,
and forty years, were interrogated as to all
the accidents they had experienced, seen,
or heard of ; and those who had sustained
losses furnished accounts of the amount.
Putting this mass of evidence, hearsay and
all, together, we are satisfied that two lives
and 3,000*l.* per annum, would be a very
high estimate of the loss of life and property
at London Bridge ; and that not the bridge
itself, but the rashness and impatience of

the sufferers, caused the great majority of the accidents.

But admitting this amount of damage (or any other amount that any one may please to assume) to be a cogent argument for an enlargement of the water-way, two other questions arise : First, are there no counter-vailing reasons, from probable damage of other kinds, resulting from such enlarge-ment? and secondly, Could not the requisite enlargement have been obtained by altering the old bridge, as effectually, as securely, and more economically, than by building a new one ?

The certain consequence of the enlarge-ment of the water-way will be, that the tide above-bridge will ebb lower and flow higher : there is much difference of opinion as to the degree. Some have calculated that the spring-tides will flow two feet higher : others, that the additional rise will be eight inches only.

The difference of level on high water spring tides, at a little eastward and west-ward of London Bridge, was stated as an established fact in the Report of Dance and others to the Bridge Committee in November 1814, to be two feet.* This statement was followed by a decided opinion, that no in-jury to the upper banks would result from

* *Commons*, 1821, pp. 89, 90.

the additional rise. The report, indeed, contemplated a great enlargement, but not a total opening, of the water-way.

The late Mr. Rennie thought, in 1810, that

> If London Bridge were removed, some part of the river banks, from Westminster up to Chelsea, would require to be raised from twelve to eighteen inches ; but that it would not be attended with any great expense. He did not think that the higher flow would fill any warehouses or cellars, but if so, he would be glad to raise his own wharf for the sake of the improved navigation.—*Commons*, 1821, p. 99.

"For the sake of the improved navigation ;" not for the sake of having a hand in the new bridge : which would, however, afford very good compensation for the expense of raising a wharf.

"The high-water line," says Professor Barlow,* "has a fall from London Docks to London Bridge of $1\frac{1}{2}$ inch at spring tides, but it is a dead level at high-water neap tides, as it is also between the London Docks and Blackwall. And from London Bridge to Richmond, the high-water mark is, according to the survey of Mr. Giles, the city surveyor, one dead level :" . . . "so that, at a medium spring-tide, we may expect the high-water mark from the bridge upwards to Richmond, to be higher by

* Jameson's *Edinburgh New Philosophical Journal.* 1826-7, ii. 49.

LONDON BRIDGE

about 13 inches than it is at present." This proceeds on the supposition that 13 inches are penned up below London Bridge at the high water of medium spring-tides. There is, however, much more than is here noticed to be taken into consideration.

It is not a question of medium spring-tides, but of the highest spring-tides : those which follow the autumnal, and precede the vernal equinox, and which are the highest of the year under ordinary circumstances ; and those of any of the intermediate winter months, when a great land flood meets the top of a spring-tide ; as in December 1821, when, even with the mighty rampart of the old bridge keeping back a great mass of tide-water, immense damage was done, all along both sides of the river, from Westminster upwards on the Middlesex side, and from London Bridge upwards on the Surrey side. The question to be asked is, whether disasters of this kind, which have hitherto been rare, will not probably become frequent when the dam of the old bridge is removed ? If so, the banks will require raising ; and if so, by whom is such raising to be paid for ? By those who cause the damage ? By those who sustain it ? Or (as we shall see the new bridge is to be paid for), by some unfortunate third party who has nothing to do with it ?

LONDON BRIDGE

" I shall not enter farther," says Professor Barlow, " into the probable changes which the removal of the bridge may occasion. A short time will decide the question by the best of all tests, actual experience."

No doubt: "Experience teaches," and so forth. But it will be poor consolation to a man, who sees the best part of his property suddenly laid under water, that philosophers, who could not foresee the case in its causes, will be able, when it is past remedy, to expound it in its effects.

The committees of 1820 and 1821, did not take the right way to seek, and certainly did not obtain, any evidence calculated to satisfy a rational man, whether scientific or practical, of the probable difference that will be made in the rise of the tides above bridge by the removal of the dam. One person had measured the difference of the high-water line on each side of the old bridge, and found it to be eight inches : another had measured it on another occasion, and found it to be thirteen inches : others were satisfied, that from some little distance below the bridge to some little distance above it, the difference was two feet: putting all which together, we should set down the difference of level at a medium of fifteen inches ; we should opine that fifteen inches additional rise would be considered too much by those who had the spring-tides at their doors, or on their premises, already ; and we should still see, that the mere difference of level, within a limited space above and below an obstruction, is only one element in the computation of the probable flow of the tide : and if the examinants do not appear to have thought of any other, it only shews, that " there are more things in heaven and earth than are dreamed of in their philosophy."

The flow of the tide up a river is the propagation of a wave : and the higher the tide ascends, (though with occasional variations) the greater is the height of the high-water line above that of the high water of the sea.* The high water at London Bridge, as ascertained by experiments during the trigonometrical survey, is eighty feet above the high water at the Nore. Any great obstruction diminishes or destroys this natural ascent of the high-water line, by breaking the impulse at the point of obstruction, and lessening the volume which passes it.

By removing the dam of the old bridge, the impulse will be greatly increased, and the volume of water passing upwards will

* Vide *Newtoni Principia*, Tom. III., Propos. 24 : Theor. 19, pp. 92-98 : Ed. Glasg. 1822.—Buat, *Principes d'Hydrauliques.*—Articles " Tide " and " River "; *Encycl. Brit.*—Robison's *Mechanical Philosophy*, vol. iii. p. 357.

be doubled. The area at high water will be increased from 7,360 feet to 14,500.* The high-water line from London Bridge to Richmond is at present a dead level. The obstruction is the only cause that can be assigned, for the ascent of the high-water line stopping at the bridge. The dead level will be raised about fifteen inches, but the unbroken impulse, and the double volume of water, will in all probability cause the high-water line to ascend from London to Richmond in the same proportion as from the Nore to London. This is at least highly probable : and if experience should confirm the theory, the mischief that will ensue defies calculation. Logs of mahogany will swim about Bankside ; kitchen-fires will be extinguished in Lambeth ; cabbages will be submerged, and melon-frames floated off at Millbank ; the Duchess of Buccleugh's beautiful villa at Richmond, will become a " house of pleasaunce " for Naiads : and our two-tailed friends will be set paddling about Westminster Hall, and sending forth sounds as choral, though not as musical, as those which Aristophanes puts into the mouths of the Frogs of the Styx.

The effect on the ebb will be, that during several hours of every tide, the river above bridge will be at least as low as it now is

* *Commons*, 1821, pp. 104, 105.

at the lowest water of spring-tides. These several hours, the latter half of the ebb, are those during which it is now dangerous to pass the bridge : but what will the navigation have gained, by having that which is now dangerous made impossible ?

The long existence of the dam has also had the effect of raising the bed of the river above bridge. There is a point just above the old bridge where the bed of the river becomes suddenly lower : and at this point there will be, in the latter ebb, a shallow rapid, till the upper channel is deepened. It may be deepened by dredging; if not, the current will wear it down, and the result of this will be, to endanger the stability of all the other bridges, and to incur the risk, that their piers may be gradually undermined, unless protected by costly operations.

Now let us suppose all these objections over-ruled, and the necessity of an enlarged waterway established ; the necessity for a new bridge remains to be proved.

Sir Christopher Wren was of opinion, that eighteen arches of the old bridge, might with perfect safety be thrown into nine ; by removing every alternate pier. Mr. Labelye, in 1746, proposed removing the starlings and casing the piers with three or four feet thickness of Portland stone.

LONDON BRIDGE

In the year 1759, the present centre arch was constructed, by removing a pier and throwing two arches into one, and it has been, at subsequent periods, proposed to extend this process to two, or three, or four new arches, or even to the full extent of nine proposed by Sir Christopher Wren. The evidence in favour of the safety and efficiency of this operation is abundantly sufficient to satisfy every mind not pre-determined on a job.

The Report of Messieurs Dance and Foulds, in 1799, describes the starlings as in a state of perfect security, and certain to be kept so with due attention; and the general mass and body of the masonry as in a state likely to last for ages.*

We shall now collect a few opinions respecting the strength of the piers, and their capacity to endure the process of throwing two arches into one.

Mr. Dance, 1799, thought

The piers of the centre arch, which had already endured this operation, were still strong enough to bear the raising of the centre arch to double its actual height.—*Commons*, p. 469.

Mr. William Chapman, Civil Engineer, gave his opinion, (1821) : that

The waterway of the old bridge might be en-larged with perfect safety, and that the bridge, so

* *Commons*, 1799, p. 469.

208

LONDON BRIDGE

altered, would last for ages with due attention.—
Commons, 1821, p. 47.

Mr. James Walker, Engineer, the builder
of Vauxhall Bridge, being asked :—

" Would you be perfectly satisfied to try the
experiment of the alterations, without coffer dams ? "
answered, " Certainly : because those piers and
starlings have stood six hundred years, and they
do not appear to have settled, and there is no
indication of it." * * * * * * " Then you pledge
your professional reputation, that it would be a
better plan to make an alteration on the old piers,
than to build a new bridge entirely ? "—" I think
it might be made as secure upon the present
piers and starlings, as the foundation of any new
bridge."—*Commons*, 1821, p. 64.

Mr. Thomas Piper, Stone-mason to the
Corporation of London, was asked :—

" After eighteen years experience, and this
[recent] examination, have you, or have you not,
any doubt of the foundation of London Bridge
supporting the proposed superstructure ? "—" I
have no doubt at all upon the subject ; and the
reason of my feeling confident is, that, whatever
imperfections or blemishes there may be in the
bridge, there is not the least indication of any
having arisen from the yielding of the foundation ;
and I think the experiment which has been made,
in turning the present great arch, fully justifies
the belief, that the arches that are now proposed
to be turned may be so turned with safety ; but
I am more disposed to think so, from the circumstance, that when the present large arch was

turned, for about twelve or thirteen feet on each face of it, it was put upon foundations that had never sustained any such weight; therefore, in turning arches as they are now proposed, we have better means of knowing that the foundation is competent, than they had who turned the present large arch; and I also think, that very little, if any, additional weight will be put upon the piers by making this alteration, because the spandrils will not, as I understand, be filled up solid." * * * * * * "Supposing this work to be done according to the best of your judgment, and under your own directions, what is your opinion as to its duration?"—"I think it quite probable, that the bridge would stand as long as it has already stood."—*Commons*, 1821, p. 66.

We cannot afford space to multiply citations, but the whole tendency of the opinions given before the committee of 1821, (Mr. Rennie's excepted) is to the effect, that the foundations of the old piers were fully adequate to sustain any additional weight that the enlargement of the arches might throw upon them. And it must be borne in mind, that during several centuries, a street of very large houses existed on the bridge, including a chapel and fortified gates.

And what was set against the mass of opinion on this side? Nothing but Mr. Rennie's doubts on the other, his statement that he had poked a boat-hook into a fissure, (which fissure had existed unaltered for at least half a century) and his saying, that he should not like to risk his reputation in the construction of new arches on the old piers, without having previously examined the piers through the means of coffer-dams.

The proposed alterations in the old bridge, would have cost 92,000*l.* without the coffer-dams : these would have cost 20,000*l.* each : and if six piers had been so examined, the cost of the examination would have been 120,000*l.* But we are satisfied, and we think our readers must be, that no such examination was necessary. Therefore, the water-way of the old bridge might have been enlarged for 92,000*l.* ; and there would have been no material interruption to the traffic over it, and no destruction of property.

Mr. Rennie's estimate for the new bridge was 430,000*l.* ; with an additional 20,000*l.* for a temporary bridge. The new bridge was to be built on the site of the old one, to obviate the necessity of new approaches, "which would lead," said Mr. Rennie, "to a very heavy expense." He gave his opinion, however, that the expense of new approaches, would be "very, very much less indeed than that of the new bridge itself ; " less, that is to say, than 430,000*l.* It appeared, also, in evidence, that the expense of keeping the starlings and the old bridge in repair, was about 4,000*l*. per annum.

The committee decided that an enlarged water-way was necessary to the navigation ; and that a new bridge was necessary, from the dangerous state of the old one. The corporation of London advertised for plans for a new bridge ; received many, and gave the offered premiums for the first, second, and third in merit ; of which three Mr. Rennie's was not one. The Act, however, which passed in 1823, stated specifically that Mr. Rennie's plan should be adopted, and it was adopted accordingly. Messieurs Jolliffe and Banks were the contractors, as augers and aruspices had foretold they would be.

The work proceeded. The coffer-dams of the new bridge contracted the water-way, and obstructed the navigation more than ever. Four arches were therefore thrown, or rather torn into two, by removing in two places an intermediate pier, and throwing plank-work across from the piers on each side. This being done without the precautions that would have been taken for a more permanent purpose, was the severest test to which the old piers could be subjected ; and the manner in which they have stood it is to us the strongest possible confirmation of the opinion, that the proposed alterations of the old bridge might have been made with perfect safety, and with every probability of the structure enduring for ages.

With respect to the removed piers, they ought, according to the theory of their insecurity, as soon as the piles of the starlings were withdrawn from around them, to have been carried clean away from their foundations by the force of the current. So far from this, however, they were, with infinite difficulty and delay, got down below the low-water of spring-tides. This was stated in the last published report respecting them, (December, 1826*) and for anything we know to the contrary, there they are still.

The work being in fair train, and past recalling, it was in due time discovered that the bridge would cost more, and the approaches much more, than had been dreamed of. An extra million or so was peremptorily required at the end of 1829. It was proposed, that this sum should be raised by loan, the interest to be defrayed by a tax on all coals passing up the river. It was held to be unbecoming to put a land-toll on the bridge, because there had never been one, and it was so great a thoroughfare ; it was very unbecoming that those who used it should pay for it ; but

* *Lords,* 1829 : Appendix, p. 873.

the consumers of Newcastle coal, all the way up the river to the westward : the old ladies of Maidenhead, for instance, who enter London at Hyde Park Corner, and to whom the Bridge can never be of any earthly service, were deemed the most eligible parties to bear the cost of a good transit for the citizens, from Gracechurch Street to Blackheath. The Lords' Committee of 1829, sat on this proposal. The first person examined was the present John Rennie, esq., and his evidence is not only highly instructive, but the most amusing, that ever fell under our observation in a parliamentary paper.

The original estimate for the bridge and approaches was 906,000*l*. : (506,000*l*. for the bridge, 400,000*l*. for the approaches). 575,552*l*. had been expended, 166,745*l*. were in hand, and 999,766*l*. were wanted : in all 1,742,063*l*. The excess beyond the original estimate was caused by departures from the original plan. The plan was, to build the new bridge on the site of the old one, first building a temporary bridge above it : but the Committee of the Corporation had decided, as they had power to do, that it should be built 180 feet to the westward. He thought the original plan best : he believed he had said so : but it was not his business to remonstrate or to ask reasons : he had nothing to do but to carry the decision into effect. They had asked if it was practicable to build the new bridge 180 feet to the westward : he had answered that it was : they had exercised their own discretion, and he had obeyed them. In the original plan there was no arch over Thames-street. He did not know whether any other plan, which included an arch, had been rejected on the score of the expense. His attention was confined to his own plan. The arch-way would get rid of the cross traffic of Thames-street. Waggons from Thames-street, to cross the bridge, would have to go round, undoubtedly. Persons from Billingsgate market, and from the fruit-warehouses in that line, crossing the bridge with loads on their heads, a good number certainly, (the question said "an immense number") would find it not so convenient to ascend the steep and narrow stairs, which will be the only approach for them. It would be not so convenient : it would be very inconvenient, certainly. The old bridge was in a very precarious state : it had been so for half a century and more : it had been made much worse by the throwing of four arches into two : he had done this in obedience to the committee : they had asked if it was practicable : he had said that it was practicable ; but that he would not be responsible ; and he was not responsible. He had obeyed orders : it was not his business to make representations. In one of the new arches, the low water had deepened from four feet to twenty-three, and the entire superstructure had been in danger of falling down. This had been prevented by throwing in rubbish. The alterations had cost nearly as much as the temporary bridge would have done. The expense of the temporary bridge had not been saved by the departure from the original plan. He did not know that the Act of Parliament prescribed Fish-street-hill as the avenue to the new bridge. He had nothing to do with Acts of Parliament, and had really not looked into it. Fish-street-hill would certainly not be the main avenue. He had altered the plan of the approaches on the authority of the Corporation Committee. He did not know that they had no authority to alter the plan of the approaches. He did not know that they had only authority to carry the Act into effect. He knew nothing of their authority. He had never thought of inquiring into it. He knew they were connected with the Treasury. He thought the letting of the dry arches, and the increased frontage of the streets, would pay for contingencies, but he was not sure.

He would not say that a still further sum of money would not be required.

All this was in the form of costive answers to questions. Our limits have compelled us to deprive it of its dramatic effect, which is great ; but it is altogether a very pretty story. A commission of lunacy would not sit very long on any individual who had managed his private affairs as this public affair has been managed. But by whom ? By the Parliament ? By the Treasury ? By the Corporation Committee ? Nobody is responsible. We do not blame Mr. Rennie. He has taken the only course to bear himself harmless. But this Corporation Committee makes an exquisite figure, fixing the site of the new bridge without thinking of the approaches ; ordering the alterations of the old one without thinking of the consequences ; violating the provisions of the Act which they were empowered to carry into execution ; spending all the money they had in getting their job half-finished, and proposing to raise more by taxing all consumers of sea-borne coal who happen to dwell westward, and who have no more to do with the bridge than the man in the moon.

In 1821, the estimated expense of this job was 600,000*l.* In 1823, it was 900,000*l.* In 1829, it was 1,740,000*l.* At a mean of these rates of progression, it will have grown to 2,600,000*l.* in 1832. The plan of approaches has, while we are writing, been altered again, after an immense destruction of property according to the plan of 1829. There will be much more demolition (including the old church of St. Michael, which is to be abolished utterly) ; and what with this, with making and paving the new roads, with clearing away the old bridge, and with all the contingencies of so complicated a mass of operations, we have not the slightest doubt that the entire expenditure will be THREE MILLIONS.

The whole affair is an instructive specimen of the way in which public business is done, and public money expended. Evidence is collected, and conclusions are drawn in the teeth of it. Plans are collected, and it has been predetermined whose plan shall be adopted. Tenders are called for, and the contractors have been already chosen. Estimates are prepared, and the expense doubles, triples, quadruples, in the progress of the work. Millions are thrown away in buildings, in colonies, in baubles and incumbrances of all kinds, in order to put a few thousands into the pockets of favoured individuals.

And what if the low ebbs and the high floods should create a clamour for restoring

LONDON BRIDGE

the dam, and on that clamour should be founded a new job for contracting the waterway of the new bridge ? Nobody will be responsible. Successively, from the sagacious engineer, to the discerning Corporation Committee, to the enlightened Treasury, to the scrutinising Treasury-bench, to the wise and incorruptible Parliament, to its free and independent constituents, Responsibility, in this, as in all other cases, like a shallow stream descending from a lofty mountain, bounds with decreasing force from ledge to ledge, and is lost in vapour before it reaches the bottom.

We have not touched the question as a matter of sentiment. But, even on this ground, we do not like these sweeping changes, which give to the metropolis the appearance of a thing of yesterday, and obliterate every visible sign that connects the present generation with the ages that are gone.

LORD MOUNT EDGCUMBE'S MUSICAL REMINISCENCES

LORD MOUNT EDGCUMBE'S
MUSICAL REMINISCENCES *

THE first edition of this work was published seven or eight years ago ; but being brought down to the present time, we may regard it as a new publication.

The Italian Opera is an affair that wants reforming ; but after the signal failure of a professing reformer, three seasons ago, no one will again make the profession for fifty years to come with the slightest chance of obtaining belief that the promise will be fulfilled.

Lord Mount Edgcumbe's Reminiscences extend over a period of sixty years—a term nearly equivalent to one-half of the entire existence of the Italian Opera in England ; and in the conclusion of them he thinks that, in every point of view—music, poetry, singers, audience—the Italian theatre in

* *Musical Reminiscences ; containing an Account of the Italian Opera in England from 1773.* 4th edit. Continued to the present time, and including the Festival in Westminster Abbey. By the Earl of Mount Edgcumbe. London : Andrews. 1834. pp. 294.

England has changed for the worse. " First impressions," he says, " are the most lasting." This is true ; and they are also the most agreeable. There is no one object to which we have attached sufficient interest to make it an uniform pursuit, of which we may not say with Byron—

No more, no more, oh ! never more on me
  The freshness of the heart can fall like dew,
Which, out of all the lovely things we see,
  Extracts emotions beautiful and new,
Hived in our bosoms like the bag o' the bee.
  Think'st thou the honey with those objects grew ?
Alas ! 'twas not in them, but in thy power
To double e'en the sweetness of a flower.

Herein lies the foundation of the *laudatio temporis acti*, which is inseparable from advancing years in all cases but in that of the philosophical few, who are satisfied that "every generation grows wiser and wiser," and that the progress of the useful in one way is more than a compensation for the loss of the agreeable in another. We shall not discuss in this place how far the useful and agreeable are identical or opposite. Medicine is useful, and not agreeable ; and it may, at some periods, be very desirable for the ultimate benefit of mankind that they should be subjected to a course of moral and political medicine, drenched with mental cathartics, and restricted, for their greatest indulgence, to potations of intellectual toast and water. This we shall not gainsay ; but our present business is with an article of mental luxury, in which we shall restrict our view of the useful to that which is useful for the accomplishment of the object proposed, leaving the great question *de finibus* to those who have already settled it to their own satisfaction.

The object proposed by the Italian Opera is to present the musical drama in the most perfect possible form. To this end there must be, in the first place, a good drama : an interesting story, intelligibly told in good poetry, and affording ample scope for strong and diversified expression : good music, adapting the sound to the sense, and expressing all the changes and trains of feeling that belong to the ideas and images of the drama : good performers—persons of good figures and features—picturesque in action, and expressive in countenance— with voices of fine tone and great power, having true intonation, scientific execution, and above all, or rather as the crown of all, expression — expression — expression : the one all-pervading and paramount quality, without which dramatic music is but as a tinkling cymbal : elegant and appropriate dresses—beautiful scenery—a chorus, each of whom should seem as if he knew that he had some business of his own in the scene, and not as if he were a mere unit among thirty or forty automata, all going like clock-work by the vibrations of the conductor's pendulum : a full orchestra of accomplished musicians, with a good leader —and especially without a conductor keeping up, in the very centre of observation, a gesticulation and a *tapage* that make him at once the most conspicuous and most noisy personage in the assembly, distracting attention from the sights and sounds that ought exclusively to occupy it—an affliction to the eye, and a most pestilent nuisance to the ear. But, with all this, there should be (as there used to be) an audience regulating its costume and its conduct by the common conventional courtesies of evening society ; not with men wearing hats among well-dressed women, and rubbing dirty boots against white petticoats ; nor with an influx of late comers, squeezing themselves between the crowded benches, and sitting down in the laps of their precursors, as we have both seen and suffered. We are aware that some advocates for universal liberty think that the morning liberty of the streets should be carried into all evening assemblies ; but, looking back to the Athenians, we cannot consider that cleanliness and courtesy are incompatible with the progress of freedom and intelligence.

Now, by following out the principal points which we have enumerated a little in detail, we shall see what we have had, and what we have wanted—what we are likely to have, and what we are likely to continue to want—for the bringing together of the constituent portions of a perfect musical drama. Lord Mount Edgcumbe touches all these points. We shall content ourselves, on the present occasion, with citing a few of his observations, and expressing our own opinions in a subsequent commentary :—

The opera in England, for the period of ten years after the departure of Catalani, will afford much less room for observation than any of the preceding, as far as the singers are concerned ; for, with one or two exceptions, there were not any of whom I feel inclined to say much, because there is not much to be said in their praise. But so great a change has taken place in the character of the dramas, in the style of the music, and in its performance, that I cannot help enlarging a little on that subject before I proceed farther.

One of the most material alterations is, that the grand distinction between serious and comic operas is nearly at an end, the separation of the singers for their performance entirely so. Not only do the same sing in both, but a new species of drama has arisen, a kind of mongrel between them, called *semi-seria*, which bears the same analogy to the other two that that non-descript the melo-drama does to the legitimate tragedy and comedy of the English stage. The construction of these newly-invented pieces is essentially different from the old. The dialogue, which used to be carried on in recitative, and which in Metastasio's operas is often so beautiful and interesting, is now cut up (and rendered unintelligible if it were worth listening to) into *pezzi concertati*, or long singing conversations, which present a tedious succession of unconnected, ever-changing motivos, having nothing to do with each other, and if a satisfactory air is for a moment introduced, which the ear would like to dwell upon, to hear modulated, varied, and again returned to, it is broken off before it is well understood or sufficiently heard, by a sudden transition into a totally different melody, time, and key, and recurs no more : so that no impression can be made, or recollection of it preserved. Single songs are almost exploded, for which one good reason may be given, that there are few singers capable of singing them. Even a prima donna, who would formerly have complained at having less than three or four airs allotted to her, is now satisfied with one trifling cavatina for a whole opera.

The acknowledged decline of singing in general (which the Italians themselves are obliged to confess) has no doubt, in a great measure, occasioned this change. But another cause has certainly contributed to it, and that is the difference of the voices of the male performers. Sopranos have long ceased to exist, but tenors for a long while filled their place. Now even these have become so scarce, that Italy can produce no more than two or three very good ones. The generality of voices are basses, which, for want of better, are thrust up into the first characters, even in serious operas, where they used only to occupy the last place, to the manifest injury of melody, and total subversion of harmony, in which the lowest part is their peculiar province.

These new first singers are called by the novel appellation of *basso cantante* (which, by the bye, is a kind of apology, and an acknowledgment that they ought not to sing), and take the lead in operas with almost as much propriety as if the double bass were to do so in the orchestra, and play the part of the first fiddle. A bass voice is too unbending, and deficient in sweetness for single songs, and fit only for those of inferior character, or of the buffo style. In duettos, it does not coalesce well with a female voice, on account of the too great distance between them, and in fuller pieces the ear cannot be satisfied without some good intermediate voices to fill up the interval, and complete the harmony. Yet three or four basses now frequently overpower one weak tenor, who generally plays but a subordinate part.—pp. 118-123.

We shall begin with the drama itself—the dramatic poem, the libretto.

Rousseau has admirably described what the lyrical drama ought to be :—

On sentit qu'il ne falloit à l'Opéra rien de froid et de raisonné, rien que le spectateur pût écouter assez tranquillement pour réfléchir sur l'absurdité de ce qu'il entendoit ; et c'est en cela surtout que consiste la différence essentielle du drame lyrique à la simple tragédie. Toutes les délibérations politiques, tous les projets de conspiration, les expositions, les récits, les maximes sentencieuses, en un mot, tout ce qui ne parle qu' à la raison, fut banni du langage du cœur, avec les jeux d'esprit, les madrigaux, et tout ce qui n'est que des pensées. Le ton même de la simple galanterie, qui cadre mal avec les grandes passions, fut à peine admis dans le remplissage des situations tragiques, dont il gâte presque toujours l'effet : car jamais on ne sent mieux que l'acteur chante, que lorsqu'il dit une chanson.

The business, indeed, of the lyrical dramatist is to present, with the most perfect simplicity, the leading and natural ideas of an impassioned action, divested of all imagery not arising from spontaneous feeling. A heroine in distress must neither demonstrate her misery by an accumulation of evidence, as in an old French tragedy, nor dress it out in a complication of heterogeneous figures, as in a modern English song, in which everything is illustrated by a chaos of images which never met in the organized world : for instance, in a Venetian serenade, in the opera of *Faustus*—

Lucy dear, Lucy dear, wake to the spring,
Hark ! how the village-bells merrily ring.

Village bells in Venice ! and, moreover, peculiar to the spring—a sort of tintinnabulary efflorescence, characteristic of the season, like the cowslip and the cuckoo !

Or in a song which we have heard Braham
sing fifty times,—

> Is there a heart that never loved,
>   Or felt soft woman's sigh ?
> Is there a man can mark unmoved
>   Dear woman's tearful eye ?
> Go bear him to some desert shore,
>   Or solitary cell,
> Where none but savage monsters roar,
>   Where man ne'er deign'd to dwell.

Here is a solitary cell, of which the grievance
is, not that none dwell in it, but that none
roar in it except savage monsters, whose
presence makes it solitary. Or in a song
which we have heard as often from half-a-
dozen female singers,—

> Meet me by moonlight alone,
>   And then I will tell you a tale
> Must be told by the moonlight alone,
>   In the grove at the end of the vale.
> You must promise to come, for I said
>   I would show the night-flowers their queen :
> Nay, turn not away that sweet head,
>   'Tis the loveliest ever was seen.

The reason for the lady meeting the gentleman by moonlight is, that he has promised
to show the night-flowers their queen,
videlicet herself ; and the lady must do
something very incongruous, because the
gentleman must keep his word with the
night-flowers.

We have put down these specimens from memory. They are the first that occur to us, but they are fair samples of modern English musical poetry—astounding and impertinent nonsense—answering no purpose, if it happens to be heard, but to distract the attention from any degree of natural feeling and expression which may belong to the music or the voice. We had much rather that the words were in the language of Otaheite. We could then at least guess at something that suited the music.

The poetry of the Italian Opera is quite the contrary of all this. It gives, with little or no ornament, the language of passion in its simplest form : a clear and strong outline to be filled up by the music : which is itself the legitimate ornament and illustration of the leading ideas and sentiments of the scene. The essentials of style, in the composition of dramatic poetry for music, are simplicity and severity. It may be said, that the same rhymes and phrases are of constant recurrence ; but though they are the same to read, they are not the same to hear. The cor and amor, fedeltà and felicità, of *Desdemona*, are not those of *Medea*. The music paints the difference. There is nothing in any Italian libretto at all resembling the egregious rigmarol of our modern English songs.

MUSICAL REMINISCENCES

To illustrate what we have said, and to avoid even the appearance of selection, we will point to the words of Rubini's most popular airs : "Ah ! così ne'dì ridenti," and "Vivi tu, te ne scongiuro" in *Anna Bolena :* "Pasci il guardo" in *La Sonnambula*—and "Tu vedrai la sventurata" in *Il Pirata.* We will quote a few lines from two of them :—

> Nel veder la tua costanza
> Il mio cor si rasserena :
> Non temea che la tua pena,
> Non soffrì che il tuo soffrir.
> L' ultim' ora che s'avanza
> Ambidue sfidar possiamo,
> Che nessun quaggiù lasciamo
> Nè timore nè desir.
>
> *ANNA BOLENA.*

> Ma non fia sempre odiata
> La mia memoria, io spero ;
> Se fui spietato e fiero,
> Fui sventurato ancor.
> E parlerà la tomba
> Alle pietose genti,
> De' lunghi miei tormenti,
> Del mio tradito amor.
>
> *IL PIRATA.*

These are fair specimens of Italian airs, and serve to prove what we have alleged respecting the simplicity and even severity with which the leading ideas are presented unencumbered with ornament. Our old English songs were models of simplicity, but our modern songs are almost all false sentiment, overwhelmed with imagery utterly false to nature, like the night-flowers and solitary-celled monsters quoted above. Mr. Moore, with his everlasting " brilliant and sparkling " metaphors, has contributed to lead the *servum pecus* into this limbo of poetical vanity : but the original cause lies deeper : namely, in a very general diffusion of heartlessness and false pretension. We will not now pursue the investigation—but as we are speaking of English theatrical songs, we will observe, that the introduction, always objectionable, of airs not belonging to the piece, is nevertheless usually managed on the Italian stage with a certain degree of contrivance, and fitted by a new scena into the business of the drama. The same thing is done in English operas, in a manner marvellously clumsy and inartificial. For instance, Henry Bertram, in *Guy Mannering*, loses his way among rocks, expects to be attacked by thieves—resolves to fight manfully—recollects how manfully Nelson fought at Trafalgar, and strikes up—" 'Twas in Trafalgar bay ! "

A singular instance of the obtuseness of our English opera song-makers occurs in the opera of *Rob Roy*. Some of Words-

MUSICAL REMINISCENCES

worth's verses were adopted, including the well-known passage,

the good old rule
Suffices them ; the simple plan,
That they should take who have the power,
And they should keep who can.

The opera-wright thought it would improve these verses to make the first and third lines rhyme, and actually altered them as follows :—

the good old maxim still
Suffices them ; the simple plan,
That they should take who have the will,
And they should keep who can.

He could not see the essential difference between the *will* and the *power* in this matter of taking.

Lord Mount Edgcumbe quotes a passage from Schlegel's Lectures :—

A few only of the operas of Metastasio still keep possession of the stage, as the change of taste in music demands a different arrangement of the text. Metastasio seldom has chorusses, and his airs are almost always for a single voice : with these the scenes uniformly terminate, and the singer never fails to make his exit with them. In an opera we now require more frequent duos and trios, and a *crashing* finale. In fact, the most difficult problem for the opera poet is the mixing the complicated voices of conflicting passions in one common harmony, without injuring their essence : a problem however which is generally

235

solved by both poet and musical composer in a very arbitrary manner.

and adds—

The consequence of this is that all the new dramas written for Rossini's music are most execrably bad, and contain scarcely one line that can be called poetry, or even one of common sense.

This sweeping condemnation is by no means merited. Some of Rossini's libretti are detestable enough ; but there is much good dramatic poetry in some of them, *Tancredi* and *Semiramide* especially. It is true, that in these dramas the Italian poet had only to condense the essence of Voltaire's tragedies, but the task is well executed. The libretto of Donizetti's *Anna Bolena* is an excellent dramatic poem.

It is seldom that we are enabled to judge fairly either of an Italian libretto, or of the music of an opera as a whole. For example, in 1832 Mr. Monck Mason professed to bring forward Pacini's *Gli Arabi nelle Gallie.* He first cut it into halves, and put the second half aside, or into the fire. He then cut away the beginning and substituted that of Rossini's *Zelmira.* He then tacked a strange air, we forget from whence, to the middle, by way of an end, and thus presented to the public both author and composer literally without head or tail. The critics discovered that the drama was non-sense, and that much of the music was stolen ; and Pacini and his poet bore the blame which belonged to the manager. This mode of murdering reputations ought to subject the offender to an action for damages. " I was induced, unfortunately," says Lord Mount Edgcumbe, "to go one night to see *Gli Arabi nelle Gallie*, a very poor opera by Pacini." What he saw was poor enough, but it was not Pacini's opera. In the same season Bellini's *La Straniera*, which has much beautiful melody, and an interesting and intelligible story, founded on the Vicomte d'Arlincourt's *L'Étrangère*, was presented in such a chaotic fashion, that the intentions of both poet and composer remained an unfathomable mystery.

These liberties are taken more or less with the works of all masters, from the greatest to the least. Mozart himself does not escape them. Interpolation indeed he does escape. The audiences of the King's Theatre are justly strict in this one point only, that they will not permit the sewing on of an extraneous purple shred to any of his great and sacred textures. But garbled and mutilated his works are abominably, to fit the Procrustean bed of an inadequate company, or to quadrate with the manager's notions of the bad taste of the public. A

237

striking instance of this is in the invariable performance of *Il Don Giovanni* without its concluding sestetto. Don Juan's first introduction to a modern English audience was in a pantomime (at Drury Lane we believe), which ended with the infernal regions, a shower of fire, and a dance of devils. Mozart's opera has, properly, no such conclusion. Flames arise—a subterranean chorus is heard—Don Juan sinks into the abyss—the ground closes above him—Leporello remains on the stage : a strongly-marked modulation leads from the key of D minor into that of G major, with a change from common time andante to triple time allegro assai ; and the other characters, ignorant of the catastrophe, rush in to seek their revenge :—

> Ah ! dov' è il perfido,
> Dov' è l'indegno ? &c.

Leporello explains the adventure, and after a general exclamation, a solemn pause, and an exceedingly sweet larghetto movement, in which the dramatis personæ dispose of themselves, " Or che tutti, o mio tesoro," the opera is wound up by a fugue in D major—" Questo è il fin di chi fa mal : " one of the very finest things in dramatic music, and the most appropriate possible termination of the subject ; and yet is this

most noble composition, this most fitting
and genuine conclusion, sacrificed to a
dance of devils flashing torches of rosin,
for no earthly reason but that so ended the
Drury Lane pantomime.

Le Nozze di Figaro and *Il Flauto Magico*
both require a better and more numerous
company than is ever assembled in this
country. If we have in the former an
Almaviva, a Figaro, a Contessa and a
Susanna, it is the usual extent of our good
fortune. We have seldom an endurable
Cherubino ; Marcellina is generally a non-
entity : Barbarina always so ; Bartolo,
Basilio, and Antonio take their chance,
which is seldom good for any of them,
and never for all ; and Don Curzio is for
the most part abrogated.

Il Don Giovanni and *Le Nozze di Figaro*
are both specimens of excellently-written
libretti, separating most effectively the action
and passion from the ratiocination of the
originals ; but we have seen the latter
especially performed in such a manner,
that if we had known nothing of it but from
the representation, we should have found it
incomprehensible ; and this sort of experiment on things which we know well should
make us cautious of pronouncing summary
judgment on things of which we know nothing
but from the showing of the King's Theatre.

Il Flauto Magico is a well-written libretto, but the subject is too mystical to be interesting, or even generally intelligible ; and this is a great drawback on its theatrical popularity, which has never approached that of the *Giovanni* and *Figaro*, though the music exhausts all the fascinations of both melody and harmony, and may be unhesitatingly cited as the absolute perfection of both. It requires more good singers than either of the others, and it requires them the more imperatively, as it depends more exclusively on the music. It requires seventeen voices besides the chorus. The music which is assigned to the three nymphs and the three genii is almost supernaturally beautiful : for this alone there should be six good voices, and there are, without these, six principal and five secondary parts. We may therefore despair of ever hearing this opera performed as it ought to be.

The works of Italian composers do not require, in any instance that we remember, so many performers. Those of the most modern composer of any name—Bellini— are singularly restricted in their principal parts. He seems to endeavour to defend himself against the caprices and jealousies of the performers by giving them nothing to quarrel about. A prima soprano, a primo tenore, a primo basso, and the ordinary components of a chorus, can perform his *Pirata*. There can be no dispute here about pre-eminence, but the general effect is necessarily meagre. But the progress of self-conceit among singers has made this result inevitable. A prima soprano is now to be found everywhere, and a seconda nowhere ; and though many who assume to be first are scarcely fit to be second, they will not be content with what they are fit for, but will be first or nothing. There appears to be this great difference between a German and an Italian company—that the Germans will co-operate to the production of general effect, and the Italians will look to nothing but their own individual display. We have seen, in a German opera, the same person taking a principal part one night, and singing in the chorus the next. We have seen the same with the French ; but with the Italians this never occurs. A German author and composer may therefore give fair scope to their subject ; but the Italians must sacrifice everything to their company, and all in vain, except for the first production—for to the whims and inefficiency of every new company the unfortunate opera must be refitted and garbled. Bellini's is the true plan for his own reputation. A soprano, a tenor, a bass, and a chorus, there must be in every company, and they can have nothing to quarrel for ; but the musical drama must be ruined if this were to become the rule of its construction. And the scheme, after all, is not always successful : for in 1830 the prima donna transposed the middle and end of *Il Pirata*, in order that she might finish it herself instead of the tenor.

" Ma femme, et cinq ou six poupets," will not make a company in the opinion of any one but Catalani's husband. No one, indeed, who has seen and heard Catalani, or Pasta, or Malibran, or Giulietta Grisi, would willingly dispense with one such prima donna ; but the single star should not be worshipped exclusively to the sacrifice of the general effect. She can be but a component, however important, part of it ; and if the general effect fails, the star will fall.

But with us, though the star cannot shine if the general effect be bad, no general effect, however otherwise excellent, will produce attraction without a star. In 1832, though the star of the French opera of *Robert le Diable* (Madame Cinti) was but one of the fourth magnitude, yet with her eclipse the opera fell. We thought the general effect improved by the substitution of Mdlle. Schneider, but the public resolutely abstained from sitting in judgment on the question. Madame Cinti's voice was not powerful—Mdlle. Schneider's much less so : both had sweetness and good execution ; but Madame Cinti was as cold as an icicle, and Mdlle. Schneider was all feeling and expression. For example, in the Princess Isabella's duet with her lover Robert, in which he begins—

> Avec bonté voyez ma peine
> Et mes remords,
> Et n'allez pas par votre haine
> Punir mes torts,

the princess echoes the words, " Et vos remords ! " " Punir vos torts ! " In Madame Cinti's performance we had merely the musical echo : in Mdlle. Schneider's we had an expression of the deepest tenderness. Her " Et vos remords " seemed to imply that his remorse was an expiation of his offences : her " Punir vos torts " seemed to imply, that for her to punish his offences was impossible. Now this is the expression which is the soul of music, of which Madame Cinti had not a particle, and of which Mdlle. Schneider was full to overflowing ; but everybody went to hear Madame Cinti, and nobody went to hear Mdlle. Schneider. We formed our secret opinion in the solitude of an empty theatre, and now communicate it to the public in especial confidence.

We do not agree in opinion with Lord Mount Edgcumbe that the decline of singing in Italy has conduced to the composition of melodramas and the frequency of *pezzi concertati*. There has been an increase of excitement in the world of reality, and that of imagination has kept it company. The ordinary stage deserted the legitimate drama for melo-drama before the musical stage did so. The public taste has changed, and the supply of the market has followed the demand. There can be no question that Rossini's music is more spirit-stirring than Paësiello's, and more essentially theatrical : more suited to the theatre by its infinite variety of contrast and combination, and more dependent on the theatre for the development of its perfect effect. We were present at the first performance of an opera of Rossini's in England : *Il Barbiere di Siviglia*, in March, 1818. We saw at once that there was a great revolution in dramatic music. Rossini burst on the stage like a torrent, and swept everything before him except Mozart, who stood, and will stand, alone and unshaken, like the Rock of Ages, because his art is like Shakspeare's, identical with nature, based on principles that cannot change till the constitution of the

human race itself be changed, and therefore secure of admiration through all time,
as the drapery of the Greek statues has
been through all the varieties of fashion.

Whether singing in Italy has declined is
another question. Lord Mount Edgcumbe
received his first impressions in the days
of " the divine Pacchierotti." We, who
received ours at a later period, cannot sym-
pathize with him in his regret for the musici.
We are content with such vocal music as
the natural voice will allow us ; we listen
with unmixed pleasure to such a basso as
Tamburini. The whole compass of the
human voice finds its appropriate distribution in concerted music, otherwise the
distribution is wrong, and not the principle
of admitting the bass voice. The basso-
cantante does not take the lead in the pezzo-
concertato, any more than the double bass
takes the place of the first fiddle in the
orchestra. The one has its proper place in
the instrumental, and the other in the vocal
distribution. And if much of the dialogue
which was formerly carried on in recitative
is now carried on in concerted music, it is
because it is found more agreeable and more
suited to the changes and varieties of
passion, and is at the same time readily
followed by the majority of the audience,
who would now find an old opera consisting

of only recitative and single airs, with at most one or two duets, or a duet and a terzetto, a very insipid production. The favourites of a century, or even half a century back, could not be successfully reproduced without ripienimenti.

Lord Mount Edgcumbe's first impressions make him partial to thin and shrill tones. This is evident to us, in his praise of Camporese and Caradori ; but with the decline of the musici, a fuller volume of tone in the female voice has been more and more required to satisfy the ear in concert with tenori and bassi. Tosi, the idol of Naples, with her soprano-sfogato voice, was not endured in England in 1832. The perfection of our domestic musical instruments has also contributed to this result. We have lost all relish, and even all toleration, for the tone of the harpsichord, since we have received our first ideas from that of the piano-forte.

A good opera well performed is a great rarity with us. Good operas there are in abundance ; but there are seldom either sense or knowledge in the management to select them, or power or good-will in the company to do them justice. The best singers come here for only a portion of the season : they sing morning, noon, and night, at concerts ; they have no time to rehearse.

MUSICAL REMINISCENCES

The manager has collected stars, but not a company : there is a soprano too much, and a contralto too little—a tenor wanting, and a basso to spare : they patch up a performance as they may—altering, garbling, omitting, interpolating—and the result is, a bad concert instead of a good opera. A good opera is a whole, as much in the music as in the poetry, and cannot be dislocated and disfigured by omissions and interpolations, without destruction to its general effect.

Lord Mount Edgcumbe justly observes that

a mean economy prevails in all the inferior departments, with regard to secondary singers, the chorus and orchestra : the scenery, decorations, and wardrobe, are in every respect unworthy of the largest theatre in the country.—p. 176.

But the enormous expense of the principal singers and dancers would not alone render this mean economy necessary, if it were not for the enormous rent exacted for the house. By a rough calculation which we made the other day, it appeared to us that the Italian Opera has been carried on in England for about a century and a quarter, at an average net loss of 5,000*l.* a year ; but of late years the Opera has yielded what would have been a liberal profit to the proprietors of the theatre, if it had been carried on by the proprietors, and not by a lessee, saddled with a disproportionate rent.

Lord Mount Edgcumbe reprobates the novel introduction of a conductor into the orchestra, not playing himself but beating time with a noisy bâton. Assuredly our Italian opera conductor verifies the remark of Dr. Burney :—

> Rousseau says, that the more time is beaten the less it is kept ; and it is certain that when the measure is broken, the fury of the musical general, or director, increasing with the disorder and confusion of his troops, he becomes more violent, and his strokes and gesticulations more ridiculous in proportion to their disorder.—p. 235.

Lord Mount Edgcumbe makes some observations on the change which has taken place in the appearance and conduct of the audience of the King's Theatre, which we fully agree with him is a change altogether for the worse. We confess we have a prejudice in favour of sitting at our ease among well-mannered company, and we have been elbowed and annoyed out of all endurance of the pit at the Opera. Amongst the principal causes of this change is the profuse admission of orders ; and on what ground these are given we saw the other day some curious evidence in a case in the Court of Requests. One of the former managers of the Opera had set up a paper

called the Theatrical Critic, which did not
succeed, and had left off in debt to the
editor two guineas, for which important
amount he was summoned ; and it appeared
that, in postponing the payment, he had
told the editor a box was always at his
service. After this we need not wonder at
the heterogeneous composition of the audience in the pit. Assuredly those who pay
have a right to complain, if they find all
the places pre-occupied by those who do
not. They do not complain, however, but
they exercise another right more fatal to
the management, and more just to its mis-
conduct—-the right of staying away. In
short, as Lord Mount Edgcumbe justly
observes,—

The whole system is radically bad ; and nothing
can restore the Opera in this country to its former
respectable and agreeable footing, or the performances to that excellence which a public paying so
dearly has a right to expect, but a total reformation,
an entire change of proprietors, of managers, of all
parties connected with the theatre, I had almost
said, hampered and embarrassed as it is, of the
theatre itself.—p. 186.

We should be sorry to change the theatre,
because it is the finest vehicle for sound in
Europe ; but we wish to see it thoroughly
reformed in all the points to which we have
adverted, and in another very important

matter—that of its exits and its entrances. It was not intended for a crowd, but it is now often crowded, legitimately or artificially ; and the occurrence of a fire on a crowded night would ensure the destruction of the audience. It is surrounded, or rather built in, by shops and taverns, and even the alarm of fire in any one of these would occasion incalculable mischief.

But it is vain to anticipate any reform of this theatre while it is in the hands of the assignees of a bankrupt estate, who think only of exacting the utmost possible rent within the year—(a double rent, in short : first, a fair return on the capital ; and, second, a most unfair and unjustifiable tax on the monopoly of the license)—from an impresario who is only an annual tenant, who can, therefore, make no prospective arrangements—who is always taken unprovided at the beginning of the season—who thinks of nothing but how to make both ends meet at the end of it—who trusts to his skill in the " detection of a star " to redeem himself by a temporary attraction in the course of it—and who, if he can fill the theatre by a fiddler or a dancer, is content to let the opera take its chance. It is true that we are indebted to him for some operatic stars, as well as for heroes of one string, and heroines of one toe ; but he has done nothing, or worse than nothing, for the musical drama, about which he neither knows nor cares anything. Last year he had five admirable performers : Giulietta Grisi, Rubini, Tamburini, Ivanoff, and Zuchelli—the first three the best soprano, tenor and bass, perhaps, in the whole musical world. What these five could do was done transcendently well, but he had no contralto, or one too inefficient to be a principal, and too conceited to be a second ; and *La Gazza Ladra* was performed a dozen times with a walking Pippo. Half a dozen most familiar operas, and one indifferent novelty, were the entire performances of the season : still it was much to have such singers, especially with the exquisite acting and personal fascinations of Giulietta Grisi, and they carried the season profitably through, with the help, indeed, of Taglioni, *la Déesse de la danse.* The present manager has an advantageous foil in the impresario of 1832, who, having professed to reform the Italian Opera, did not present a single good Italian performance throughout his entire management ; but a manager of the Italian Opera should be—

conversant with the Italian stage, a good judge of music and of singers, acquainted with foreign languages and foreign usages, of liberal ideas, not sparing of expense, but judicious in the application of it ; knowing what is right, and firm in exercising his authority to enforce it : in short, one who can act for himself, and not be dependent on the ignorance or bad faith of subordinate agents. Such a one only can carry on the business of the theatre with success, and give to the English public a really good Italian opera.—pp. 176, 177.

Such is Lord Mount Edgcumbe's idea of what an Italian Opera manager ought to be : it is unquestionably just ; but it is unfortunately a portrait to which we may long continue to apply the words of Juvenal,—

— qualem nequeo monstrare et sentio tantum.

FRENCH COMIC ROMANCES

FRENCH COMIC ROMANCES

It is our intention, in a future Number, to give some account of the popular French novelist Paul de Kock, whose works have extended in fifteen years to the number of seventy-seven volumes ; and are proceeding at the same rate with undiminished, or rather with progressively increasing, success. But before doing so, we have a few words to say of one or two of his predecessors in this branch of literature.

Paul de Kock is the legitimate successor of Pigault le Brun ; and though he is, like his predecessor, *un écrivain un peu leste*, his works are, of all modern French novels, the most popular among English fashionable readers. In one respect, his writings present a striking contrast to those of his predecessor. Pigault le Brun began as a writer with the beginning of the French revolution : his successive works are impressed with the political changes of the day : they carry their era in their incidents ; the actions of his heroes and heroines are

255

interwoven with the great events that are passing around them ; we live with the living witnesses and agents of the Constituent Assembly, the Legislative Assembly, the National Convention, the Executive Directory, the Consulate, and the Empire. The political and religious opinions of the author are kept always prominent ; and we find him a sturdy enemy to priestcraft and tyranny throughout : with this modification, that prudence, during the Empire, restraining his politics, he gave a more undivided range to his theology. In the writings of Paul de Kock, a theological opinion is here and there slightly indicated, but a political opinion never ; the era of his narratives is marked by manners only, not by political events and opinions. We are made aware that there is a government, but the only use that is made of it is to provide the hero, or one of his friends, with *une petite place dans l'administration :* there is nothing to show whether the head of it be a president, a consul, a king, or an emperor. The Sunday excursions of the Parisians—the village dances and gaieties of Sunday evening—imply a striking negation of Sir Andrew Agnew : but ecclesiastics, who cut a very conspicuous figure among the buffoons of Pigault le Brun, as they had done in French comic tales of all ages, from the Fabliaux of the twelfth century to the romances of the revolution, are never exhibited by Paul de Kock, either for good or for ill. In short, Church and State, which are always in the foreground of Pigault le Brun's pictures, are scarcely seen through the most dim perspective in those of Paul de Kock. Whether the regular succession of disappointments which have been inflicted on the friends of liberty, in the persons of Robespierre, Napoleon, the Bourbons, and Louis Philippe, has, amongst a very large class of readers, converted the bright hopes of the earlier days of the revolution into a sceptical indifference to their possible realization, is a point which we reserve for future consideration. In the meantime, we think it worth noticing, as a matter of fact, that two authors, having so many points in common, evidently not differing in opinion, and the second not less liberal than the first, present in this particular so remarkable a difference ; and which is the more remarkable, because, though no preceding writers have poured forth comic romances in such abundance as these two, yet all the works of this kind which preceded the revolution—works, that is to say, illustrious in their kind—embodied opinion in a very cogent and powerful form.

FRENCH COMIC ROMANCES

In respect of presenting or embodying opinion, there are two very distinct classes of comic fictions : one in which the characters are abstractions or embodied classifications, and the implied or embodied opinions the main matter of the work ; another, in which the characters are individuals, and the events and the action those of actual life—the opinions, however prominent they may be made, being merely incidental. To the first of these classes belong the fictions of Aristophanes, Petronius Arbiter, Rabelais, Swift, and Voltaire ; to the latter, those of Henry Fielding, his Jonathan Wild perhaps excepted, which is a felicitous compound of both classes ; for Jonathan and his gang are at once abstractions and individuals. Jonathan is at once king of the thieves and the type of an arch whig.

To the latter class belong the writings of Pigault le Brun. His heroes and heroines are all genuine flesh and blood, and invest themselves with the opinions of the time as ordinary mortals do, carrying on the while the realities of every-day life. There is often extravagance both in the characters and the actions, but it is the mere exuberance of fancy, and not like the hyperboles of Rabelais, subservient to a purpose. Rabelais, one of the wisest and most learned, as well as wittiest of men, put on the robe of the all-licensed fool, that he might, like the court-jester, convey bitter truths under the semblance of simple buffoonery.

Such was also, in a great measure, the purpose of his contemporary Bertrand de Verville, who, although he introduces *Frostibus, Lieutenant-Général de tous les diables*, apostrophising Luther, in an exceedingly whimsical oration, as *Monsieur de l'autre monde*, was not one of the least strenuous, or least successful, supporters of the cause of the Reformation.

It would be, we think, an interesting and amusing inquiry to trace the progress of French comic fiction, in its bearing on opinion, from the twelfth century to the Revolution ; and to show how much this unpretending branch of literature has, by its universal diffusion through so many ages in France, contributed to directing the stream of opinion against the mass of delusions and abuses which it was the object of those who were honest in the cause of the Reformation, and in the causes of the several changes which have succeeded it to the present time, to dissipate and destroy. If, as has frequently happened, the selfishness and dishonesty of many of the instruments has converted the triumph of a good cause into a source of greater iniquities than the triumph overthrew ; if use and abuse have

259

been sometimes swept away together, and the evils of abuse have returned, while the benefits of use have been irretrievably lost ; if the overthrow of religious tyranny has been made the pretext for public robbery ; if the downfall of one species of state-delusion has been made the stepping-stone to the rise of a new variety of political quackery ; if the quieting of civil discord has been made the basis of military despotism ; * if what has been even ultimately gained in the direct object proposed, has been counterbalanced by losses in collateral matters, not sufficiently attended to in the heat of the main pursuit—(a debtor and creditor account well worthy the making out, if the requisite quantity of leisure, knowledge, and honesty could be brought to bear upon it) ; if the principles which were honestly pursued have been stigmatized as the necessary causes of effects which did not belong to them, and which were never contemplated by those by whom those principles were embraced ; and if those who were honest in the cause have been amongst the first victims of their own triumph, perverted from its legitimate re-

* Lepidi atque Antonii arma in Augustum cessêre : qui *cuncta, discordiis civilibus fessa,* nomine principis, sub *imperio* accepit. TACITUS, Ann. i. *Weariness of civil discord* founded the despotisms of Augustus, Cromwell, and Napoleon.

sults ;—we shall find, nevertheless, in the first place, that every successive triumph, however perverted in its immediate conse- quences, has been a step permanently gained in advance of the objects of the first authors of the Reformation—freedom of conscience and freedom of inquiry ; and we shall find, in the second place, not only that comic fiction has contributed largely to this result, but that among the most illustrious authors of comic fiction are some of the most illustrious specimens of political honesty and heroic self-devotion. We are here speaking, however, solely of the authors of the highest order of comic fiction—that which limits itself, in the exposure of abuses, to turning up into full daylight their intrinsic absurdities—not that which makes ridicu- lous things not really so, by throwing over them a fool's coat which does not belong to them, or setting upon them, as honest Bottom has it, an ass's head of its own.

Ridicule, in the first case, the honest development of the ridiculous *ab intrà*, is very justly denominated the test of truth : but ridicule, in the second case, the dis- honest superinduction of the ridiculous *ab extrà*, is the test of nothing but the knavery of the inventor. In the first case, the ridicule is never sought ; it always appears, as in the comic tales of Voltaire, to force itself up obviously and spontaneously : in the second case, the most prominent feature of the exhibition is the predetermination to be caustic and comical. To writers of the latter class most truly applies the axiom—*homines derisores civitatem perdunt.* But an intense love of truth, and a clear apprehension of truth, are both essential to comic writing of the first class. An intense love of truth may exist without the faculty of detecting it ; and a clear apprehension of truth may co-exist with a determination to pervert it. The union of both is rare ; and still more rare is the combination of both with that peculiar " composite of natural capacity and superinduced habit," which constitutes what is usually denominated comic genius.

We shall not lose sight of the progressive inquiry we have indicated, and shall perhaps return to it on a future occasion : but to execute it properly would require much more continuous leisure than will be readily suspected by those whose studies have not been directed into disquisitions *de rebus ludicris.* Our present purpose is much more limited.

Among the works of the successors of Rabelais, one of the most remarkable is *Le Compère Mathieu.* The design of running a tilt at predominant opinions is manifest throughout this work ; but it is by no means evident what use the author, Du Laurens, proposed to make of his victory, or what doctrines he wished to exalt in the place of those he aimed to overthrow. He was himself an ecclesiastic, but his mother church was so little grateful for his labours, that she shut him up for several years in a convent of penitential friars, where he had ample leisure to meditate on the wisdom of a resolution formed by one of his own heroes, never to live in a country in which the Catholic was the dominant religion. We shall give one or two specimens of this work, which we believe has never been translated.

Le Compère Mathieu is the history of a little society of five individuals, presenting a very clearly-defined and graduated scale of energy and intellect. At the head of this society is Le Révérendissime Père Jean de Domfront, who, on his first meeting with the other principal characters at an inn, recognises Mathieu for his nephew, and gives an account of his own education, adventures, and principles.

Le Révérendissime Père Jean has very early discovered that he was born free, and not under any natural subjection to either parent or prince ; that nothing but his own consent could make him submit to any

power on earth ; that vice and virtue, good
and evil, justice and injustice, and all that
depends on them, are terms significative
only of the opinions of those who invented
them for their own interests : and accordingly, having torn asunder the veil of illusion,
and thrown off the yoke of misery, servitude,
and superstition, he finds himself brought
into frequent collision with kings, priests,
and ministers of justice, who uphold their
legal right as he does his natural right, by
the ultimate arbitrament of might. " I have
everywhere encountered," he says, "treacher-
ous and powerful enemies, but I have
triumphed over them by my foresight, my
address, and my firmness. On these virtues, which have never abandoned me, I
have founded that tranquillity of mind
which I enjoy, and which accords so well
with that liberty of thought which I have
adopted, as well as with that unalterable
sang froid which has never quitted me,
even when I killed the Capuchin who interfered in my amour with the abbess, or the
marquis, who was going to run me through
for not getting out of his way. I have the
comfort of a good conscience, never disturbed by any of that foolish sort of reminiscence called remorse, which is a mere
fruit of ignorance and prejudice."

The second in this worthy fraternity is

FRENCH COMIC ROMANCES

Le Compère Mathieu, who, like his uncle, the Révérendissime, has thrown off the yoke of all the prejudices belonging to religion and law, but has some philosophical notions of right and wrong of his own, which he wishes to substitute for the opinions by which the mass of mankind is misled. He makes it his pride to be the martyr of the most sublime philosophy, and quadrating his practice with his doctrines, gets into as many scrapes as the Révérendissime ; but having less foresight and less firmness of purpose, he does not bear reverses with the same equanimity, nor elude them with the same dexterity, as Père Jean.

The third and fourth persons of the drama are Vitulos and Jérome : the former an unfrocked friar and thorough-paced knave ; the latter a very honest, simple-minded, and well-meaning person : both of that description of characters who cannot find their own way in the world without a leader, and therefore become necessarily attached to some one cleverer than themselves. Thus Vitulos cleaves to Père Jean, and Jérome to Le Compère Mathieu ; and the honest man and the knave are, by the mere force of circumstances, drawn into precisely the same line of conduct, and participate in the same good and evil fortune—being not themselves the immediate causes of anything of which they feel the effects, but merely blind tools and victims of the good or evil stars of Le Révérendissime and Le Compère. It is Jérome who narrates the history of his Compère Mathieu.

The fifth and last personage is Don Diego-Arias-Fernando de la Plata y Rioles y Bajalos, a most bigoted worshipper of relics, and of all the saints in the calendar, but a most faithful servant of the Compère, and still more of the Révérendissime, who is to the poor Spaniard as sublime a mystery as any in his hierology, and whom he never fails in any difficulty or distress to invoke with his other saints : " Oh St. François ! oh St. Ignace ! oh très redoutable et très secourable Père Jean ! "

The adventures of these worthies are worthy of their finely-graduated characters. We shall not follow them through their adventures, but shall give two specimens which will exhibit them with some distinctness as reasoners and moral agents.

They undergo a severe persecution in St. Petersburgh, in consequence of having exercised the natural right of stamping such impressions as suited them on pieces of metal, and are, by way of special grace and favour, banished to Siberia. Here the Compère, who is an adept in all knowledge, geographical and else, undertakes to lead them back into the civilized world through Tartary. Having formed this plan, they seize their opportunity, and commence their march, with the addition of a Jew, an Englishman, a German, and a Swede :—

Le Compère Mathieu, by virtue of his knowledge of geography, was declared Director of the Route ; the respectable Père Jean was proclaimed Captain-general of the Troop ; Vitulos, Lieutenant-colonel ; the Jew, the Englishman, the German, the Swede, Diego, and myself, were anything we pleased.

Having found the means of providing ourselves with three fowling-pieces, powder, ball, two bows, arrows, a hatchet, a bill, and a kettle, we committed ourselves to the auspices of fortune.

We ascended the left bank of the Oby to the environs of Kalami, where we passed the river on a raft of branches, constructed under the direction of Père Jean. When we had reached the river Kieka, we coasted it, traversing Grutinski and Lucomiria, and we gained the mountains of Krabia, where they join those of Sania and Belgian. Having passed these mountains, not without risk of perishing through cold and hunger, we found ourselves on a desert, across which the Compère determined to direct our course upon Samarcand, which he calculated we could reach in about eighty days by traversing Samariki, Karacathai, Chanaket, Charbian, and some other countries of Western Tartary. That might be ; but having advanced about one hundred and sixty miles in the desert, our progress was arrested by streams, marshes, and other obstacles, which compelled us to determine on passing the winter, which was near, on that spot. We proceeded to knock up a rough habitation, and to lay in a stock of game, fish, and wood, that we might not be taken unprovided by the snow. We acted very prudently; for eight days after we had housed our store, the snow fell in such quantities that the earth was covered to a depth of six feet.

*　*　*　*　*　*　*

With the return of the spring we resumed our march; but having found the line of Samarcand impracticable, the Compère determined to direct our course south-east.

Having travelled about forty-five days over mountains, and through vast forests abounding in all sorts of animals, the country became less fertile. The Compère having warned us that we were about to enter on the desert of Samoio, we thought of the future. We made a hunting excursion, and brought in six hundred pounds of flesh, which we dried in the smoke of wood: we then entered on the desert, hoping to find on our route some occasional supplies, which, added to our store, would enable us to traverse it without fear of famine.

After proceeding some days we found no more trees, and were out of sight of the mountains: all around us was a vast plain of reddish sand, covered with dry moss, and with a few plants of a species of bulrush, different from that which grows in Europe. There were neither rivers nor rivulets: all the water to be found was here and there a small, green, stagnant, fishless pond; and the only animals that seemed to inhabit the desert were a sort of weasels, that appeared very rarely, and very seldom within gunshot.

FRENCH COMIC ROMANCES

As we advanced, the desert became more sandy, more dry, more sterile, and the weasels more rare. A few days more, and the sun became obscured : we knew not which way to travel : we resolved to await the re-appearance of the sun, but after ten days of vain expectation and constant diminution of provisions, the Compère determined to lead us by chance, in the hope of discovering some more fertile spot.

We wandered three weeks without once seeing the sun. We were reduced to two pounds of bread amongst us eight ; then to one : we were exhausted by hunger and fatigue. The Compère preached philosophy : Père Jean was a model of adamantine fortitude ; Diego vowed a pilgrimage to the shrine of St. James, and to present with his own hands a wax candle to our Lady of the Pillar ; but all in vain. We were as deaf to the lessons of philosophy and heroism as the saint and the lady were to the vows of Diego.

After many days of wandering they find themselves in a forest of pines, in which, when they are all reduced to extremity, the Révérendissime kills a bear, of which he boils a portion, restores his exhausted companions with moderate doses of the broth, and eats the meat himself. Then they find a rabbit-warren, which supports them a few days ; but the stock diminishes rapidly—

We did not despair of finding another warren ; it seemed impossible that there should be only one spot of the forest inhabited by those animals, which, as I have said, had restored courage to

us all except to the Englishman, who appeared
absorbed in such profound melancholy, that he
never opened his lips to speak, and seldom to take
food, which he did with apparent reluctance, slender
as was his ration.

We had determined to remain three or four days
near the warren, partly to make the most of it,
and partly to rest. On the second day, the Englishman appeared more disturbed than ever. Sometimes his cheeks were inflamed, his eyes sparkled,
and he walked rapidly up and down; sometimes
his face was pale, his eyes wandered, he walked
slowly, stopped, sat down, and showed by all his
actions the terrible state of his mind.

At the close of the evening he lay down near
us on the grass; but he could not rest: he tossed
and turned, arose and lay down continually, and
every now and then cried out like a madman.
Towards morning he was more tranquil; he even
appeared to repose. But soon after he started up
suddenly, walked a few steps with great precipita-
tion; then lifting his hands and eyes to heaven,
he exclaimed, " Fortune and I have been fighting
all our lives; she has fairly beaten me; I shall
now place myself for ever out of her reach." At
the same time he seized a cord, passed it round
his neck, and was proceeding to hang himself on
the first tree, when the Compère seized him by
the arm and addressed him thus :—

" My friend, I have often heard that the English
were liable to be seized by a passion for suspending
themselves from the end of a string, but I was told
at the same time that they set about it with the
utmost possible *sang froid*—but your preliminaries
have been the agitations and grimaces of a demoniac.

FRENCH COMIC ROMANCES

Not that I prefer the mode of proceeding of your countrymen to your own; for if the mania of funipendulism should seize upon me, I should adopt neither fashion, but should proceed to it deliberately, after a process of reasoning, which should have been convincing to my understanding, and without having surrendered myself illogically to that fatal despair, which manifests itself in some subjects with the symptoms of morbid melancholy, and in others with those of rabid frenzy.

"It is true that your life has given you no ground to thank fortune for her favours; it is also true that your recent sufferings have been enough to shake the constancy of the most intrepid; it is, finally, true that we have no assurance of ever escaping from this dreadful desert. But the past is past, and no more to be thought of. For the future our prospects have brightened. We have reached a spot where the earth shows signs of vegetation, and where we have found a few rabbits and fuel to roast them; and we may still find more in our progress, till fate, weary of persecuting us, shall conduct us to a more fertile country.

"Our death is either near or distant: if near, it is not worth while to hasten it; if distant, we have still time to see the event of our misfortunes. Life is the best present nature has made us: it is too good a thing to be lightly thrown away. If the sage ought not to be dazzled by glory and prosperity, neither should he be beaten down by mischances. Pain and misfortune are the aliments of virtue, as their opposites are the touchstone of philosophy. There is more fortitude in wearing than in breaking the chain—more firmness of mind in Regulus than in Cato. It is cowardice, not

courage, to shrink out of fortune's way into a hole
under a stone. All the troubles of life in one scale.
are not worth as much as life alone in the other ;
and there are so many sudden changes in human
things, that it is impossible to determine the precise
point which is the end of our hope. There is
always hope, as the proverb has it, while there is
life.

"I do not deny that there are circumstances in
which death is preferable to life. There are some
occasions in which voluntary death is glorious ; but
they should be carefully weighed and thoroughly
understood. To avoid swelling the triumph of a
despicable enemy, and gratifying a tyrant and a
rabble with the spectacle of a cruel and ignominious
death, is such an occasion, and perhaps the only
one. Our position is far removed from it."

"I should like to know," said Père Jean, "why
my dear nephew arrogates to himself the privilege
of preventing those who are so inclined from
suspending themselves in any manner they think
proper, and interrupting them in their way to a
convenient peg with his farrago of impertinent
commonplaces ? He has preached a thousand
times against tyranny of all sorts ; but I know
no tyranny more atrocious than that of preventing
a man from following his fancy in a matter which
concerns nobody but himself.

"Do not listen to my nephew," he proceeded,
addressing the Englishman ; "he likes the sound
of his own voice, and talks without knowing what
he says. He sets up for a philosopher, and has
never found out that he has much more to learn
than to teach. He says life is the best present
that nature has made us ; but each man is in his

FRENCH COMIC ROMANCES

own case the best and sole judge of the value of the present. If there be courage in bearing misfortune, there is at least prudence in getting out of its way ; and there are no more effectual means to this end than a string round a branch of a tree. Death, says Seneca, is the solution and end of all troubles, beyond which our sufferings do not extend, and which replaces us in that tranquillity in which we were before we were born."

Père Jean proceeded, in his capacity of generalissimo, to interdict every one of the party from interfering with every other's right to suspend himself. But by a singular effect of the spirit of inconsistency and contradiction, the Englishman, who had seemed more resolute than ever during the speech of the Compère, lost courage at that of the Révérendissime ; his transport evaporated, and was succeeded by an evident embarrassment, arising from remorse at having gone so far, and shame at drawing back.

The Révérendissime perceived it, and said— " Do you tremble, and at what ? Are you no longer the English hero ? Tired of waging war with fortune, you were running to seek refuge in death, but all at once you hoist sail, and fly from the friendly port. What is to become of you if you can neither bear misfortune nor get rid of it ? Look death in the face, and its mask will fall ; it is terrible only to those who fear it. A man subdued by calamity, and seeing no end to it, has nothing to do but to die. If the cause of his despair is well-founded, it is a clear case, let him hang himself : if ill-founded, it is still a clear case —let him hang himself, because he cannot bear the present and has neither hope nor fortitude to await the future."

These last words re-animated the Englishman's courage : he walked calmly and tranquilly to the tree to which he had before run in desperation, climbed up the stem, and dropped himself from a branch with as much gravity as if he had been merely discharging one of the everyday functions of life.

As soon as he was dead, Père Jean cut him down, and, turning round to us with a look of great composure, said—"Here is provision for eight days."

We pass over the sequel of this adventure, and all the other adventures of this hopeful party, to the close of the history. They are then in Paris, living in common on the contents of a strong box, well filled, it matters not how. The Compère is taken ill, and, finding his last hour approach, is seized with repentance, and desires to die in the arms of the Church. Diego is sent to bring him a confessor, and, to make sure of the matter, runs to three different places, and applies for a confessor at all three.

First comes a Récollet, by whom, after being duly confessed and exhorted, the Compère is informed that he has no hope of mercy but in giving a third of his wealth to the poor, a third to the souls in Purgatory, and a third to the Church. This the Compère promises to do ; but as the deed is worth more than the word, the Récollet insists, and the Compère directs his companions to

bring him his share of the common purse.
They tell him that Père Jean has the key of
the chest, and the Récollet, awaiting his
return, proceeds to direct the Compère, if
he should recover from his malady, to
enter into the order of St. Francis. The
Compère inquires if it would not be safer
for him, if he should die, to die in the
habit of that order :—

The Récollet answered yes ; but as he could
not provide him with the habit on the instant,
he added that his cowl would suffice. In pursuance
whereof he encowled the Compère, and girdled his
loins with the seraphic cord. The Compère, thus
accoutred, began to look on death with courage
and resignation, and entreated us to join our prayers
to his that the venerable signs with which he was
invested might be the proofs of his triumph over
Satan.

Diego, who had gone out as soon as he had
introduced the Récollet, now re-appeared with a
Carmelite and a Jacobin.

As soon as the new-comers saw the Récollet
and each other, they asked the Spaniard if he had
been making game of them ? The Récollet asked
if they were not making game of him ? The three
monks were all in a rage ; and, after making the
whole house ring with their quarrel, they were
on the point of coming to blows when Père Jean
re-entered.

The Révérendissime doubted if he was awake.
The sight of the three monks in hot dispute, and
his nephew in a cowl, made him recoil with amaze-

ment, but recovering his senses, he seized a broomstick, and proceeded to lay it so vigorously over
the three ghostly brethren, that he would have
broken all their bones if Vitulos and I had not
interfered. The terrified Carmelite took refuge
under the bed—the Jacobin fell on his knees, and
cried mercy—and the Récollet proceeded to
exorcise the Révérendissime, whom he took for
the foul fiend.

Père Jean dragged out the Carmelite by the leg,
and ordered the three monks to embrace each
other. " Come," he said, " you who make a trade
of reconciling sinners with heaven, reconcile yourselves on the spot with each other." " Alas! worthy
sir," said the Jacobin, " do you not know that
our differences are irreconcileable ? These good
fathers have to uphold the honour of their order—
I that of mine—and all three that of the Church.
Kill us if you please : we will not be guilty of
any baseness." " Out with you, then, generation
of vipers ! " said Père Jean, " and finish your
quarrel in the street." " My cowl," said the
Récollet. " Out with you, vermin ! " said the
Révérendissime, flourishing his broomstick ; and
the three monks had nearly broken their necks in
bounding down the stairs.

"So, my friend," said the Révérendissime,
turning to the Compère, " there you are, prettily
equipped with your cowl. I always expected that
you would play some foolery at the hour of death ;
but I never thought it would be that of dying
encowled. You have made it the boast of your
life to be the martyr of the most sublime philosophy,
and you end it by being that of the most vile
superstition,—an end truly worthy of those who,

like you, have always reasoned at random and without principles, and rather from the desire of making a noise in the world, than from that of instructing mankind."

Upon which the Révérendissime walks off, and no solicitation can induce him to see his nephew again. The Compère dies ; and the Révérendissime becomes a captain of dragoons,—a process which, to the infinite advantage of the church-militant, has been, in our own days, reversed by some of our own half-pay captains of dragoons, who have become Révérendissimes.

It will be seen, by the specimens we have given, that to stir up and play with opinions is the main business of the author of *Le Compère Mathieu*. In the well-known work of Louvet, written before the revolution, amidst all the levity of the subject and characters, the opinions which subsequently predominated may be often seen rising, playfully, and sometimes seriously, into collision with those by which they were then repressed.* In this work, as in those of

---

* Faublas fut achevé dans les premiers mois de 1789. C'est sans doute un ouvrage bien frivole ; pourtant je crois pouvoir répéter ce que j'ai dit ailleurs, qu'à travers les légèretés dont il est rempli, on trouve, du moins dans les passages sérieux où l'auteur se montre, les principes de philosophie et ceux d'un républicanisme encore assez rare à l'époque où ce roman fut écrit.— *Mem. de Louvet.* Coll. de Mem. de la Rév. Fr., liv. xiii. p. 329.

FRENCH COMIC ROMANCES

Pigault le Brun, the play of opinions is incidental—sometimes frequent, sometimes rare ; but none of Pigault le Brun's works are without them, though they are always pertinent, and chime in naturally with the progress of his characters. Of this characteristic of his predecessors in the school of humorous romance Paul de Kock is altogether divested. We shall not, however, anticipate what we have to say of this author in an article which we purpose to devote wholly to him. We were desirous to take some preliminary notice of those of his predecessors whom, *à cela près*, he most resembles ; and we shall close this preliminary view with a specimen of the style of Pigault le Brun, from his romance of *Monsieur de Roberville*, which we select the rather, because we believe that, like the *Compère Mathieu*, it has not been published in an English version.

Monsieur de Roberville is a schemer, who makes and loses fortunes by successive projects and speculations, and passes through all varieties of fortune, and all sorts of accidents, tragic and comic, till, having dissipated the last relic of fortune's last favour, he dies at the gate of an hospital. We shall introduce him to our readers in one of the later passages of his eventful history, when he has lost an arm, and has just been wounded in an eye, and, having at the time the means, determines to renounce a world by which he has been so maltreated, and to finish his days in philosophical solitude.

"I have lost an arm," soliloquised Roberville, in a *fiacre*, "for having conducted a journal. I have just lost an eye, for having arranged a marriage. Some poor devils are born unlucky; their most virtuous projects turn against them. I will do nothing more; that is the only way to escape my evil star. I have some money; I will invest it safely, and I will live tranquil and unknown by mankind—always envious, often wicked. Already I see myself alone, in my simple and comfortable retreat. A few chosen books interest and amuse me, develop and adorn my understanding, which I have too much neglected. I study the exact sciences; they have neither sects nor systems. I am clear that two and two make four; and it is most satisfactory to be in possession of a truth which nobody disputes. My knowledge extends and advances. I discover the quadrature of the circle. My reputation extends throughout the world. Everybody seeks me. I deny myself to everybody. Wrapped in my damask dressing-gown, with my velvet cap on my head, shut up in my library, I communicate only with my books, my spheres, and my secretary. Those who present themselves at my gate believe my merit exactly proportioned to my modest pride; and as nothing is so sublime as what is out of reach, I shall be placed by the side of Archimedes, and be admired on trust, as he is. Ah—but a secretary—is that exactly what I want?—No! a housekeeper—an attentive, careful housekeeper—that is the thing. I will take her young; she will grow old in my service: pretty; as I have only one eye left, it should look only on pleasant images: gentle and obedient to my will; yes; but my will must be only that of a man devoted to the high sciences. Oh, but my eye—it torments me horribly. Coachman, set me down at the first oculist's." "I don't know one, sir, or I couldn't drive my *fiacre*. That wants both eyes and both arms, and good ones too." "Here's a rascal, who thinks me not fit to drive a *fiacre*.—Inquire." "Of whom, sir?" "Ask anybody: ask the groom there at the corner." "Sir." "What is the matter?" "Here's your man, much forwarder in your business than yourself." "How so?" "He has already a plaster on his eye, and you have only your handkerchief on yours." "Good—speak to him."

The man with the plaster was an old lieutenant of grenadiers, who had had the light of one eye gloriously extinguished at the battle of Minden, and who was walking slowly and painfully under the weight of years and laurels. "Pray, sir, direct me to your oculist." "It is the surgeon of the regiment." "Where does he live?" "At Besançon, with the officers." "What shall I do for my eye?" "Is it hurt?" "I have just had the point of a sword in it." "It must have been a very clumsy fencer that hit you in the eye instead of running you through the body." "That would not have mended the matter." "Well, there is no oculist who can restore a lost eye. Put on a poultice of brandy-and-water:

leave it off in eight days, and if you are disfigured, wear a plaster like me. I love brave men, and I offer you my services for the first dressing." " Sir, you are very good. On, coachman."

They arrive at Roberville's : the lieutenant looks around him with amazement—" *Corbleu!* I never saw a barrack-room furnished like this. Lacquey! some brandy. With all the necessary, and so much of the superfluous, you can spare an eye and an arm. Lacquey! linen and scissors. I am another Belisarius—brave and a beggar, though only half-blind. *Diable!* you are a lucky fellow. The thrust a little straighter, and you were a dead man! Soldier in 1710 ; corporal in 1720 ; sergeant in 1730 ; sub-lieutenant in 1737 ; lieutenant in 1750—covered with seventeen wounds ; I have just been refused a company because they pretend that a captain of infantry ought to have the use of his legs." " Refused !—shameful !—you shall have it." " Bah ! " " And you shall command on horseback." " That is not the custom." " Custom is made for the contempt of the wise." " Faith, you are right. You have patronage, then ? " " I have a chief clerk of the war-office under my thumb, through a rich marriage which I arranged for his brother. Meanwhile, you shall live here." " I desire no better." " I am going to live a retired life. You shall share my solitude. What can be a more noble employment of wealth and credit than to employ them in the service of merit in distress ? It is much more satisfactory to live in the company of a worthy man, and to live in the consciousness of doing good, and in the enjoyment of friendship and gratitude, than to sit poring over Euclid, whom, however, I do not renounce. Are

you a mathematician ? " " No, I am an Artesian."
" Mathematics are the art of judging by demonstration : their subjects are extension and number."
" What is the use of all that ? " " Do you not
perceive the advantage of knowing exactly how
many miles you are from the sun ? " " I am
content with its warmth and light." " In knowing
how long a cannon-ball would be in reaching it,
travelling with undiminished velocity ? " " What
is the use ?—I am content to know the consequence
of a cannon-ball reaching me, and in the meantime
to enjoy myself as I may. Seek your happiness
in the earth, not in the sun." " You do not yet
conceive the sublimity of the things we shall study
together, and when we have overcome the first
difficulties "—" I have no inclination to combat
them." " You are content to remain ignorant."
" And happy. When I was young, I made love ;
and it was more important to me to know the
height of my mistress's window than that of the
stars, with which I have no concern. Now I am
old, I have given up love for a faithful friend,
who annihilates distances and brings about me all
I wish to hear and see. This dear friend makes me
forget the indifference of women, the injustice of
men, the pain of my wounds—lifts me above myself ; makes me a new man ; gives me boldness to
undertake anything, and confidence to carry it
through ; secures me the favours of beauty—the
baton of a marshal—the throne of France—the
throne of the world. I wake from my dream, but
my friend is still there, to give me happiness in a
new form, again and again. Wine !—wine !—let
us drink ; and if we must have a head-ach, let us
earn it by Burgundy and not by ciphering. The

water-drinkers despise us : they think it a great
matter to stand firm on both legs, and hold themselves very superior to those who balance on one
at a time ; but their heads are always empty of
pleasant images, and the head of the wine-drinker
is full of nothing else." " Faith, master lieutenant,
I think you are right."—" Lacquey ! a couple of
bottles, and of the best." " Oh what pleasant
projects I shall have presently." " Projects !
realities !—Here's to you ! " " Here's to you."
" This is good. Have you much more of it ? "
" About five hundred bottles." " Enough for a
month—drink ! "

The new friends drank *tête-à-tête*, but spoke
little at first. The lieutenant was not over-stocked
with ideas, and only got warm when talking of
his friend or full of his influence. By degrees the
warmth began to circulate in his veins. Roberville
was younger, but wanted practice : thus the ther-
mometer of the two brains was always at the same
degree. By the third bottle, their imaginations
began to inflate. " They refuse me a company,
damn their ingratitude ! " exclaims the lieutenant ;
and Roberville pours out projects, finishing by
lodging himself in great glory on the top of a
mountain. " Now I shall build on the top of
my mountain "—" Of our mountain, as we are to
have all in common." " Right, of our mountain ;
a palace, where we will live together. There we
breathe a pure air, and drink without fear of being
disturbed." " We must not be disturbed ; but
we must receive visiters." " We will receive all
who come, and keep whom we like—drink, lieutenant ! "—" Here's to you, one-arm ! But how shall
we feed them ? " " I stock the top of my moun-

tain."—" Of our mountain."—" Hé, yes, that's understood."—" With what ? " " With goats : we will eat the kids, and drink the milk of their mothers."—" I hate milk : we will make cheese of it." " I hate cheese."—" It relishes wine."— " I'll have no cheese ! "—" I'll have no milk ! drink, one-arm ! don't let us dispute." " So be it ; I give up the goats at the top, and stock the bottom of the mountain with rabbits."—" I hate rabbits."—" I love them."—" No rabbits."—" No cheese."—" I insist on cheese ! "—" I insist on rabbits ! "—" You shall not have them ! "—" I will have them ! "—" *Sacrebleu ! corbleu ! ventre-bleu !* you shall not ! " " You are an impertinent rascal ! "—" You are a puppy ! " " Scoundrel ! " —" Coxcomb ! say another word, and I will throw you from the top of your mountain into the sea ! " And the lieutenant, who had two arms, seized Roberville, who had but one, and threw him, not into the sea, but into the middle of a large looking-glass, which fell to pieces with a tremendous clatter. Roberville's servant rushed in to part the disputants ; and the lieutenant, resolving himself immediately into Marshal Saxe, fighting Cumberland and Waldeck at once, proceeded to overturn chairs and tables, and to fire away candlesticks, ornaments, china, glasses, and full and empty bottles, at the heads of master and man. The master, capering over the ruins, amidst the shower of missiles, too drunk to find the door, fell at last prostrate in a corner ; while the lieutenant was knocked down in the opposite corner, and buried under chairs and tables by the valet, who left them to subside as they might into sleep, one roaring " cheese and no rabbits," and the other "rabbits and no cheese."

This scene is perhaps a little *outré ;* but many of the main incidents of Pigault le Brun's stories are marked by a character of startling extravagance, which, to an English reader, appears at first sight out of nature ; yet it is scarcely out of French nature. The movements of society in France seem to have no definite aim but the production of a *coup de théâtre.* When Louvet had denounced Robespierre, he had produced his *coup de théâtre :* his business was done, and, instead of following up his victory, he went home to supper, and sat down, *buvant frais*, with the chiefs of his party, till their festivity was interrupted by a friendly admonition to fly for their lives. When, after all the fire and fury —all the blood and thunder of the barricades—Louis Philippe and Lafayette hugged each other in a balcony, the first crying— " Henceforth the charter is a truth ; " and the latter—" This is the best of republics ; " *—there was the *coup de théâtre*—not the proposed, but the real, end of the tragicomedy of the " glorious three days." There was a grand chorus and fugue on *Vive Louis Philippe !—Vive Lafayette !—Vive la Charte !* —and the curtain fell on the beautiful group in the balcony, amidst the acclamations of a

* There is some doubt about the words, but none about the pantomime, of this performance.

crowded audience, who very soon found that this same *coup de théâtre* was the be-all and the end-all of the fruit of their magnificent exploits. The revolution ended like one in Pekin, where the people have the felicity of seeing Ho-Fum put over their heads in the place of Fum-Ho. The charter turned out a lie, and ' the best of republics ' the beginning of the vilest and most sordid of tyrannies.

The history of the French Revolution is a history of *coups de théâtre*, carried on with an unstudied and unconscious, but systematic and undeviating, attention to groupings, dresses, and decorations. The most overwhelming and terrific means lead to the most opposite and most farcical conclusions. *Mon Oncle Thomas*, who lays a mine under a *batterie de cuisine*, springs it with a red-hot poker, kills several dozen people, and cuts his father-in-law into halves, perpendicularly, with the lid of a fish-kettle, having no other ultimate object than that of jumping unmolested out of the window ; and the author, who buries the said *Oncle* alive for thirty years in a monastic *vade in pace*, to reproduce him as the deadly foe of monks and friars, re-appearing before his relations, who had thought him dead, with a belt of Capuchins' ears in the days of the Reign of Terror, present felicitous adaptations of means to ends in comparison with the realities of the same time ; or with those of the Three Glorious Days, when the end of the conflict was liberty of the press, and the final means chosen by the victors were Louis Philippe and an assemblage of vapouring deputies, who, having vanished at the first roll of the thunder of battle, emerged from their lurking-places to raise a hollow echo of the onset when the victory was won, and, after carefully abstaining from riding on the storm, to give a false direction to the tail of the whirlwind.

THE ÉPICIER

THE ÉPICIER

WE shall come by-and-by to Paul de
Kock, in pursuance of the promise in the
third article of our last Number ; but we
have first a few more prolegomena to dispose
of, and his works are so voluminous, that
we must give them an undivided notice.
We do not intend to give another version of
the King of Bohemia and his seven castles ;
nor to write, as Hazlitt said of Coleridge's
Friend, the everlasting prospectus of an
imaginary work : and we hope we shall not
suggest the inquiry : " Quid dignum tanto
feret hic promissor hiatu ? " for there is no
hiatus in the matter, but that of an unavoidable separation in time between the
beginning and the end of our subject. We
shall dispose, on the present occasion, of
all that remains of our preliminaries, and
shall, on the next occasion, come without
preface to the execution of our original
purpose.

The remarks which we now wish to offer
are pertinent to the question which we

mooted in our last Number :—Why the
writings of the most popular of modern
French novelists present so striking a contrast to those of his predecessors, in being
totally divested of every trace of political
opinion ? The answer, we think, is two-
fold : first, there is no demand for the
commodity amongst the great body of his
readers ; second, it does not fall under his
view as an observer of a particular class
of society.

The Greeks rejected turtle, and made a
luxury of the cuttle-fish. We make a
luxury of the turtle, and make no use of
the cuttle-fish, but to turn his one bone
into pounce. Accordingly, the cuttle-fish
is one of the least known to us of the creatures of the deep, and the turtle is in the
streets of London a sight of every day.
Thus demand regulates supply in the most
abundant productions of nature, as well as
in those of human industry.

It is the same, we apprehend, with men.
There was no demand for Cincinnatus in
the days of Augustus. There was an old
theory for Cincinnatus, but the practical
tendency was for Augustus. There was no
demand for Napoleon in the American revolution, nor for Washington in the French.
Napoleon, in the place of Washington, could
not have established a military despotism

in America ; nor could Washington, in the place of Napoleon, have established a democratic government in France. It was because each of them was precisely the man he was, that the practical tendency of events threw him to the surface.

So with religious observances. In an age which demands the show of sanctity testified by mortification and penance, there is no lack of a Simeon Stylites living on the top of a pillar, or of a hero like Voltaire's naked Faquir sitting *avec des clous dans le derrière pour avoir de la considération.* Comes an age which demands freedom of inquiry, the Saint and the Faquir vanish from the scene, and we have Luther demolishing the pope with his pen, and flinging his inkstand at the head of the devil. Come the days of Church and State, and we have no hero of any sort, gymnosophist or reformer, but a host of plump well-fed parsons, who are, moreover, justices of peace and quorum, and who would commit both the Faquir and Luther, if they should show themselves within their jurisdiction, to the treadmill as rogues and vagabonds.

So with philosophy. An age which demands free inquiry, pushed without fear or compromise to its legitimate conclusions, turns up an Epicurus or a Hobbes. In one which likes to put up at an half-way house, there will be no lack of a Dugald Stewart, or a Mackintosh, to provide it with comfortable entertainment.

So with literature. Among a people disposèd to think, their every-day literature will bear the impress of thought ; among a people not so disposed, the absence or negation of thought will be equally conspicuous in their literature. Every variety of mind takes its station, or is ready to do so, at all times in the literary market ; the public of the day stamp the currency of fashion on that which jumps with their humour. Milton would be forthcoming if he were wanted ; but in our time Milton was not wanted, and Walter Scott was. We do not agree with the doctrine implied in Wordsworth's sonnet,

> Milton ! thou should'st be living at this hour :
> England hath need of thee.

England would have been the better for him, if England would have attended to him, but England would not have attended to him if she had had him. There was no more market for him than for Cromwell. When Shakspeare was, Mozart and Rossini and Giulietta Grisi were not. The musical drama has struck down the legitimate. Shakspeare wrote plays, because it was

the best thing he could do for himself.
If he were now carrying a link before the
Teatro alla Scala, he would probably limit
his ambition to writing libretti for the next
Gran Maestro.

French literature bore the impress of
political liberty long before the Revolution,
and its tendency in that line was always on
the advance before that terrible political
eruption. Opinion had heaved with growing strength under the pressure of custom
and authority, as Typhon had tossed and
tumbled many ages under Etna, before he
threw up the first torrent of fire that deluged
the fields of Sicily.

Pigault le Brun lived in the days of the
Rights of Man, Political Justice, and Moral
and Intellectual Perfectibility. Paul de
Kock lives in the days of the march of
mechanics, in the days of political economy,
in the days of prices-current and percent-
ages, in the days when even to dream like
a democrat of the Constituent Assembly,
would be held to qualify the dreamer for
Bedlam ; in short, in the days of the *épicier*.

Who, or what, is the *épicier ?* That we
shall explain presently.

It may be said that to develop opinions is
not in the taste of Paul de Kock, though it
was in that of Pigault le Brun. But this
would be a very insufficient solution of the

phenomenon. Pigault le Brun was an observer. He exhibited the play of opinion because he found it in the society he depicted. Paul de Kock is also an observer. He does not exhibit the play of opinion, because he does not find it in the society he depicts.

The case is somewhat different with a writer of romances, who draws from books and imagination, more than from actual life. With him, the development of opinion may be a matter of personal taste. But even in this case the experiment will scarcely be repeated to any extent, without a certain degree of public sympathy and encouragement. When works of fancy run out to the extent of those of Paul de Kock, or Walter Scott, we may be sure that the authors have chimed in with the predominant tastes, as well as with the predominant opinions, or negations of opinions, of a great body of readers.

Paul de Kock makes his observations on the class of the *épicier*. From this class he draws the great bulk of his characters, and the negations of opinion which characterize that class at present are faithfully reflected in the mirror which he holds up to *la nature épicière*. We shall now see what the *épicier* is.

Épicier means, as all the world doth know, grocer ; but the Parisian is not exactly a

THE ÉPICIER

counterpart of the London grocer; he is more like what, in an English country town, would be called, saving his presence, a huckster.

The *épicier* has three phases: diurnal, general, and metaphorical; the first being positive, the second negative, and the third derivative. We shall consider him first in his diurnal capacity, following the regular routine of his avocations and recreations, wherein each succeeding year rolls over the traces of its predecessor.

> Redit labor actus in orbem,
> Atque in se sua per vestigia volvitur annus.

In this capacity, M. de Balzac shall describe him for us.

The *épicier* is the common link of all our wants, and attaches himself necessarily to all the details of human life.

"Pen, ink, and paper," cries a poet.—"Sir, there is an *épicier* at the corner of the street."

"I am ruined!" cries a gamester. "Powder and ball to blow my brains out."—"Sir, the *épicier* sells them."

"Oh for a cigar! a real havannah: to see it consuming with a slow fire, and resolving itself into smoke: like love!"—"The *épicier*."

"I must give Clara an elegant breakfast. Mocha coffee, Pekoe tea; *terrine de Nérac truffée.*"—"The *épicier*."

Would you wake through the night? The *épicier*.

THE ÉPICIER

Would you sleep through the night? Still the *épicier*.

Would you have drugs to save your life, or poison to end it? Still, still, the *épicier*.

The *épicier* sells to the child his marbles, and his kite and the string that flies it;—to the old invalid the eternal snuff, performing its inexhaustible and incessant circulation through snuff-box, nose, and handkerchief, making the nose of an inveterate snuff-taker an image of infinity;—to the priest his wafers and tapers;—slates to the schoolmaster;—sugar-plums to the god-father;—scented-soap to the bride;—liqueur to the bridegroom;—paper for the elector;—fire-works for the deputy. The *épicier* has sold himself to the public, like a witch to Satan. He is the alpha and omega of all human society. You cannot travel a league,—you cannot commit a crime,—you cannot do a good action,—you cannot make a meal,—keep up an orgy,—carry on a work of art,—or pay court to a mistress,—without having recourse to the *épicier*. He shows you the way when you inquire at his door, and follows you with his eye, with an anxious solicitude to see you go right. He is the abstract and quintessence of ever-smiling politeness. He is civilization behind a counter, society in whited-brown paper, necessity armed from head to foot;—life itself distributed into drawers, bottles, bags, jugs, boxes, kegs, and cannisters. If you are abandoned by all the world except one *épicier*, you may live with him like a mouse in a cheese. When you read in golden letters *épicier du roi*, you may ask yourself with terror, " which is most the sovereign, the *épicier* of the king, or the king of the *épicier* ? "

THE ÉPICIER

Thus far we have seen the *épicier* in that part of his positive phasis which belongs to his occupation. We have yet to see him in his relaxation and recreation. But on these points Paul de Kock has so admirably pourtrayed him in his M. Dupont, that we shall reserve this view of him till he turns up again in his proper order.

In the mean time the reader may depict to himself a jolly *bon vivant, totus teres atque rotundus*, all smooth and round, morally as well as physically, making, with a neighbour, a brace of wives and a brace of children, one of six in a *fiacre*, with a hamper wedged in the midst of them, followed by two or three more vehicles similarly stowed, to enjoy a *fête champêtre* in the environs of Paris ; on his way to which we shall leave him, and look at him hereafter when he has unpacked his hamper in the Bois de Romainville.

This is the *épicier* in his diurnal functions. We must now look at him in his general or negative capacity, as a component part of the body politic, in which he stands for the representative of the whole class of dealers in whatsoever commodities, from funds to rushlights, and figures as the personification of the great clog or drag-chain on the wheels of the movement. In this his more curious and important phasis we shall

THE ÉPICIER

exhibit him from a French MS. communication with which we have been favoured.

POLITICAL PHYSIOLOGY OF THE ÉPICIER

Since the Restoration the *épicier* has become the type of a class of men very widely diffused in France. There are coarse and narrow understandings which have neither the creed and feelings of the past, nor those of the future, and which maintain a fixed middle point amid the movement of ideas. This is what we call *l'esprit épicier*. Applied to literature, to the arts, to the mode of living, and manifesting itself in manner, style, and taste, by something obsolete, vulgar, and awkward, tinged with the ridiculous, this spirit has created what we call *le genre épicier*.

The *épicier* has formed his political opinions, if he has any, in the school of the *Constitutionnel*. He has not emerged from the narrow principles of the old liberalism of the Restoration. His nationality is a prejudice, without ideality, and without grandeur. He thinks himself a friend of liberty, and he sacrifices it daily by lending an unintelligent support to power. His ruling passion is the love of " order," because he has observed that in the days of political disturbances there has been a fall of a per-centage on his operations. The apprehension of anarchy, or, to speak more correctly, the fear of diminished sales and falling prices, has made him a fanatic of " l'ordre public." It would be impossible to make him comprehend that the best means of consolidating public tranquillity would be to labour for the reconciliation of all the interests of society. He cannot conceive, even in moral order, any other interests than those of his

300

THE ÉPICIER

trade. For him, order is a positive result which must be obtained at any price, without regard to the causes which may have produced a feverish over-excitement in any portion of society.

Abstractedly from this passion for public order, he cares little for either the monarchical form of government, or the new dynasty. In the rare instants in which he is troubled with the fancy of being witty, he makes himself merry at the expense of our rulers, their *pots-de-vin* and their *tripotages de bourse*. But while he condemns the governing body, he upholds the established order, rather than undergo the consequences of another change. He had rather keep an open account with this bad debtor, than get rid of him by settling with him at a fixed loss once for all.

It is not, therefore, any enthusiasm for the monarchical principle, it is mere self-defence that has turned him into a hero against the *émeute*, and decorated him with the cross of honour for his achievements in the campaigns of the streets. If he has still later been stimulated to the pitch of marching against the barricades of the Cloître St. Méry, it was because he could not contain his rage against the republicans, who on that day, in risking their lives for the triumph of a principle, had made him lose the sale of some pounds of sugar or coffee. The next day he overflowed with stupid astonishment at the madness of those young men who had got themselves killed for an idea. It had never happened to him to have an idea in the course of his life.

Entrenched behind his counter, the *épicier* has never been carried away by the current of popular opinions : since he has seen the consequences of

301

THE ÉPICIER

the Revolution resolve themselves into public calamities, he affects a superb disdain for politics. By an inconceivable confusion of ideas, he has taken effects for causes ; in other words, he attributes to the ruled the faults of the rulers. He thinks himself so clear-sighted and so well-informed, that he remains deaf to all the proofs you can give him of his error.

He will not hear of the debates in the Chambers, nor of the discussions of the press, being persuaded that it is the organs of publicity which keep up perturbation in the minds of men, and, consequently, in the operations of trade. He has stereotyped the dogmas of shopkeeping indifferentism—" I never look at the papers ; I have no time to read them." " I never meddle with politics : they do not concern me." If by chance he tells a customer a piece of current news, he adds immediately—" I merely heard my young man mention it." In fact, his lowest shop-boys are better informed of the course of public affairs than their master. He goes to the coffee-house to take his *demi-tasse*, and play his game of dominoes ; but he no longer reads the newspapers, not even the Constitutionnel, since the old journal has committed the oversight of giving itself a few airs of independence. In short, while he is, of all men, the most harassed by political changes, he is the one who thinks the least about them.

Nevertheless, since the last triumph of *citizen royalty* in the streets, political scepticism has made an irruption into the obtuse mind of the *épicier*. He has asked himself how it can have happened that France has been more agitated under the reign of public order, than in that of public disturb-

ance ? There is a palpable contradiction in the
terms of the question, which he would try to
resolve, if it were not that above all things he
anticipates with the greatest alarm the consequences of thinking. But with all his predetermination against inquiry, doubt having once
crossed his conviction, cannot wholly pass away
and leave no trace of its progress. The time will
yet arrive when the *épicier* and the republican will
meet side by side on the route of the movement.

About two years ago, at a winter evening-party
in Paris, a large part of the company had gathered
round the great national lyrist Béranger. All
agreed that the monarchy was wearing itself out
by its own excesses, and consuming, in a short
space, through impatience of enjoyment and mistrust of futurity, the little vitality which remained
to it. They repeated, with Napoleon, that the
time must come when republicanism would profit
by the errors of the monarchy ; but they differed
as to the probable distance of the time when the
republic might obtain the majority of suffrages,
and establish itself with the strongest chances of
permanence.

The moderates anticipated this result as the
necessary consequence of the diffusion of knowledge.
Béranger, who was of that opinion, summed it up
at once, by a touch at once witty and profound.
" Believe me, gentlemen," said he, " you must
arrive at the republic in company with the *épicier*."

We have here seen the *épicier* in his
general phasis, as a great political negation;
one whom the fall of a *centime* in the price
of a pound of sugar, if he should connect it

as an effect with the cause of a "glorious revolution," would establish, for the rest of his days, as a dead wall in the way of an *émeute populaire*.

We may now contemplate him, in his third phasis, as an emblem. And in aid of this purpose, we shall draw upon an article in the *Revue Encyclopédique* for February, 1833, entitled *Études Politiques sur l'Épicier*. The article is long. We shall present so much of its essence as is needful to our purpose.

On the 29th of July, 1830, Claude Tarin (the fictitious hero of the *Studies*) poured out to Benjamin Constant the overflowings of his enthusiasm in the cause of the three glorious days.

In the beginning of November, Claude Tarin accompanied Benjamin Constant to a sitting of the Chamber of Deputies. It was a deplorable spectacle for Claude Tarin to see the collective impersonation of false pretences, dreading either to fulfil their mission, or to betray the cause of the heroes of July, and manifesting, in every word and gesture, the anxiety and irresolution of a rider astride on a fiery steed, fearing alike to relax or tighten the reins, and doubting whether his courser's next movement will be horizontal or perpendicular.

Benjamin Constant walked home from the

THE ÉPICIER

assembly leaning on the arm of Tarin. In the middle of a street he stopped and said : —" My young friend, you have just seen a number of persons who have been called to exercise a good or evil influence on the progress of events. Orators, legislators, administrators, apparent chiefs of parties, have passed before you at the tribune. Yet, on my conscience, you could not see, in the faces of any of them, any such signs of an immediate and powerful authority, as you may in the face at that door on the opposite side of the street. At first sight, perhaps, he appears nothing remarkable. But look attentively. Do you not discover a singular air of prudent penetration in those little round and shaded eyes ? Do not those fat cheeks of coarse and insipid air, hanging in great soft wrinkles, express an invincible pertinacity ? Is not that pursed-up mouth the index of an unalterable self-satisfaction? Would it not indicate small skill in physiognomy not to recognise, in the fixedness of that equivocal smile, all the characters of impatient desire to enjoy the present, and of indifference and incredulity with respect to the future ? Would it not be insanity to suppose that any great Utopia was lodged under that low and narrow forehead, rising up into a point under that high and abundantly curled wig ? Do you see nothing in those

305

inflexible eyebrows ? Are you not struck
by the confident air of those arms, falling,
with all their weight, at his sides, and by
that massive corpulence ? Can you not
read a futurity about that man ? "

" But," said Claude, " that is an *épicier*."

" Yes, yes, it is an *épicier*. Now walk
straight on, and do not look round ; he has
noticed that we have observed him ; and
the moment is not distant when his power
will be more and more formidable."

" That *épicier* ! " said Claude. " *Allons*,
you are a child ! " said Benjamin Constant,
smiling with some bitterness.

Benjamin Constant died sad and dis-
enchanted, as every body knows.

Many, who had seen the most renowned
among the defenders of public liberty
successively corrupted by power, said,
" Benjamin Constant has died in time." But
Benjamin Constant had died simultaneously
with the death of his last cherished illusion.
He had dreamed of popular power—great,
majestic, beneficent : he had seen it little,
abject, ridiculous, selfish. The reality stared
him in the face : he closed his eyes, and
died. He who has lost his last illusion,
who has used up his ideality, has nothing
to do but die.

Claude Tarin remembered the last words
of his deceased friend : he took a lodging

THE ÉPICIER

in the house of the identical *épicier* pointed out by Benjamin Constant, and devoted himself to the physiological study of the *épicier*. The result of his studies was, that in the whole world of French political power—deputies, counsellors, ministers, and king—there was but one spirit, the spirit of buying and selling, on a larger or smaller scale ; but regulated by no more enlightened or extensive views than those which regulated the dealings of his little landlord in coffee, treacle, and fish-sauce. He found, in short, that within the circle of the *épicier's* dealings and opinions were comprised all the aims, views, tendencies, and aspirations of the citizen-monarchy.

" It is not," he says to some of his comrades, whom he finds seeking the means of extrication from the abyss of political despair, in which France seems to be plunged— " it is not an invisible power that governs you—it is not a prophet, not a legislator, not a tribune, not a statesman, not even a citizen—it is the *épicier !*—the palladium, the tabernacle, the labarum of France, the centre of all things—the alpha and omega— the elect of the great cycle of eighteen hundred and thirty !

" Enthusiasts would overthrow him. It is in vain. They might break him into atoms, they might bray him in his own mortar, they might bury him in the ruins of his counter—he would rise like the phoenix from its ashes, flourishing in portly corpulence, to reign and smile on till he shall have fulfilled his mission.

" If you think it desirable to deliver the genius of our national destiny from his actual incarnation, and to give him a more noble one, so be it : I think with you. But show me the signs of power to accomplish your purpose. Exorcise the *épicier ;* trace your circle ; evoke the new form which society should wear ; invest it with features of moral and intellectual beauty. But in the meantime desist from evil lamentations and fruitless struggles ; move not weapons that will recoil on yourselves. For the present, acknowledge yourselves conquered; bow down to the *épicier ;* bend in homage to your king."

With this peroration terminate the *Études Politiques*.

We have now seen the *épicier* in his three phases—commercial, political and emblematical ; and we can now easily understand that the grand incarnation of *l'esprit épicier*, the citizen-king, sits safe on his throne, because the *épicier* is not now, as in 1790, an *enfant de la patrie* singing the Marseillois hymn, or at least listening approvingly to those who sang it ;

THE ÉPICIER

but a *gendarme* determined to uphold
whatever is uppermost, provided it will let
him deal without molestation ; not because
he likes or admires what is uppermost, or
would cross the street to fetch it back if
it were once fairly turned out, but because
he has had sufficient experience of change of
masters to desire to change no more. He
remembers the sayings and doings of 1789 ;
he has asked himself what good he and his
class have gained by any past political
change, which, placed as a solid gain in
one scale, would counterbalance his loss
by a single fall of a denier in the price of
any one of his commodities, when his
boutique was stored, on the other ? and he
has answered—*Nil.* In politics he dis-
cusses nothing, aims at nothing, anticipates
nothing. He acquiesces and maintains.
He is the great *vis inertiæ* that presses down
anarchy, and upholds the colossal mass of
brute physical force, embodied in military
power, which supports the existing order of
things. He is the broad-backed tortoise
that stands upon chaos, and carries the
elephant that carries the world—the world
of France : on which, like Eblis in his hall,
sits enthroned *le grand épicier*—the Citizen-
King : the grand master of the order of
L'Épicerie : the king of the sugar-market,
and the autocrat of the stock-exchange : the

THE ÉPICIER

embodied spirit of the age, and of all the ages of all the exchanges of the world—broker- ages, agiotages, mortgages, averages, and per centages : the reverse of " no waiter, but a knight templar," being in truth no knight, but an *épicier*.

But the *épicier*—passive substratum as he is—is, like the great passive substratum, his mother earth, " one shape of many names," * as Æschylus has it, diffusing his own life through all that lives above him. The influence of his spirit is everywhere positive and predominant. The *épicier* votes—the *épicier* elects ; the *épicier* does not discuss, but the *épicier* decides, and the *épicier* administers. The *épicier* rules the court and the camp, the bourse and the bureau ; the *épicier* wields the sword of the national guard, and the sceptre of the citizen-king. In short, the whole existing political system of France is one *grande boutique d'épicerie*.

Thus there is in France a mass of fiery youth tending perpetually to a republic ; a government, no matter how called, or on what principles and professions originally based, repressing this tendency by force ; the progressive increase of the opposite pressures, every now and then generating an explosion ; and the *épicier*, with his con- firmed habit of order, satisfied with any

* Πολλῶν ὀνομάτων μορφὴ μία.

form of government under which he may buy and sell in peace, bringing the vast bulk of his own dead weight to the upholding of any mode of authority which accident has made uppermost at the end of the turmoil, and which seems to him likely to keep prices looking up, and to throw no cloud over his Sunday enjoyment of the suburban picturesque.

We are now, we think, sufficiently deep in the *physiologie de l'Épicier* to understand why writings, founded mainly on observation of this class of society, do not meddle with political opinions, or beat time in any way to the march of the movement.

Since writing the above, we have received and read Paul de Kock's last novel, *Ni Jamais, ni Toujours*,—in which, for the first time, we find an indication, but a very slight one, of political opinion : it amounts to nothing more than an expression of regret that destruction has been so much more vigorous than construction : a position, however, which, carried out into its practical, or rather into its non-practical results, will be found to furnish the basis of *la philosophie épicière*.

BELLINI

BELLINI

THE composer Bellini, who died in the vicinity of Paris on the 23rd of last September, is as great a loss as the musical stage, in its present circumstances, could well have sustained. His style had many beauties, but its chief characteristic was a deep and touching pathos ; and his death comes unfortunately in support of a theory on which we have frequently meditated, that the faculty of pathetic musical composition, possessed in a pre-eminent degree, is the song of the swan—

—prophetic of the doom
Heaven gives its favourites,—early death.

Need we mention Mozart and Weber ? Bellini, at least, adds another name to the list of those whose music has sounded the very depths of feeling, and who have passed away while the blossom of their genius, though expanded to maturity, if judged by its actual development, could scarcely be regarded as more than a promise of the future, if judged by the ordinary relations of time.

Vincenzo Bellini was born in 1804, at Catania, in Sicily. His grandfather, father, and brothers were all composers of music, but had not the genius of Vincenzo, and wrote only church music with moderate ability.

At the age of thirteen, Bellini was placed in the Royal Musical Academy, or Conservatorio, at Naples, where his talents immediately acquired for him the title of Maestrino —a name given instead of that of pupil to those scholars who are advanced in the art, and are capable of giving the first instructions to the junior students. The celebrated Maestro Zingarelli conceived a warm attachment to the young Bellini ; and under his paternal instructions Vincenzo soon produced compositions in ecclesiastical music, and in all the strict forms of counter-point, simple, double, and fugued.

Before he left the Conservatorio, Bellini evinced great intellectual aptitude, and eminent musical genius for dramatic composition, and composed the music of a melodrama called *Adderson e Salvina*. This, his first production, was performed with great success by the pupils of the Academy, and Zingarelli exclaimed, " *Ecco un Maestro che farà epoca !* "

BELLINI

His first production after leaving the Academy was the opera of *Bianca e Fernando*, which is composed with his peculiar style of sweet and pathetic melody. In the remaining nine years of his life he composed *Il Pirata, La Straniera, Zaira, Beatrice di Tenda, I Capelletti, La Sonnambula, Norma, I Puritani*—in which he enriched the Italian stage with those exquisite melodies of sweet, impassioned, melancholy tenderness, some of which *must* live till music itself shall be forgotten.

His operas from the first arrested the attention of the public of Italy, who would before listen only to Rossini. In Milan his popularity was so great from the production of the *Pirata* and *Straniera*, that he was called the spoiled child of La Scala.

Bellini was melancholy, sensitive, generous, and high-minded, and greatly beloved in the circle of his friends. After the success of his *Puritani*, he was living in retirement near Paris, and studying the prosody of the French language, with the intention of composing an opera for the Académie Royale, when a malignant intestine disorder carried him off in a few days. He preserved his serenity of mind to the last, excepting for a few moments of delirium before death, when he sprung from his bed, and called on his mother, father, and brothers—" *Mia madre, mio padre, miei fratelli—vi abbraccio ancora una volta !* "

His friends honoured his obsequies with a magnificent funeral at their own charge, remitting all his property to his relations. The funeral was attended by an assemblage of the *élite* of Parisian society, and of all that was eminent in the arts ; and the same friends are preparing in the same manner to erect a monument to his memory. It is, however, a trite saying, but strictly applicable to Bellini, his best monument is in his works, which are diffused throughout the world.

Of Bellini's operas, six have been performed in England : *Il Pirata, La Sonnambula, La Straniera, Norma, I Capelletti e i Montecchi*, and *I Puritani*.

The first of these was strangely garbled on its first production in 1830 ; and was moreover the unfortunate vehicle of introducing a prima donna (Madame Lalande) who had been fearfully bepuffed, and whose performance fell far short of her note of promise. But the *disjecti membra poëtæ* were apparent, and it was obvious that at least some of the music had grace, expression and originality.

La Sonnambula was produced for the first time at the close of the season of 1831, when the recent success and great popularity of Donizetti's *Anna Bolena* had left little space for a competitor. Pasta was the heroine of both : both parts had been expressly written for her : but all who know the great actress must be aware that she was much more at home in afflicted majesty than in a village girl walking in her sleep over pantiles. There were but two or three nights of the season left, and the theatre was thinly attended ; but some of the melodies gave great delight to those who heard them, especially Rubini's air in the last act. We were then told by some of the superlatively knowing, that real judges did not admire this air, (real judges being those who judge like the parties who call them so,) and that it was only pleasing to the admirers of Rubini's " vicious style : " but it delighted English audiences night after night when it was sung at Drury Lane by Templeton. This opera had in its English dress a run of almost unexampled popularity. This success we were told was owing to Malibran, and not to the music ; but Malibran, in all the splendour of her genius and beauty, could not give the same attraction to any other opera. The truth is, the entire performance of Malibran, histrionic and musical, was as nearly perfect as any-thing mortal can be : but it could not have produced its astonishing impression if the composer had not given to the afflicted village maid melodies that came home at once to the understandings and feelings of the audience. The unsophisticated English audience thought the music beautiful, because it abounded with expressive and intelligible melody : and it happens very fortunately for the production of the simply and naturally beautiful in all branches of art, that pedantic orations, proving to the mass of mankind that they ought not to like what they do like, have been in all ages and nations thrown away.

La Sonnambula in the English theatres, and *I Puritani*, last season in the King's Theatre, may be regarded as the two triumphs of Bellini. *Il Pirata* never thoroughly recovered the effect of its first misrepresentation : *Norma* was admired, and Pasta was truly great in it ; but the main subject and character were too like *Medea* and *Anna Bolena* to have much effect of novelty, and the melody was too much buried in harmony, often more ambitious than appropriate. *I Montecchi e i Capelletti* was in spite of Pasta a total failure ; but no English audience even in the King's Theatre, can ever endure such an affair as the Italian *Romeo and Juliet;* though the libretto would appear to be a favourite in Italy, being, with a few unimportant differ-

BELLINI

ences to suit the composer, the same in the compositions of Zingarelli, Guglielmi, Vaccaj, and Bellini.

Bellini's great force is in melody. Those who have called him an unscientific harmonist have contented themselves with the allegation and adduced no proof of it. But his harmony wants depth and variety : he rather multiplies the repetitions of the chord than gives distinct business to the several components of the score. We do not go so far as to apply to him Ritson's favourite saying : " The only use of the harmony is to spoil the melody ; " but his harmony often smothers more than it adorns the melody : it has neither the splendid variety of Rossini, nor the consummate combinations of Mozart, nor the torrent of sound of Beethoven, with its mysterious current of murmured undersong which creeps on in such delicious and marvellous intermixture with the vast mainstream of harmony. In all these composers there was genius for harmony. In Bellini there is only genius for melody. He was a melodist by nature, and a harmonist by education. The deep and touching pathos of the simple ballad was more accordant to his tone of mind than the sublime and spirit-stirring volumes of sound which shake the modern musical stage.

321

BELLINI

Bellini had a genius for melody, and chiefly for pathetic melody, which is always the more touching, the more singly and simply it is presented. Johnny Armstrong's " Last Good Night," or the " Cruelty of Barbara Allen," with which the dairy-maid so touched Goldsmith's feelings in his youth, that in his latest years the finest modern music was dissonance to him in comparison with its mere recollection, a difference which he ascribed solely to the tendency of age and knowledge to sour our dispositions, would even in his youth have affected him little with a full orchestral accompaniment. Sorrow is solitary. The voice of the nightingale is most affecting when it is single in the twilight. It is only in funeral hymns, and on other rare occasions that allow the expression of a common grief, that sorrow can be properly choral : even then the accompaniments are necessarily softened and subdued, and in the general effect, much is lost to the pathetic and given to the sublime. Rubini, who possesses, more than any singer we ever heard, the power of identifying the redundancies of ornament with the overflowings of feeling, gives to Bellini's melodies a force of pathetic expression, which seems to be the genuine echo of the composer's soul.

BELLINI

Pasta, Malibran, and Tamburini have developed in passages the full strength of the recondite feeling ; but generally speaking, we have, in a quiet apartment, from, of course, very inferior, but still correct and expressive execution, felt more of the true intrinsic pathos of Bellini's music, than we have felt from all the appliances and means of theatrical decoration. Bellini has written melodies with which future maids may charm the ears of future Goldsmiths, who will afterwards think in the Italian theatre, that they hear nothing so touching as they heard in their youth.

We are desirous of enabling our readers to form their own judgment on the correctness of our opinion of Bellini's genius for pathetic melody. We shall present three specimens, each from a different opera : the first from *Il Pirata*. The drama is taken from Maturin's tragedy of *Bertram*, and the passage we select is adapted to the last words of *Gualtiero*, the Bertram of the opera, before he stabs himself. He addresses the confidante of Imogine (the object of his first love, whose husband he has killed, and who has become a maniac), in the presence of the assembled knights. They are the last words of love, despair, and remorse, not unmixed with a feeling of self-vindication and gratified revenge.

BELLINI

Ah! non fia sem - pre o - dia - - ta la
mia me-moria, io spe - ro se fui spie-ta-to e
fie - ro fui sven - tu - ra-to an - cor, e
par-le - rà la tom - ba al - le pie-to-se
gen - ti, de' lun-ghi miei tor-men - ti del
mio tra-di-to a - mor, e par-le - rà del - -
mio tra - di - to a-mor, e par-le-rà del - -
mio - - tra - - - di-to, tra-di-to a - mor.

BELLINI

The second specimen we shall take from *La Sonnambula :* it is the air to which we have previously alluded. The words are those of Elvino, distracted between love for Amina, and conviction of her infidelity.

Allegro moderato.

Ah! per-chè non pos - so o - diar - ti in - fe-
del, com' io vor'- re - i! Ah! del tut-to an-cor non
se - i can - cel - la - ta, can-cel-la-ta dal mio
cor. Possa un al - tro ah pos - sa a-
mar - ti qual t'a-mò que - st'in - fe -
li - ce! Al - tro vo - to o tra - di -

tri-ce, nò, ah! non te-mer non te-mer dal mio do-

lor. Al - tro vo-to non te- mer non te-mer dal mio do-

lor, Al - tro vo-to ab! non te - mer non te-mer dal mio do-lor.

The third specimen we shall take from
La Straniera; and as this opera is less
known than the two others, and the story
was not at all understood when it was performed here in 1832, we will give a brief
sketch of the preliminary matter. The
subject is from the Vicomte d'Arlincourt's
L'Etrangère. La Straniera is an unknown
beauty, who resides in mysterious solitude
among the mountains. Arthur, the betrothed of Isoletta, the daughter of a
neighbouring baron, sees, loves, and pursues
the fair unknown, who calls herself Alaide.
The passion is reciprocal, but some fatal
secret enslaves the lady. His friend Valdeburg pleads with him the cause of Isoletta.
In justification of his passion, he takes
Valdeburg to the dwelling of La Straniera.
Alaide and Valdeburg recognize each other

BELLINI

with marks of affection, which madden Arthur with jealousy.—Watching round her dwelling in a stormy night, he sees Valdeburg come forth, and overhears from them a determination to depart together in secret. He falls upon Valdeburg—refuses to listen to explanation :—they fight ; Valdeburg is wounded, and falls into a lake. Alaide calls on Valdeburg as her brother, and the rage of Arthur is turned into repentance and grief. His disappearance causes inquiry,—suspicion falls on the lady, and she is placed on trial for his murder. Arthur appears, and takes the crime on himself. The judge is about to pass sentence, when the wounded Valdeburg enters the hall, and exhorting his sister to depart with him, tells her that fate allows her nothing but to live and die unknown. This is the subject of the air, which we select from *La Straniera*.

Me - co tu vieni o mi - se - ra,

lun - ge da queste por - te, o - ve ce - lar le

la - grime ti scor - ge - rà la sor - te, ti

327

BELLINI

scor - ge - rà la sor - te: tomba ove i-gno-ta

scen - de - re la terra a te da-

rà: ah! vie - ni: sî vie - ni:

tomba ove i-gno - ta scen - de-re la

ter - ra a te da - rà - - tom - ba i-

gno-ta a te da - rà, tom - ba i-

gno-ta a te da - rà, a te da - rà.

We always thought this opera extremely
beautiful. On its first production it was
received with enthusiasm in Italy, and we
think it deserved it. The sequel contains

328

some very striking effects, both musical and dramatic. Alaide exacts from her lover a promise to marry Isoletta, to which, after many struggles, he accedes, on condition of receiving his bride from the hands of his mistress. She consents, and having absolved her promise, issues alone from the church, and leaning on a tomb in the adjoining cemetery, gives vent to her affliction in strains of impassioned melody, which mingle in touching contrast with the pealing organ and choral song within the church. Arthur breaks from the unfinished rites, and renews his suit in an ebullition of unavailing remonstrance and passionate despair. The grand prior and the nuptial train enter in disorder. The grand prior recognizes the Straniera, who has thrown back her veil, which she has worn in the ceremony, hails her as queen, and informs her that she is recalled to the throne by the king her husband, from whom she had been unjustly separated. But in the midst of the salutations of honour which rise around her, Arthur stabs himself at her feet—she falls on his body, and dies of a broken heart.

The heroine of this story is Agnes de Méranie, the unfortunate wife of Philip Augustus of France. This did not appear in the libretto, as presented here, in which the name of the heroine was kept as profound a state secret as it might have been in the beginning of the thirteenth century ; and the whole story was made thoroughly incomprehensible, which must have been the fault of our worthies at the King's Theatre, and not of the Italian dramatist : for *La Straniera*, so much of it as was correctly given, had all the characteristics of an excellent poem. It was, as well as the *Pirata* and the *Sonnambula*, written by Signor Felice Romani, the author of *Anna Bolena*, who has shown in all those instances a talent for dramatic poetry far above the present general level of the Italian musical stage.

Bellini's forte was in the pathetic ; but he has many charming melodies of a more lively character, all tinged, however, in some degree with the tone of melancholy which was natural to his mind. There is another quality which we have remarked in his compositions, a peculiar beauty and almost classical simplicity in the rhythm of his compositions. We say almost classical, because, to be perfectly so, it is essential that metre and music should correspond syllable for note. This was indisputably the characteristic of the ancient Greek music ; and from this acknowledged premise some writers have jumped to the

conclusion that the great charm of ancient
music, to which such wonders were ascribed,
must have consisted in the accurate beating
of time. They cannot imagine that music
could have been brought to much perfection
without the modern liberties of exuberant
ornament. The pleasure which is derived
from mere perfect metre is familiar to all
who are familiar with classical poetry. The
infinite variety of the Greek lyric metres
must have afforded some scope for variety
in music ; but we are inclined to think that
the perception of that kind of harmony
which resulted from the intimate correspondence of music and metre, (adorning,
in their connexion, the most perfect lyrical
poetry human genius has ever produced,)
must have caused a degree of intellectual
delight, for which the complete independence
of both metre and meaning, which modern
music has assumed, may be but an indifferent compensation. It has occurred to
us to try on one of those airs of Bellini,
which we have called almost classical, the
experiment of making it quite so ; and by
fitting it note for note to the pure metre,
to which, with some difference, it naturally
belongs, to try how far what it loses in
musical ornament is compensated by the
perception of metrical symmetry. We have
tried this experiment with the melody of

BELLINI

the last air of the *Sonnambula*, which runs thus :—

BELLINI

This melody suggests at once the Ionic *à minori* metre :—

⏑ ⏑ — —

And, with the omission of some of its ornaments, resolves itself into four pure Ionic *à minori* tetrameters, or measures of four feet, the first and third being acatalectic, or consisting of four perfect metres :—

⏑ ⏑ — — | ⏑ ⏑ — — | ⏑ ⏑ — — | ⏑ ⏑ — —
πολύχειρ, καὶ | πολυναύτας, | Σύριόν θ'ἄρ | μα διώκων.

Æschylus in Persis.

(Horace's ode to Neobule (iii. 12) consists of ten of these tetrameters, which are sometimes arranged in four decapods ;)—the second and fourth being catalectic, or consisting of three perfect metres, and one, of which one syllable is wanting :—

⏑ ⏑ — — | ⏑ ⏑ — — | ⏑ ⏑ — — | ⏑ ⏑ — —
τόθεν οὐκ ἔστ | ιν ὑπέρ θνα | τὸν ἀ-λύξ αν- | τα φυγεῖν.

Æschylus in Persis.

333

BELLINI

To this metre Bellini's melody may be fitted somewhat as follows :

The bar takes the place of the metrical arsis. The arched lines discriminate the metres.

We give this as an experiment merely. *Valeat quantum valeat.* But we conceive it is not very discrepant from such a melody as might have been sung in the Athenian theatre. The harmony, if it had been so sung, would, according to the received opinions of Greek music, have consisted wholly of unisons and octaves. We have some reasons of our own for thinking that the Greeks had the harmony of the fifth in their choruses, which we shall hereafter endeavour to develop if we can find leisure.

To return to our subject.

Musical critics, who hear by rule, have laboured to discredit Bellini. Fortunately reputations grow in despite of these systematical doctors. The feelings of the ordinary unsophisticated and unprejudiced hearer are always in advance of their rules ; and that which has, in despite of them, been once stamped with popular favour, becomes a standard to the same class of critics in the next generation.

We have on occasions been very much amused by some of these gentry. Listening one evening with great pleasure to some beautiful modulations in one of the operas of Rossini, we were edified by a learned Theban near us, who could hear nothing but a profuse use of the diminished seventh. And we have somewhere fallen in with another variety of the same genus, who, when the whole theatre was electrified by a bold and striking effect most appropriate to the scene, could only expatiate on the harmonic atrocity of consecutive fifths, by which in a great measure the effect had been produced.

It is fitting that there should be rules in science, because they are the collected and concentrated experience of ages ; but they

335

are not to be converted into pedantic fetters to bind genius through all future time. As there is no possible sequence of sounds to which human passion does not give utterance, so there is no possible consonance or dissonance which will not find its fit place in dramatic music. Nothing was more appalling than Mrs. Siddons's scream. There was no weapon in the armoury of her art which she used so sparingly ; but when she did use it the occasion demanded it, and the effect was proportionate to the occasion. Rossini has taken many liberties in opposition to rules—generally because they were appropriate in their place ; but sometimes, we verily believe, with mere malice prepense, to make the hair of the disciplinarians stand on end at sequences of perfect fifths or sevenths resolved by sevenths.

Akin to the pedantry of inflexible rules is that of entrenching the want of tact and feeling behind the authority of great names— saying, " This is nought, because it is not like Mozart, or Haydn, or Beethoven, or Handel ; " and thus sweeping away all modern music as with the fire of an impregnable battery. All the great names thus used had, in their own day, precisely the same sort of artillery pointed against themselves. When Beethoven was first heard of in England, it was as a madman who wrote crazy music which nobody could perform : and even where he was better known and more justly valued, all the transcendent and unrivalled dramatic talent which his *Fidelio* demonstrates, did not give him sufficient theatrical encouragement to write a second opera. Truly says Montaigne, " Les evénements sont très maigres témoins de notre prix et capacité." Mozart was long unknown in Paris, and has never been relished in Italy, where the anti-national use which factious pedantry has made of his name has caused him to be looked on as a sort of national enemy. Handel and Bononcini ; Gluck and Piccini ; Mozart and Rossini ; the world of music has, in all these cases, been wide enough for both ; yet it seems a necessary condition of society that there must be faction in all things.

But to be entrenched behind great names, which already bear the stamp of immortality, is an exceedingly safe position. It is an excellent *locus standi* for the fulmination of dogmas. The oracle shakes his head, and the profane take for granted that there is something in it. They give him credit for having approached the pure source, and drank from the same fountain with the great spirits with whom he seems so familiar. If we take the liberty to throw a shell into

BELLINI

this oracular entrenchment, it is not against the great names which are misused in its construction, but against those who so misuse them, that we wish to be understood to direct it.

We stake our opinion of Bellini on the airs which we have selected, and of which our limits do not permit us to give more than the subject-melodies. But they are melodies that cannot die. They have been, are, and will be, felt and admired wherever unsophisticated perceptions sit in judgment upon them. But, as we have said, musical critics, *soi-disant par excellence*, who hear by rule, and whose chief seat of feeling is in their fingers, have so unworthily disparaged Bellini, that we have felt it a mere act of justice, as well as of gratitude, for the delight which those melodies alone (even if there were nothing else) have given us, to pay this passing tribute of honour to his memory.

GASTRONOMY AND CIVILIZATION

GASTRONOMY AND CIVILIZATION

Two conditions are necessary to the cultivation of the science of gastronomy, national peace and individual taste. Wherever these have existed, the science has progressed, with more or less credit, limited by temperance and rational festivity where men were refined, and degraded into fantastic gluttony where they were licentious. The greatest abuse of this science has been under the monarchical form of government from ancient Egypt to modern Russia. Republican virtue has thriven on simple fare, from the turnips of Cincinnatus to Andrew Marvel's cold shoulder of mutton.

In Egypt, where luxury was carried to the greatest excess, superstition spoilt many a goodly mess, by interdicting the use of onions and leeks, of which restriction Juvenal writes,

Porrum et cepe nefas violare, et frangere morsu,

while to gratify their ambition for costly and unheard of delicacies, the rulers of this

341

people misapplied things intended to minister to other senses, by forcing them into the service of the palate, as exemplified in Cleopatra's extravagant beverage seasoned with melted pearls.

In ancient Greece, temperate enjoyment administered unrivalled hospitality. When Phœnix, Ajax, and Ulysses, at the head of Agamemnon's deputation, waited on Achilles, Patroclus, himself the son of a king, cooked the dinner and attended to the fire ; and though camp performances may be no standard for ordinary practice, yet, as Homer particularizes the skilful carving of Achilles, it is probable he intended to represent the best manners of the period, which, though simple, were not rude, as it is evident that careful arrangement and courteous attention, the primal elements of scientific festivity, presided at the unexpected banquet. (*Iliad*, ix.) It is remarkable that there should be no mention of either fish or fruit in the Homeric repasts. It is evident that both must have been used when the *Iliad* was written, as a description of the angler drawing a heavy fish to shore is used as a simile in the 16th Book ; and as fruit is mentioned growing in the garden of Alcinous, it may safely be inferred that it was eaten. Athenæus accounts for the omission of these

CIVILIZATION

articles on the supposition that Homer did not think it dignified to particularize them at the meals of his heroes. It is worthy of notice, however, that when Nestor returns to his tent with Machaon, after the latter has been hurt in battle, Hecamede gives the wounded warrior green honey, sacred flour of barley, probably made into little cakes, and an onion relish, previous to presenting him with a strengthening draught composed of Pramnian wine, in which goat's-milk cheese and barley are grated. (*Iliad*, xi.) It may be that the meal of a wounded man being medical as well as gastronomical, and requiring more than ordinary skill in its arrangement, made Homer think it worth while to give these particulars. Salt, apparently a more superfluous article, is sometimes mentioned, but then it bore a triple signification of sanctity : first, it was held sacred, because it possessed the divine power of preserving meat from putrefaction (*The Scholiast*) ; secondly, because it was used at sacrifices ; when Chryseïs is given back to her father, salt is sprinkled with barley between the horns of the hecatombs as they are going to be slain (*Iliad*, i.) ; and lastly, because it was used at meals, and was therefore regarded as a bond of union between men. (*The Scholiast.*) In the repast given by Achilles to the deputa-

343

tion sent by Agamemnon, Patroclus sprinkles salt over the meat he is cooking; but this is an exception to the general rule : it is usually flour that is strewn over the roasting meats in the *Iliad*.

The only method of preparing the Homeric repasts is roasting, yet, as there is an allusion to pork boiling in a pot, used as a simile in the 21st Book of the *Iliad*, it was clearly a mode both understood and practised. Several striking examples of the ready hospitality of Greece occur in the *Odyssey*. It is effectively illustrated when Telemachus invites Minerva to share the banquet preparing in the palace of Ithaca ; as the invitation is not given to the goddess either in her divine character or in the assumed one of Mentor, both of which are unknown to Telemachus, but simply to a stranger as such, with whose name, position, and purpose he is entirely unacquainted. (*Odyssey*, i.) It is exhibited under a different phase when Telemachus, and Minerva, under the form of Mentor, come upon Nestor and his sons sacrificing to Neptune on the Pylian shore, and are promptly invited to join the rite and the feast without any preliminary questions of their names or business. (*Odyssey*, iii.) And again, in another aspect, when Ulysses, journeying on foot as a poor old beggar,

CIVILIZATION

is received into the house of Eumæus, the
steward of the swine, where he is entertained and lodged in the best manner his
host's circumstances allow. (*Odyssey*, xiv.)
These features of the old heroic ages were
the basis of social life in Greece, and
expanded into the fullest development in
her wonderful republics, where enjoyment
was ministered by courtesy, tempered by
sobriety, graced by art, and dignified by
science.   The luxury of the Greeks has
been much misunderstood and exaggerated.
Gluttony was a rare thing amongst them,
and never, at any period of their independent
existence, a national characteristic.   In the
times of Socrates, there were three meals
which answered respectively to our breakfast, luncheon, and dinner.   The first usually
consisted of bread dipped in wine, which
gave it the name of ἀκράτισμα.   The luncheon,
ἄριστον, was a simple meal, of which the
substance varied according to the circumstances of different families ; the time for
it was also uncertain ; but in the regular
life of cities it was probably about noon, as
Philocleon describes the satisfaction of going
home to lunch after the business of the
courts of justice was over, and gives a
lively description of the manner in which his
wife and daughter pressed him to try several
things. (Aristophanes. *Vesp.* 605-612.)

The principal meal, δεῖπνον, occurred late in the day, sometimes at sunset. In the houses of wealthy Athenians, this meal consisted of two courses : the first comprising fish, flesh, fowl, vegetables, bread, and the invariable μάζα, a preparation of flour and wine ; and the second, which combined the features of our third course and dessert, was composed of confections, fruits, and sweetmeats. The Athenians were a very social people, and seized on every good excuse for dining together, such as religious festivals, family anniversaries, or the natal days of illustrious men. The young men, as early as the time of Homer, had an entertainment something like the modern pic-nic, being a joint-stock meal, to which each person contributed a share of the provisions, or subscribed an equal portion of money to purchase them. On ordinary occasions, the dinner was cooked, or superintended, by the mistress of the house, but for great banquets a professional man cook was engaged. The Athenians bathed and dressed with care when they went out to supper, and reclined while taking their meals. It has not been ascertained when reclining superseded sitting ; it has been conjectured that this mode was adopted when baths were introduced, but this explanation cannot be supported, as the Homeric heroes invariably sat, and they took the bath before supping. (*Iliad*, x.)

The Greeks have the reputation of being great drinkers, which is an exceedingly mischievous error, built up into a popular doctrine from some such conclusive evidence as that their great solemnities were bacchic, and that Anacreon and Cratinus were jolly fellows. Even Alexander, who has the most suspicious character in this respect, has been very unjustly aspersed. It is certain that if he ever exceeded at all, it was only when the duties of the day were over, and never till the latter part of his life ; but it is probable that the violences attributed to this part of his career rose from ungovernable pride and unrestrained temper, rather than from intoxication. It is certain that he was remarkable for his temperate eating; and though he was very particular in providing a good supper for his guests, and careful in helping them attentively, he disregarded dainties himself, and when rare fish and fruit were brought to him from a distance, he divided and distributed them among his friends, seldom retaining any for himself. The grateful Queen of Caria frequently sent him delicacies and choice viands, but when she forwarded some of her best cooks and bakers to him, he declared he had no use for them, as his tutor Leonidas had supplied him with far better, a march before day to get his dinner ready, and a light dinner to prepare his supper. His habits were simple and soldierly ; he never reclined till supper, when the day and its work were dispatched, but sat to his dinner like the Homeric heroes. Plutarch says he sat long after supper, not to drink, but to talk, which is in perfect harmony with the character of the soldier in every age.

Bacchus, and the festivals in his honour, come in for a large share of this misrepresentation. This god was the most chaste, temperate, and beneficent of all the heathen deities : he taught men the use of the vine and the cultivation of the earth, and achieved the conquest of India chiefly by the introduction of these benefits. He instructed in the use of the fruits of the earth, but did not sanction their abuse. It has been well distinguished by an American poet, who has read the mythic meaning with a gifted eye, that " Bacchus was the type of vigour, and Silenus of excesses."

The excitement which possessed people during the Dionysia was the result of religious enthusiasm, and not of intoxication. The Bacchantes were animated by inspired fervour alone, therefore the beautifully executed figure of the drunken

Bacchante in the French department of the Great Exposition perpetuates an erroneous conception. The priestesses were not admitted to the mysteries of the Anthesteria, one of the most ancient Attic festivals, until they had undergone especial preparation and purification ; and as men were excluded from these mysteries altogether, it is easy to see that these rites could not have deserved the character for licentiousness which some have affixed to them.

In private life, the Greeks did not drink unmixed wine till the first course was removed ; after which they washed their hands, and poured out some wine as a libation before tasting it themselves. Excess of every kind was discouraged in Greece, both by the precept and example of philosophers, and by the enforcements of law. In Sparta, men were obliged to dine at the public tables, supplied with very simple fare, in order that luxury might not creep into the state through the home habits of the citizens. In Athens, the laws of Solon, which flourished 400 years, excluded the debauched from the right of public speaking ; and though Plato permitted men after the age of forty to become intoxicated at the Bacchic festivals, yet, as he prohibited wine altogether to youths under eighteen, and from that age till thirty allowed but a moderate quantity, the tendency of his indulgence is clearly to establish sobriety, as no man who had cultivated temperance till he was forty years old, would be likely to become a toper afterwards. Yet, even during this elevated condition of public and private morality, the cant of an austerer virtue sprang up, and the cynics asserted that the perfection of human life consisted in a total subjugation of the flesh. They substituted mental for physical excess, and disgraced virtue by the manner of their protest against vice. " I see your vanity through your rags," said Socrates to Antisthenes, the founder of the system. Finding it easier to suppress their desires than to regulate them, they made an ostentatious boast of the abstinence which emanated from the vanity and weakness of their natures ; and so, like some of us, turned their failings to a profitable account. They taught nothing, they only railed. Diogenes, who made himself the most conspicuous of the sect, indemnified himself for the discomfort of his self-imposed renunciations by snarling at the comforts which he had not the temperance of spirit to enjoy with moderation. He received a well-merited rebuke from Plato, when, stamping on the decorations of the divine philosopher in presence of some noble guests who were supping with him, he exclaimed, " Thus I trample on the pride of Plato ! " " And with greater pride, Diogenes," answered the temperate Athenian.

The Greeks did not disregard dietetics, nor did their greatest philosophers neglect to warn against the use of unwholesome articles of food, while inculcating simplicity of diet. Their gastronomy was simple, as contradistinguished from rude on the one hand, and gluttonous on the other.

It is singular that the popular conception of the sensualist refers his parentage to precisely that philosopher who had the most temperate doctrines and practice. Free from all extremes, Epicurus inculcated moderation in all things : he taught that only in the equal exercise of all his faculties could man attain happiness, by which he understood the happiness of his whole life, not the exaggerated felicity of any one moment. In the chosen retreat of his Attic garden he enjoyed tranquil speculation, the social intercourse of his friends and followers, and dispensed simple hospitality to all who needed it. Wonderful days in the world's history were those of republican Greece, where all that was lofty, heroic, beautiful, and good, met in one place and at one time, to be a pattern and a glory for ever. Who would not have lingered over his wine to drain the richer draughts of wisdom from Socrates, to drink the sublime eloquence of Plato, the calm philosophy of Epicurus, and listen to the rare melodies of that lost music, whose recorded effects have become a fable and a dream ? The Romans, although they imitated the Greeks in many arts and practices, did not get their licentiousness from them, as the vulgar error supposes. Livy traces the degeneracy of Rome from the introduction of luxury by the Asiatic army after the triumphs of Cn. Manlius Vulso, A.U.C. 565, and sets down amongst its worst effects, that cooks were then for the first time held in value, and that what had formerly been esteemed as the meanest of service, began to be considered an art : *" tum coquus, vilissimum antiquis mancipium, et æstimatione et usu, in pretio esse : et quod ministerium fuerat, ars haberi cœpta."* The Romans became more remarkable for gluttony than for rational gastronomy : their *grands gourmands* combined the voraciousness of a Justice Greedy, and the fantastic fancies of a Cleopatra, with the impudent foppishness of a Brummel. Horace illustrates the two first of these characteristics, in his satire on the supper given by Nasidienus to Mæcenas, amongst the component parts of which, in addition to various wines and many sub-

CIVILIZATION

stantial dishes, he mentions broiled flounders' entrails, and gander's liver stuffed with figs ; the host, during the entire feast, ostentatiously bragging of the superiority of his wines, viands, and inventions, and setting forth their varieties and qualities in a strain of endless dulness. Horace is a more just and credible satirist than either Seneca or Juvenal, because his sympathies are more extensive and his judgment more lenient : jovial and social himself, he is more likely to censure abuse fairly, because he is better qualified to distinguish it from use ; and we may conclude, from the general tone of his writings, that his own opinion is expressed when he makes Ofellus condemn the nonsensical preference given by his contemporaries to a poor-flavoured peacock, on account of its gay plumage, over a fat pullet :—

> Vix tamen eripiam, posito pavone, velis quin
> Hoc potius, quam gallina, tergere palatum,
> Corruptus vanis rerum.

The doctrine which he puts into the mouth of Alphius, who declares his preference for simple diet, giving easy digestion and cheerful spirits, and affirms that neither curious fish nor rare birds are so acceptable to him—

> .... quam lecta de pinguissimis
> Oliva ramis arborum,

Aut herba lapathi prata amantis, et gravi
Malvæ salubres corpori ;

may also be presumed to be the opinion of
Horace himself, as the apostasy of Alphius,
at the conclusion of the satire, throws discredit on his own tergiversation, and does
not affect the principles he assumed.

But the fullest and most curious account
of Roman luxury is that given by Petronius
in his *Feast of Trimalchio*. This elaborate
supper began with ripe and unripe olives,
by way of stimulants, with which were
served dormice seasoned with honey and
poppy juice ; sausages accompanied by
Syrian plums and pomegranate seeds ;
and a wooden hen fashioned as if sitting on
eggs, which when examined, proved to be
made of paste containing each an ortolan
surrounded by yolk of egg sprinkled with
pepper. The second service was served
entire on a round repositorium. It consisted
of twelve dishes, representing the signs of
the Zodiac, on each of which some emblematical article was placed ; and while the
guests were testifying by their abstemious-
ness their disappointment at such meagre
fare, the upper part of the repositorium was
lifted away, (just as we would take off a
dish cover,) and exposed a goodly service
of meat, game, and fish, the most noticeable
articles being a hare so arranged as to

represent Pegasus ; and at the four corners of the tray a statuette of a satyr pouring garum—a sauce probably very similar to our Anchovy—Brillat Savarin thinks it was Soy,—over fish, which in a vessel at his feet seemed to be swimming in the Euripian sea. Next followed an enormous wild sow, out of which flew a flock of live thrushes, and from whose tusks depended two palm baskets filled respectively with Theban and Syrian dates. She was surrounded by a litter of little pigs, made from some kind of cake-paste. When this course was removed, three pigs of different ages, decorated with handsome bells, muzzles, and halters, were marched into the banquet-hall, and Trimalchio having selected the largest, it was carried off to be killed, and re-appeared cooked in as short a time as it would have taken an ordinary cook to prepare a fowl. But it is remarked that this pig is larger than the wild sow that had been previously served, and Trimalchio observing it intently, discovers that it had not been opened ; whereupon he sends, in a towering passion, for the cook, who arrives in fear and trembling, and pleads as an, excusable oversight that he had forgotten to eviscerate the animal ; but Trimalchio, regarding the omission in a very serious light, desires him to strip (*despolia*), like Vatel in Scribe's admirable vaudeville of that name, who visits his son's culinary errors in the same severe manner—*Dépose tes insignes, je te dégrade!* Trimalchio's cook is being marched off between two torturers, when the company intercede for him, and the courteous host pardoning him at their request, orders him to open the pig, and remedy his forgetfulness in public, which, having re-donned his tunic and knife of office, he proceeds to do, when, from the first incisions, hog's puddings and sausages bound out in all directions. The servants compliment their master with loud acclamations on the success of this farce, and the cook, who had so cleverly performed his part, receives a silver garland and the honour of drinking a goblet with the company. Then follows a boiled calf; and while the guests are engaged in dispatching him, the whole *triclinium* trembles, the ceiling cracks, and while the affrighted company are rising in consternation, a vast hoop descends through the opening, with garlands and pear-shaped boxes of perfumes attached to it; and during the time that each person is helping himself to these, a light service of cakes and fruit is placed on the table, which yield a delicious odour of saffron on being touched. This is succeeded by a course called *matteæ*, consisting of delicacies and choice dainties. In this instance it was composed of fat pullets dissected and boned, surrounded by thrushes, and goose's eggs surmounted by a paste crown. Then followed an after-course (*epidipnis*), brought in on fresh tables, containing some curious specimens of culinary achievements. Thrushes stuffed with a peculiarly light kind of wheat (*siligo*), flour, raisins, and nuts of some kind, probably walnuts. Quinces stuck full of prickles, to resemble sea-urchins, similar to that well-known ornament of our own re-fined supper-tables—a sponge-cake hedge-hog, sprinkled with cut almonds. These are accompanied by a goose, various fish, and many kinds of birds, all of which Trimalchio assures his astonished guests are made out of pork by his skilful cook. This making one thing out of another was a favourite achievement, probably originat-ing as an expedient, and perpetuated as a diversion, as it is related that when Nico-medes, king of Bithynia, being three hundred miles from the sea, longed for fish, his cook contrived to produce something which satis-fied both his eye and his palate, so exactly did it represent the object of his desires. While this course of transformations is being examined, two slaves enter the hall, disputing with such intensity, that they pay no attention to Trimalchio's remonstrances, and presently each breaks the other's *amphora*, from which oysters and all sorts of shell-fish roll out ; these are collected by a serving-boy, and presented to the guests. The cook, so ingenious in masquerade dishes, then enters singing, carrying little shell-fish smoking hot in a silver gridiron : and this would have concluded the repast, but that just as Trimalchio is delivering a " won't go home till morning " * sentiment, he is interrupted by the crowing of a cock, which is instantly caught and cooked.

The manners throughout this long feast are deserving of notice ;—first, it is observable that Trimalchio enters the hall and takes possession of the seat that has been reserved for him, after his guests are placed, with a regal air worthy of a colonial court. Petronius mentions that this was a newly-introduced fashion. When settled on his be-cushioned *triclinium*, he makes use of his

---

* *Quare tangomenas faciamus, et usque in lucem cœnemus.* There has been much discussion about this word *tangomenas*. We have little doubt that it is a corruption of the two first words of the well-known fragment of Alcæus : τέγγε πνεύμονας οἴνῳ, ' Moisten your lungs with wine.' ' *Quare*, τέγγε πνεύμονας *faciamus* ' is, therefore, equivalent to, ' So let us sing, *Soak your clay.*' Naples being a Greek colony, the colloquial phrases abounded with corrupted Greek. The writing of Petronius is extremely pure, and his manner the very perfection of style ; but the dialogues throughout his satire are sprinkled with bastard words of the kind in question.

tooth-pick very elaborately and ostentatiously before touching anything : a silver tooth-pick being a mark of luxury, he is anxious to exhibit his wealth in this very disagreeable manner, and it is to be regretted that many modern Trimalchios make an equally reprehensible display of an instrument which, while designed to relieve its possessor, should not be made an infliction on his neighbours. An accidental and more favourable opportunity for display occurs in the course of the festival, when one of the attendants lets a silver dish fall to the ground, and Trimalchio will not let him pick it up, but desires the groom of the furniture to sweep it away with the refuse. The bread was handed round as at our own tables, and no water was allowed ; and when Trimalchio perceived that some of that simple beverage found a place at his costly board, he ran round the table vociferating that it should be carried away. There were professional carvers, and this important art was performed to the sound of music, and with appropriate gesticulations. We wish our modern gourmands would follow the very good example of Trimalchio, in this respect, and if they must have their viands carved on the sideboard by servants, take care that, like his carvers, they are trained to the art.

GASTRONOMY AND

Luxurious and debauched as the Romans were, Trimalchio is, even for one of them, a very absurd and exaggerated person, bearing about the same proportion to one of the nobles of his time, as a new city lord of these days does to the cultivated gentleman. All his devices to entertain his guests are of the tight-rope merry Andrew order, scenic shows, pre-arranged and perhaps rehearsed between himself and his servants, like those of the pretended unopened pig, the mock fight resulting in the broken *amphora*, and the shower of shellfish, and the "four-and-twenty blackbirds baked in a pie" effect, when the live thrushes fly out of the gigantic sow. He is, nevertheless, seen to be a good-natured kind of person, and when any of the servants or slaves commit any real fault, his threats of punishment generally begin a sentence which ends with their forgiveness. The servants sometimes venture to get up a little scene on their own account, which they would not have dared to do if he had been as fierce and relentless as he thought it dignified to appear. They turn his pretensions and foibles to their own profit with impunity. A young slave, desirous of obtaining his liberty, tumbles over Trimalchio, who, though wounded, instantly gives the youth his freedom, in order that it might not be

360

CIVILIZATION

said that so illustrious a personage as himself had been hurt by a slave. When half-seas-over, at the end of the feast, he quarrels with his wife, Fortunata, whom he had extravagantly lauded at its commencement, and after throwing a cup at her in the heat of the moment, he gravely decrees that she shall be punished by not being permitted to kiss him when he is dead, and that her figure shall not be carved on his tomb. The artistic entertainments are of the most vulgar kind, tumblers, tricks, recitations of nonsense, and music and singing performed by his slaves : his own philosophical and historical dialogues are as ridiculous as Mrs. Malaprop's phraseology; but the conversation of his guests is very amusing, and the whole satire conveys a most graphic and minute picture of Roman manners. Petronius was held in such esteem by the learned German Meibomius, that seeing in a letter from Bologna the words *Habemus hic Petronium integrum*, (" we have here Petronius, entire,") he took it for granted the complete manuscript of Petronius was there, and posted off in search of it ; when he arrived, he asked where Petronius was to be found, and on being informed he was kept in the church, he expressed his surprise at such a place being chosen to deposit him in ; upon which his informant asked what fitter place could be found for a sacred body than the church ; and the discomfited scholar found he had travelled with such infinite diligence only to discover the mummy of Saint Petronius !

As we have said so much about Petronius, we will add that, with all deference to Niebuhr, we agree with those who assign him to the age of Nero, and rejoice with Otto Jahn (*Prol. ad Pers.* xxxiv.), that Studer has re-vindicated him to that period.

It is to be regretted that the bill of fare which Cicero gave to Julius Cæsar has not come down to us, when Cicero, who had expected his guest to show himself very unamiable, was agreeably surprised by the justice Cæsar did to his hospitality, in eating a great deal more than he found it convenient to keep on his stomach. (*Ep. ad Att.* 13, 52.) Roman gluttony became so excessive, that laws were framed to repress it ; a decree passed interdicting the use of pork, sweetbreads, cheeks, &c., at their public suppers, and the Emperor Hadrian issued an edict prohibiting all persons from bathing before the eighth hour, to prevent the abuse of the bath, which was systematically used after immoderate eating, to give relief by assisting the digestion : the

CIVILIZATION

Emperor Titus is said to have died from this cause.

Between Greek and Roman luxury there was a wide distinction ; the Greeks were infinitely more refined, temperate, and artistic ; in their states, individuals were not able, as in Imperial Rome, to amass extraordinary riches ; of what they did possess, they expended more upon art, and less upon indulgence. The Romans had no social arts, and endeavoured to supply their deficiency by profusion. They hired dancers, singers, musicians, and jokers to amuse them ; the Greeks amused themselves, for though they also possessed professional singers, dancers, and musicians, the most illustrious of their warriors, poets, and philosophers were versed in one or more of the festive arts, without which society would lack grace and animation, and festivity become rude and licentious. Epaminondas was a skilful dancer, an accomplished singer, and a clever performer on the harp and flute. Pelopidas was celebrated for his graceful dancing and musical skill. Socrates reproached Alcibiades because he had not learned to play on the flute ; and Themistocles had to excuse himself in the zenith of his popularity for his want of accomplishments, by pleading his naval achievements, by which he had saved his country from the Persian invasion. The Romans had no sympathy with this artistic culture ; their musicians, even if they were citizens at all—which is by no means certain—were very lightly esteemed ; they were low, vicious and greedy.

The Romans were not, like the Greeks, persuaded of the immense power of music upon the mind. Cicero ridicules Damon (in Plato) for dreading lest the city itself should be altered if the kind of music which distinguished it were to be changed. Among the Arcadians a man might be ignorant of every art but music—not to know which was a disgrace. Throughout Greece, it was esteemed a grievous reproach not to know how to play, sing, and dance ; music was introduced at banquets, and the guests were expected to sing to it. The arts and graces were innate in the Greeks ; the Romans only borrowed them, and endeavoured to make up by profusion and exaggeration what they wanted in taste and quality. Their one animus under every form of government had been to conquer other nations and enlarge their own. Consequently when they sat down to enjoy the fruits of conquest, they proceeded in a very rough, unscientific manner, having given all their best energies to the arts of war, and very small attention to the graces of peace.

CIVILIZATION

But when we speak of the degeneracy of Rome into luxury, we must not forget the remark of Voltaire—" As if virtue consisted in robbery, and vice in enjoying the spoil."

We remark such a close affinity between the Roman and German cookery and festive habits, that we believe all that now remains of Roman gastronomic art must be sought only in modern Germany. The agro-dolce sauces, by which the former was characterized, still distinguish the latter : the *bizarre* admixture of meat and fish, of sweet fruit sauces with meats, the large proportions of wine used in their dishes, the marinated viands having boiling vinegar poured over them just as they are ready to be served, and the vast assortment of sausages— including those made of fish, which are said to have been invented by the Emperor Heliogabalus—all tend to establish a Roman origin. Added to which, there is the additional presumptive proofs of several Roman games and habits, having synony- mous representatives in the Zollverein. The ancient pastime, *micare*, still survives there ; and the wealthy Frankfort merchants sometimes have a kind of lottery at their magnificent parties, entitling each guest to some present inscribed on the ticket which he obtains ; after a fashion identical with the *apophoreta* of Petronius and Suetonius.

In the German Christmas-tree, we probably see Trimalchio's hoop (*circulus ingens*), with its presents of garlands and perfumed boxes.

Though the light of the kitchen fire was probably the brightest spot in the dark ages, yet as its reflection has not come down to us, we can only conjecture that barbarian kings would feast, as they did everything else, coarsely and ravenously. The continental nations preserved traditional traces of Roman luxury ; and Eastern festivity, extinguished by a long series of invasions and disasters, revived in a much more agreeable form under the Saracens. Dr. King relates that the maid of an inn served a poisoned shoulder of mutton to Mahomet himself, remarking, with Oriental nonchalance, " If he is a prophet, he will discover it ; if he is an imposter, no matter what becomes of him." No authority is given for this anecdote, *ma se non è vero, è ben trovato*.

The *Arabian Nights* furnish vivid and picturesque accounts of the gay, light, and graceful banquets of the true believers, to which flowers and perfumes were as necessary as food. Tinged and coloured meats and grains ; snowy pullets, reposing on plains of verdant rice, chickens, looking as rosy as the flowers that surrounded them ;

the permitted wine of dates, and, occasionally, the forbidden vintage of the infidel; with the variety and quantity of fruit, sweetmeats, and cakes, which formed the basis of all their entertainments, are described over and over again, with all the honours of Oriental recapitulation. But it is the perfect social equality of all true Mussulmauns which strikes us most forcibly in those delightful tales. The meal of the traveller is ready in every house. Every guest that presents himself is welcome, irrespective of condition. If a man exhibits unusual perturbation, when he discovers that he has been unwittingly supping with the Caliph himself, it is not the rank that disturbs him, but the consciousness that he may have been very near losing his head—an infallible consequence, if any of his words or looks had given umbrage to the mighty potentate. With this one little drawback, all are equals. Zobeide and her sisters entertain the porter who carried home their provisions, the three Calenders, and the distinguished Caliph and his Vizier, with equal attention and hospitality. And the only difference that we perceive in the guests at this charming supper, is, that the porter appears to be the most intellectual character of the set. Where there is any demur about eating in unfitting situations, the difficulty arises from some source independent of the condition of the company. When the Vizier and Agib's grandmother are so enraged with the servant, who has taken their little relative to eat in the cook's shop at Damascus, it seems evident that the cause of their wrath must be sought elsewhere than in the different ranks of the parties, as the internal evidence throughout these tales exhibits persons of all classes dining together without demur. But as it was customary to perform ablutions before eating, and as the Orientals are very strict observers of etiquette, we conclude it was the omission of ceremonial, consequent on taking a repast at a cook's shop, which incensed the child's illustrious friends ; and this was an error which would, of course, be aggravated by the elevated position of the defaulter.

We are confirmed in this opinion by the present practice in Persia with regard to cooks' shops, to which only the common people go to dine ; for though the middle classes and shopkeepers very frequently send to them for their supplies, they take their meals at home.

As we before remarked, the Continental nations preserved traditionary traces of Roman luxury, which served in some instances as a basis, in others as an indication,

CIVILIZATION

for the creation of their respective kitchens. But England owes her characteristic dishes and drinks to her native people : it was not till the time of the Norman Conquest that any material invasion of foreign dishes took place in the British kitchen. The native Britons had an illustrious appreciation of good ale long before the Saxon invasion. Prince Aneurin's poem of the battle of Cattraeth, composed in the sixth century, in commemoration of the heroes who perished at it, attributes the loss of the battle by the Cambrian Britons to the state of intoxication in which they entered the field. Some of the oldest Welsh songs are in praise of ale, which they celebrated in conjunction with the Hirlas.

But we from the horn, the blue, silver-rimmed horn,
Drink the ale and the mead, in our fields that were
    born.

Some centuries before,

King Hardicnute, midst Danes and Saxons stout,
Carouzed in nut-brown ale, and dined on grout.

By Chaucer's time, gastronomy had made such progress that cooks were almost as accomplished in the art of cheating as those of our own highly ingenious days. Before the cook is allowed to tell his tale to his fellow-pilgrims, he is admonished of his culinary delinquencies—

369

Now tell on, Roger, and loke that it be good,
For many a pastee hast thou letten blood ;
And many a Jacke of Dover hast thou sold,
That has been twies hot and twies cold ;
Of many a pilgrim has thou Cristes curse,
And of thy perselee yet fare they the werse,
That they have eten in thy stoble goos,
For in thy shop goth many a flie loos.

This worthy " Cook of London " was
evidently at once a restaurateur, a pastry-
cook, and a baker. If the pasty had been
made by himself, he would have had no
interest to deprive it of gravy ; it must,
therefore, have been sent to him to bake.
The nature of the Jacke of Dover has been
much controverted, but as it is impossible
to ascertain what it was, we must content
ourselves with determining that it was something named after a Jacke of Dover, just
as the well-known tea-cake is christened
by Sally Lunn. It is certain the illustrious
Jacke was a celebrated character, as he is
often mentioned ; and there is besides a
biographical sketch of a portion of his
career, entitled *The Adventures of Jacke of
Dover in search of a greater Fool than himself*.

We do not know whether the French,
when they invaded Italy under Charles
VIII., in 1494, introduced new ideas of
cookery as a portion of their conquest ;
but it would seem so from Berni's *rifaci-
mento* of the *Orlando Innamorato*. Bojardo's

ideas of cookery are simple and severe. Berni has high notions of sauces and seasonings. For instance, the Giant, in Canto VI., who has Orlando in an iron net, speculating on his plumpness and the good supper he will furnish him, says—

> Intiero a cena me l'avrò mangiato,
> Sol d'una spalla vuò fare un boccone :

but in Berni he projects a recondite stuffing, and says—

> Arrosto fia un boccon dilicato,
> E l'impierò di mille cose buone.

Bojardo's Giant is a hungry glutton; Berni's is an epicure.

We have before us a comedy, which, from internal evidence, appears to have been written in the year 1450. The first printed editions appear to have been by Aldus, at Venice. Our copy is a Milanese edition of 1519. It is extremely rare. It is entitled— *Commedia Nuova composta da Nocturno Neapolitano.* There are, in the British Museum, two copies of some of the works of this author : but neither of them contains this comedy. This author, however much neglected now, seems to have been highly esteemed in his own time, as may be seen by the many editions of him, and by the Strambotti beginning :

> Dunque tu sei quel unico Nocturno,
> Che non hebbe mai par ne in ciel ne in terra.

At the end of this comedy is a marriage-feast, of which the bill of fare is given in great detail. It consists chiefly of birds and confections, no fish. Solid roast meat is mentioned, but nothing specified but veal. It is also to be observed that there are dishes *all' Inglese, alla Catalana ; alla Romana ;* none *alla Francese ;* which may confirm what we have before said, of the probable introduction of French notions of cookery after the time of Bojardo. Wine is not particularized ; but the house of the heroine is abundantly stored with it, as every servant who goes into it comes out drunk, with exuberant commendation of the excellence of the liquor. We give that portion of the scene which relates to the bill of fare. Provida and Virido are the bride and bridegroom. Scaltra is charged with the arrangement of the banquet.

Virido. Ma dimmi un poco l'ordin d'isto pasto,
In che maniera e modo il guiderai.

Scaltra. Til dirò, perchè cauto fu rimasto.
Prima, piffari e trombe,—se vorrai.
Che a te sta questo,—che agli spirti umani
Dan gran conforto, e tu gran lode avrai.
Da poi l'acqua odorifera alle mani,
E tuttavia in argenti aurati e belli,
Per non parer da rustici e villani :
E una salata minuta de occelli :
E dopo vo chel rosto sia venuto :

CIVILIZATION

Prima a guacetto giotti, figatelli,
Tordi, quagli, occellin conci a stranuto,
Lepre, cunigli, cercene e pigioni,
Ranci, limon : rosto grosso e minuto :
Il lesso poi, fagian, starne e paoni,
Conci a l'Inglese ed alla Catelana,
E il rosto de vitello con caponi :
Zelatine diverse alla Romana ;
E torti bianchi e verdi, con cupata
Da lecchar il taglier, ovver la piana :
Poi pere guaste, zucha e codognata,
Ranzato, rinci, e cedri più perfetti,
Marzapan, pignochado, e morselata :
Poi l'ultima mestura dei confetti,
Pignol, mandole, nice e fulignati,
Anesi, curiandoli e rancetti.
Così di grosso—or che ti par ? sta bene ?

Virido. Sì per mia fè ; che gli hai ben ordinato.

It is curious that of the vast numbers of
recorded and narrated festivals, it is in
most instances impossible to obtain the bill
of fare ; of real banquets it is almost
hopeless to make any researches ; and the
details of fictitious feasts are extremely rare.
Henry Machyn, citizen and merchant
taylor of London, records in his Diary, 1523,
the funeral feast of Alderman Sir William
Roche, Knight, before the Reformation :—
" After the dirige came back to his house,
and had spice-bread and comfits (confections), wine, ale, and beer. The next day
the mourners went again to church, where

they had a collacion," and afterwards returned to the son's house, where the company dined, excepting the Drapers' Company, which dined in Drapers' Hall. The first course at the son's house consisted of brawn and mustard, boiled capon, roast swan, capon and custard ; and the second course contained pidgeons and tarts, bread, wine, ale, and beer ; to which Lady Roche sent, " of her gentylness four gallons of French wine, a box of wafers, and a potell of ipocras."

The same kindly gossip records how, " on the 30th July, 1557, himself, Master Dave Gyttons, Master Meynard, and Master Draper, and Master Smyth, Master Caldwella, and Master Asse and Gybes, and Master Fackington, and mony mo, did ett alff a bushell of owsters in Aucher-lane, at Master Smyth and Master Gytton's seller a-pone hoghedes, and candyll lyght, and onyons, and red alle, and clarett alle, and muskadylle fre cope, at VIII. in the mornyng."

We infer that this jolly fish breakfast was to celebrate the season that brought oysters in again ; and allowing for the old style and the slow traffic of those days, there would seem to be very little difference between the time of their coming in then and now. We perceive also in that dark cellar

CIVILIZATION

faint glimmerings of the light which afterwards blazed into Lovegrove and Greenwich.

The old dramatists furnish the fullest details of the manners and feastings of our ancestors. Shallow's supper to Falstaff is ordered with expressive brevity :—" Some pigeons, Davy; a couple of short-legged hens; a joint of mutton ; and any pretty little tiny kickshaws, tell William cook." A more comprehensive idea of the notions respecting a good dinner in those days is expounded by Justice Greedy, in Massinger's *New Way to Pay Old Debts*—

> Puff-paste too ! Sir Giles,
> A ponderous chine of beef ! a pheasant larded !
> And red-deer too, Sir Giles, and baked in puff-paste !
> All business set aside, let us give thanks here.

He is afterwards involved in weighty disputes with Sir Giles Overreach's cook, and his great difficulty in persuading him to roast a fawn with a Norfolk dumpling for stuffing, without which, he says " we wise men know "—" 'tis not worth threepence." He is further tormented by the cook's obstinacy about woodcocks :

> —he has found out
> A new device for sauce, and will not dish them
> With toasts and butter ; my father was a tailor,
> And my name, though a justice, Greedy Woodcock
> And, ere I'll see my lineage so abused,
> I'll give up my commission.

Ben Jonson's Sir Epicure Mammon, in his anticipations of luxury, dwells almost exclusively on reviving the cookery of the ancients : though he seems to expect the invention of a new sauce :

—an exquisite and poignant sauce
For which I'll say unto my cook, there's gold,
Go forth, and be a knight.

Fletcher's " Lazarillo," though he throws no light on cookery, is too noticeable a gourmand to be passed over. This indefatigable hunter of delicacies, having discovered that the head of an umbrana, a fish, like our own sturgeon, appropriated to the royal table, is to be served at the duke's board, turns courtier for the nonce, and manages to get invited to the court dinner, but immediately afterwards hearing that the rare fish has been sent to a courtier, he makes his escape and pursues it to its new quarters, where he has no sooner overcome all impediments, than he learns it has gone elsewhere, but he still keeps up the pursuit, until he is at last obliged to contract a very disgraceful marriage in order to enjoy it. (*The Woman-Hater.*)

The introduction of French cookery by Mary Queen of Scotland is associated with a terrible history of unhallowed love, infanticide and execution. An old ballad or complainte written in the character of the

unfortunate maid of honour, thus pathetically records her approaching expiation,—

> Yestreen Queen Mary had four Maries ;
> This night she'll hae but three ;
> She had Mary Seaton, and Mary Beaton
> And Mary Carmichael and me.

The queen and her ladies frequently
amused themselves by making *petits gatels*,
but whenever after Mary Hamilton's tragic
death, any tale of palace scandal spread
among the good folks of Edinbro', the old
wives would shake their heads, and exclaim
with doleful mispronunciation, "Aye, aye,
they ha' bin playing at ' petticoat tales '
again."

We have been favoured with a copy of
the bill of fare of a feast of the East India
Company in the time of James the First,
which we give entire.

*The seruing in of the feast of the East India Comp^a at
Merchãtailors hall, 20 January, 1622 [23].*

The vpper table, 4 messe.

THE FIRST COURSE.

Grand boiled meate.
Boiled pheasants, 2 in a dish.
Boiled partridges, 6 in a dish.
Forced boyled meate.
Boiled teales, 4 in a dish.
Boiled larkes, 12 in a dish.
Soussd cappon.
Grand sallet.

Rost kidd, wholl.
Lamb, a venison pasty.
Rost mutton with oysters.
Boyled carpe, hott.
Rost pheasant, 2 in a dish.
Paris pie.
Rost hearons, 2 in a dish.
Sweet breade pie.
Ffresh salmon whole.
Made dish.
Boyled pike.
Pheasant pie.
Rost cappons, 2 wherof, 1 wth oysters.
[?] Tarte.
Sowssed carpe.
Rost Turkey.
Quince pie.
Almond leach.
Cold baked meats.
Rost turkie chickens, 4.
Gamon of bacon.
Leach of fruit.
Dowcetts.

Nota. That there a lackt 2 dishes of Turky chickens, and instead thereof were 2 dishes of rosted hare.

The Second Course.

Gelly rockt.
Rosted lambe in jointe.
Potatoe pie.
Preserued dish.
Boyled oysters.   Dicto broiled.
Rost ducks, 6 in a dish.
Oyster pie.

CIVILIZATION

Standing dish.
Marled smelts.
Rosted house pigeons, 6.
Partridge pie, 2 in a pie.
Sowssed pigg.
Orringeadoe pie.
Rost snites [snipes], 10 in a dish.
Chines of salmon broyled.
Sowssed eele.
Sett tart.
Rost larks, 2 dozen.
Dryed neats tongues.
Pickled oysters.
Anchovees.
Canded tart.
Amber leach.
Sturgion, one jowle.
Caviare.
Rabbett suckers, 6.
Dried salmon.
Pickled hearring.
March paine.

The 2 side tables, 14 messe ; and 2 messe for the gallery.

THE FIRST COURSE.

Grand boyled meate.
Forced boyled meate.
Boyled ducks, 2 in a dishe.
Grand sallet.
Rost mutton with oysters.
Rost Turkie.
Venizon or lambe pasty.
Boyled pike.
Paris pie.
Rost lamb.

Made dish.
Rost capon 2, whereof 1 with oysters.
Quince pie.
Almond leach.
Fresh salmon.
Gamon of bacon.
Boiled carp, hott.
Fruite leach.
Dowcetts.

THE SECOND COURSE.
Rost partridges, 4 in a dish.
Oyster pie.
Rost cocks, 4 in a dish.
Orrangeadoe pie.
Dryed neats tongues.
Rost larkes, 1½ dozen.
Oysters pickled.
Anchovees.
Caviare.
Pickled heringe.
Amber leach.
Sturgion.
March paine.

The wayters, 7 messe.
Leg of mutton, boyled.
Rost veale.
Calues foot pie.
Rost capon, 1 in a dish.
Custards.

Ffor the Clerke and the Beadle of the Hall, 2 messe between them.
Boyled capons, 1 in a dish.
Rost goose.
Calues foot pie.

CIVILIZATION

Rost capons, 1 in a dish.
Custards.
> *For the players, 3 messe.*

Boiled duck, 2 in a dish.
Sallets in sorts.
Rost mutton.
Calues foot pie.
Rost lambe.
Pippin pie.
Rost capon.
Custards.

*Sweetmeats wayed out from Mr. Abraham Greenway
and Mathew Bell, for the banquet.*

	lbs.	£	s.	d.
Dried cherries - - -	2 -	0	16	0
Towers apricocke, drie - -	2 -	0	16	0
Peaches of Genoa - - -	2 -	0	11	0
Peares of Genoa - - -	3 -	0	12	0
Venis green dates - - -	3 -	0	16	6
Dried goosberries - - -	1 -	0	6	0
Peaches of Marseilles - -	2 -	0	11	0
Plums of Armenia - - -	2 -	0	11	0
—— plums - - - -	2 -	0	11	0
Plums Damascus - - -	1 -	0	5	6
Genoa plums - - -	2 -	0	12	0
Dried quincces - - -	2 -	0	10	0
Venis greene apricocks - -	1 -	0	6	0
Plums provincia - - -	2 -	0	11	0
Madera figgs - - -	2 -	0	8	0
Madera almons - - -	1 -	0	4	0
Venis artichoke - - -	2 -	0	8	0
Paste of quinces - - -	2 -	0	6	0
Paste of barberries - -	2 -	0	6	0
Paste of grapes - - -	2 -	0	6	0
Valentia plums - - -	2 -	0	11	0

	lbs.		£	s.	d.
Paste of respins (raspberries) -	2	-	0	6	0
Paste of cherris - - -	2	-	0	6	0
Paste of goosberries - -	2	-	0	6	0
Paste of lymons - - -	2	-	0	6	0
Paste of greene apricocke -	2	-	0	6	0
	50	-	11	4	0
Callibas of Genoa - - -	2	-	0	8	0
Paste of muske peares - -	2	-	0	6	0
Paste of muske melleons -	1	-	0	3	0
Bucconis of Genoa - - -	1	-	0	5	0
Dried sitterns - - -	8	-	1	4	0
Paste of Genoa - - -	6	-	1	10	0
Fine candies - - - -	10	-	2	10	0
Maccarones - - - -	8	-	0	16	0
Candid oranges - - -	3	-	0	6	0
Candid lymons - - -	3	-	0	6	0
Candid eringies - - -	4	-	1	0	0
Prunellis - - - -	6	-	0	18	0
Savoy amber cum.[fitts] -	1½	-	1	4	0
Musk pine-apple cum. -	3	-	0	6	0
Prsved cherris - -	2	-	0	5	0
Prsved wholl orranges -	5	-	0	12	0
Prsved goosberries -	3¼	-	0	8	2
Almon cumfitt - - -	3	-	0	3	3
Orrange cumfitt - - -	3	-	0	3	9
Dried potatoes - - -	2	-	0	8	0
Naples bisquet - - -	3	-	0	6	0
Paste of apricotte - - -	2	-	0	8	0
Prsvd quinces - - -	3¼	-	0	8	6
Small mrch pane stuff - -	3	-	0	6	0
Orange cakes - - -	2	-	0	6	0
Paste Ryall - - -	3	-	0	12	0
	93	-	15	9	2

CIVILIZATION

	lbs.		£	s.	d.
Amber comfitt - -	- 2	-	0	8	0
Genoa apricocke can[did]	- 2	-	0	10	0
Genoa peaches can -	- 2	-	0	10	0
Gentle and noble esses -	- 3	-	0	18	0
Candid wholl orranges -	- 2	-	0	10	0
Candid artichoke - -	- 2	-	0	10	0
Candid musk mills - -	- 2	-	0	10	0
	15	-	3	16	0

More wayed out to supply ag^t neede should require.

	lbs.		£	s.	d.
Lemon cakes - -	- 2	-	0	6	0
Genoa plumbs - -	- 2	-	0	12	0
Damasco pippins - -	- 2	-	0	8	0
Towers paste of Genoa -	- 2	-	0	8	0
Dried sitterns - -	- 2	-	0	6	0
Dried plums - - -	- 2	-	0	11	0
Savoy amber - -	- 0¾	-	0	12	0
Pears of Genoa - -	- 2	-	0	10	0
Dried quinces - -	- 2	-	0	10	0
Prunellas - - -	- 2	-	0	6	0
Fine candies - - -	- 4	-	1	0	0
	22¾	-	5	9	0

[*Nota.*] Whether this were spent or not.

Messe signifies, that the dishes were so many times repeated.

Most of the sweetmeats given in this curious relic are used at Genoa at the present day. But it is not always clear what the articles specified are. For instance, by cumfitts we must understand confections : bucconis are bocconis (little mouthfuls) : sitterns are citrons : prunellas, dried plums : musk millions and mills, melons : callibas is callibash

383

a small pumpkin : can, means candied : caviare an Italian preparation of sturgeon's eggs : eringus, the roots of the eryngium or sea-holly : and marchpane, a cake made of all sorts of nuts : leach is not so clear, but it was probably a salted preparation ; we are confirmed in this opinion by the distribution of this word and amber throughout the bill before us. In the first course, we find almond leach, and fruit leach, and in the second we see amber leach ; but where amber is mentioned among the sweetmeats, it is associated with either savoy or cumfitt, or both, and not with leach. Potatoes were made into a sweetmeat, at four shillings a pound.

This bill of fare seems to have been drawn up by the most careful of stewards. He is provident to have an additional supply of sweetmeats "wayed out ag^t neede" beforehand ; and equally particular to ascertain afterwards "whether this were spent or not."

It is to be observed that the first and second course make the feast, and that the sweetmeats are distinguished as the banquet, which was equivalent to our dessert. The old dramatists confirm this distinction, and portray the very sensible practice of our ancestors in connexion with this division of the meal, of leaving the eating-room as soon as they had dined, and having the dessert in another apartment.

CIVILIZATION

We will dine in the great room ; but let the music
And banquet be prepared here.
                    The Unnatural Combat.
                    Act ii., Sc. i. (MASSINGER.)

This was unquestionably a more refined
custom than our own habit of sitting down
to delicate fruits and wines of unseizable
flavour, in an atmosphere redolent of heavy
viands, hot soups, and pungent sauces.
Another advantage suggested to us by
this bill of fare is, that the repetition of
dishes allowed every one at table to have
everything specified, affording compensation
for the infinite variety of our own system by
the harmonious equality established among
all the guests. We have been present at
some balls in France where this course
was adopted ; there were not, perhaps,
more than six articles altogether, but of
these there was an unlimited supply, and
they were all of the best quality. The
unchristened " made dish " of those days
was not more unintelligible than the *Fanchonets aux corinthes*, *Boudin au bassalique*,
and other such cognomens of our own.

We do not object to foreign names, but
to appellatives that hide the meaning they
are intended to convey, like the most
Christian distinction of knighthood in the
company of Jews and Parsees ; we protest
against *Mirlitons à la Polonaise* and *Quenelle*

de volaille en demi deuil, on the same principle that we object to a Sir Moses, and
a "Sir Jamsetgee," because neither etymo-
logical examination, traditionary research,
nor moral investigation can discover their
meaning by the help of their titles. *Mulets
à l'Italienne, Vol au vent, Croque en bouche*,
and similar distinctive names, are admis-
sible, because significant. Let us christen
dishes from every country of the earth, if
needs be ; but let it be provided that they
convey an intelligible meaning.

Quot Galli totidem coqui, might have been
applicable to monarchical France, but it
remained for the republic to diffuse amongst
all classes the good living previously arro-
gated by one.

The proprietors of cooks became suspicious characters during the great revolution ;
they were regarded as aristocratic luxuries,
and, as such, exposed their masters to danger ;
and as no one was prepared to lose his
head for the accommodation of his stomach,
they were universally dismissed, and,
quitting the inhospitable shores of France,
they distributed themselves throughout
Russia, Austria, and England. This dis-
persion produced a great change in French
social life : kitchens dispossessed of cooks
became useless, and everybody of every
class had to seek dinner at public tables.

CIVILIZATION

These were at that period few and mean,
but the supply soon answered to the demand ;
that which had heretofore maintained only
the condition of a cabaret, quickly expanded
into a restaurant, and, finally, took that
universal development which threatens to
supersede domestic life in modern France.
The fictions of the ante and post revolu-
tionary periods demonstrate this difference
with very precise demarcations. Louvet and
Paul de Kock depict, respectively, the social
and gallant life of France as it was and is,
with this difference, that while with Paul de
Kock's characters, dinner is as important
as love, Louvet's never think about the
matter. We see that Paul de Kock repre-
sents an age when the pretension to gastronomical enjoyment is as universal as liberty,
equality, and fraternity ; from the discriminating gourmetise of the young nobleman, to the expansive gourmandise of the
voracious grisette, all are more or less
gastrological. In Louvet's time luxury was
greater, but it was confined to a smaller
circle ; and although his writings aimed at
the vices of that particular class, he ignored
their general excesses, which did not come
within his mark, in his zeal to expose those
which were his peculiar object ; and as
the popular manners would not supply
the evidence which he overlooked in the

exclusive aristocracy, he passed that phase
in silence. There is no mention of feasting
with him, excepting incidentally ; when he
has given a minute account of his hero's
career for twenty-four hours, and it is quite
evident that he must be starving, Louvet
gives him a fowl or a pot of jam, and that
is all you hear about the matter.

What the culinary excesses of that period
were we learn from Voltaire's letter to the
Comte d'Autrey, wherein he expresses his
condemnation of the fashionable cookery,
and signifies his objection to see a sweet-
bread smothered in a highly salted sauce,
and a hash composed of turkey, hare, and
rabbit. He also condemns the indiscrimi-
nate use of essences and spices, by which
cooks transformed and encumbered food
otherwise wholesome. He repudiates the
soi-disant improvements, such as bread
without crust ; he declares his own rational
taste, which was, like Rousseau's, to prefer
things in their natural seasons, to adhere
to simple diet, while, at the same time,
he avoids both indifference and excess.
" Je trouve fort étranges," he writes, " les
gens qui mangent sans boire, et qui ne
savent pas même ce qu'ils mangent." Whatever the habits of others may be, the true
republican is invariably simple in his manners. Mirabeau's stomach was stronger

than his conscience, but then his convictions were unsettled : Danton and Desmoulins talked of Spartan broth and quaffed champagne. There was no more simple liver than Robespierre : no one, with so much power, ever lived or lodged so humbly as this " grand incorruptible." The Consulate and the Empire brought *recherché* dinners in again, beginning with Cambaceres, and continuing with Talleyrand. When Napoleon was First Consul, the little conciliatory dinners which he gave at Malmaison were characterized by a simplicity which could not conceal the ambition that lurked behind the apparent moderation. The poet Ducis was about to depart from one of these important little banquets in a hack coach, when Napoleon declared that such a conveyance was very unfit for a man of his age and talent, and begged to be allowed to arrange that he should have a carriage of his own. The venerable republican pointed to a bevy of wild ducks that were passing over their heads,—" There is not one of that flock," said he, " but can smell powder from afar, and scent the gun of the fowler. I am like one of those birds, Citizen General ; I, too, am a wild duck." When he afterwards refused the Cross of the Legion of Honour, Madame de Boufflers exclaimed,— " That is just like Ducis ; he is an ancient

Roman." " Not of the time of the emperors, at least," answered her husband.

It is to be lamented that the bill of the supper given by Jerome Buonaparte, on the evening of his nomination as King of Westphalia, to Pigault le Brun and another friend, at the Palais Royal, has not been preserved. When the repast was over, and the bill presented, his majesty found that neither himself nor his guests could muster enough to settle it. In this dilemma, the host was summoned, and the difficulty explained to him. He asked the names of his debtors, but when the two friends announced themselves as the chamberlain and librarian of the King of Westphalia, the host, thinking it a joke, said, " I suppose you will tell me next that your fat companion is the King of Westphalia." "Precisely," replied the newly appointed monarch. But the landlord, believing he had to do with a set of rogues, declared they should relate their pretensions to the guard ; upon which Jerome, in a terrible taking, offered his watch as a pledge, and departed. The trio were scarcely out of the house, when the restaurateur discovered the imperial cipher on the watch, and flew with it to the commissary of police ; the commissary posted to the prefet, the prefet to the minister, and the minister to the emperor. The next day his Majesty of

CIVILIZATION

Westphalia departed to enter on the government of his kingdom.

Doctor Reveillé-Parise bewails the dearth of profound gastronomers in France at the present time, and laments, above all, the decadence of his medical brethren in the social art. He celebrates the illustrious fraternity of the eighteenth century, as remarkable for their inventive and appreciative genius in culinary matters, as for their extraordinary medical proficiency. They seem to have been a very jolly set of fellows, from Chirac, the inventor of a sauce with which it might be held excusable for a man to eat his own father, to Maloët, lamenting when old and ruined, that his circumstances permitted him only two indigestions a week. We must not omit to chronicle Doctor Gastaldy, who when reminded by a lady that he was taking a large portion of macaroni after a very plentiful dinner, replied, " Madame, le macaroni est lourd, mais il est comme le doge de Venise ; quand il arrive, il lui faut faire place, tout le monde se range." Still less must we pass over the nameless *confrère*, who, precise in his sauces, learned in tit-bits, and particular in his *modus operandi*, finished his repast as the most picturesque of *convives*. " C'était une chose curieuse de l'observer après un long et succulent repas : ses yeux brillants,

un peu voilés, sa respiration légèrement
précipitée, un doux mouvement de gonfle-
ment ondulatoire abdominal, sa pose non-
chalente, déterminée par une corpulence
pansue, annonçaient l'homme plongé dans
cette torpeur digestive pleine de béatitude
pour le gastronome consommé. Quelque-
fois, néanmoins, il semblait se ranimer ;
c'est alors que, frappant légèrement du
plat de ses mains sur les parois de son
vaste abdomen, il s'écriait, plein de jubi-
lation : Dîner ! savoureusement dîner !
Ah ! que j'ai bien rempli cette loi de mon
être ! ''

The learned Doctor looks for a gastronomical index to returning order and re-
invigoration of the social body, and believing
that the flames of sedition are incompatible
with a scientific kitchen fire, he refuses,
with Henriot de Pensey, to believe in
civilization till he shall behold a cook at
the Institute. He holds that in his country
the heart may sometimes be republican,
but the stomach never : but he does not
seem to take into consideration the wonderful
versatility of the French temperament, which
can accommodate itself with Aristippian
philosophy to every variety of circumstances, as exemplified by Mathews' *Monsieur Zephyr*, who described the luxury of
his altered circumstances as only a French-

CIVILIZATION

man could :—" In Londorn I dine for von
penny, superbe," said he ; " A Monsieur
come to my door ev'vary day with his own
cabriolet, and call ca's meat ; I nev'ver
could tell vat it vas, dis ca's meat, but
it ver good."

If we examine impartially the progress of
gastronomy in England, we shall find that
we have not advanced as far as we think.
The last century was distinguished by a
generation of hungry gluttons and inveterate
topers, whose excesses do not sleep with
them in the tomb, but walk the earth, the
bluest of all possible devils, in the stomachs
and brains of their nervous, morbid descend-
ants. If we have abandoned some of their
bad practices, we have lost some of their
good ones : we no longer force our guests
to eat more than they can digest, or to drink
till they disappear under the table ; but
we have only escaped Charybdis to founder
on Scylla. We add to the business-imposed
late hour of dining the fashionable affectation of later, and offer to stomachs too
fatigued to cope with boiled mutton ambitious failures of all sorts of incongruities.
We have added to the number of our dishes,
and have forgotten how to melt butter.
We have let the beer of the people disappear,
and have grown ashamed of roast beef.
There is no set of men of whom we could

now say with Young Loveless in Beaumont and Fletcher's *Scornful Lady*,—

> Ale is their eating and their drinking solely.

Draught ale has vanished, and all the bottled compounds that go by that name are but unwholesome concoctions of drugs and camomile. We have brought chemistry into our kitchens, not as a handmaid but as a poisoner : she would have taught us the principles of assimilation, affinity, and harmony, and would have instructed us in the laws of preparation, arrangement, and the true theory of the application of heat, but we desired her to conjure bread with muriatic acid and soda, and separate osmazome from gelatine and albumen. We attempt more, and know less how to set about it. If we have got rid of our gluttons and topers, we have replaced them by a set of *nil admirari* wafers whose only art is that of a refined nothingness : we can boast some gourmands and gourmets, but very few gastronomes. We introduce foreign manners either without object or made ridiculous by misapplication. Legs of ham and mutton are always enveloped above the knuckle in cut paper. We adopted this from the French, where it was, and in the provinces still is, the custom for ladies and gentlemen to hold the leg with one hand, while they carve it with the other. We have also borrowed the fashion of leaving the table-cloth on for dessert,—a necessary ugliness with the French, who have scarcely any dining tables that are fit to be seen, but with our beautiful mahogany an unpardonable infliction. We have rose-water carried round in a finger-glass after dinner, and not two persons out of twelve know how to use it ; instead of flicking the corner of a napkin in and out, with the dexterity of a Frenchman, your neighbour probably dips his damask into the delicate fluid, and then squeezes the superabundant moisture back again, and so passes it on for your use. We have very little hospitality ; our ideas of comfort have turned our houses into impregnable castles, which no one may approach without previous notification. You arrive in town from a northern county ; you have plenty of intimate friends there, but you know that there is not one of them to whose house you may venture, and be sure of a welcome, a dinner, and a bed. Of course, if this permission were universal, it would be an abuse, but the total absence of any such familiarity deprives hospitality of all social utility, and demonstrates our very contracted view of it. Instead of expanding the comfortable to dimensions that will include the accommodation of our friends, we have contracted it to encircle our own vanity and selfishness, and that we may not be discovered with a three days' table-cloth and a cold leg of mutton, our Glasgow chum must find

His warmest welcome at an inn.

There are not many who can make their friends feel at home when they have them there. Hospitality is not to be measured by the square inch, and calculated by cubic feet of beef and mutton : it is dependent more on quality than capacity, and requires generosity, delicacy, liberty, and taste for its true administration : it preserves our own personal duties and habits intact, without inflicting any that may be distasteful to our guests, while it legislates for the free exercise of their particular comforts and practices, within the limits of general compatibility.

Our public and great city dinners, where political, scientific, and literary bonds are cemented by common enjoyment, and animosities are softened by the intermediatory offices of an unpremeditated libation, are productive of great good. Hearts expand simultaneously with mouths ; the pride of office thaws in the refulgence of the reflected kitchen fire ; genius and talent unveil themselves ; prejudices vanish before experience ; and the mahogany of a goodly table frequently becomes the bond of reconciliation between ancient feuds ; then the hitherto unperceived merit of an enemy is brought to light by aid of the magnifying powers of a jorum of claret. The complicated hatreds, jealousies, and prejudices of our social system would coat the wheels of life with invincible rust, if honourable members and learned gentlemen did not rub off with oil at dinner the asperities of public opposition.

We have thought over those of our friends who constitute the pleasantest company, and we must say we find them, with very rare exceptions, amongst those who enjoy a good dinner. It is wonderful what a humanizing effect this habit of decorous conviviality has on men who, from their studies and pursuits, would otherwise be ' as dry as the remainder biscuit after a voyage.' The practice of dressing for dinner, the cleanliness and propriety of costume, the entire arrangements of a well-ordered table, are all efficient superinducents of cheerfulness, good humour, self-respect, and reciprocal kind feeling.

We shall take the opportunity of entering our protest against an innovation which is going too far. That some of the more bulky dishes, the *pièces de resistance*,

GASTRONOMY AND

should be placed on the side-table, well and
good—though even to this Addison objected,
and not without reason ; but that the fish
and the game should be so bestowed, and
distributed like rations to paupers, by
attendants, who for the most part cannot
distinguish between the head and the tail
of a mullet, the flesh and fin of a turbot,
the breast and leg of a turkey, the wing and
thigh of a woodcock, and are totally ignorant
of the boundaries of the alderman's work in
a haunch of venison, is enough to disturb
the digestion of the most tolerant gastronome, and send him home with all the
symptoms which are precursory of nightmare. We must say, we like to see our
dinner, most especially the fish, and to see
every part of it in good hands. Trimalchio's
carvers were trained in the art. The
fashion to which we allude will render
necessary the establishment of a college
of carving ; and a professor of the side-
table, who has finished his education with
credit, and received his degree, will become
as important a person as the cook himself.

We agree with Addison, that " he keeps
the best table who has the best company
at it; " but the table must have its own recommendations to attract the best company.

The arrangement of the bill of fare is
another important matter : it should be

composite, to meet the demands of the delicate and the *bon vivant*. There is then a certain harmony of succession, which the accomplished gastronome will carefully study and pre-arrange, like the Frenchman, who, being asked what he would have, answered—" *Je n'ai pas formé mon plan*."

Despite philosophical panegyrics on plain living, practically very few even among philosophers really dislike a good dinner. Some, like poor Spinoza, prefer gruel, as the symbol of liberty, at home, to the grand repasts of others, which might have trespassed on his independence. Others, like Descartes, detected by a gay aristocrat in the act of discussing a savoury repast, will say, as he did, in answer to the Marquis's question, " What, do you philosophers eat dainties ? " " Do you think God made good things only for fools ? " Many are like Pope's Catius :—

> Catius is ever moral, ever grave ;
> Thinks who endures a knave is next a knave :
> Save just at dinner, then prefers, no doubt,
> A rogue with venison, to a saint without.

There is every shade of gastronomical proficiency, from the glutton, gourmand, and gastrolâtre, to the gourmet and gastronome ; but these are generally herded together as synonymous terms. The wise man will not assume a distinction he has not attained. The philosopher, though he may be very positive about what he does know, is equally ready to admit what he is deficient in. " I am told you are a great epicure, Mr. Hume," said a lady to the distinguished historian. " No, madam," he replied, " I am only a glutton."

Excesses degrade, but rational gastronomy is consistent with prudence and conducive to generosity. Quin, of whom it is related that the only marriage he cared about was that of John Dory and Ann Chovy, made his last appearance, for the benefit of Ryan, a brother actor, in 1752, having been on the stage forty-two years. On this occasion he acted Falstaff, and with such success that Ryan solicited a similar favour in the following year ; to which Quin replied, " I would play for you if I could, but will not *whistle* Falstaff for you. I have willed you 1,000*l.*; if you want money, you may have it, and save my executors trouble. James Quin."

We have recorded, as historical evidence, that the most incorruptible republicans were austere and abstemious ; but it is still a question whether they would not have exerted a more beneficial influence, and have been better men, if they had moistened their throats with Madeira and enlarged their sympathies with grouse. Solitary habits take away many means of forming correct opinions, and prevent opportunities of removing prejudices. The student in his cabinet is an impartial spectator, and may be a wise judge, but he is never a good governor. Austerity, as Plato says, is the companion of solitude. It is problematical whether Coriolanus would not have gained the consulship, and thereby have saved his country from war, and himself from disgrace, if he had been conciliating and social, instead of isolated and overbearing. If Robespierre had held companionship with others, he might have exercised in public the tenderness that characterized him at home, where it was never believed that he had committed the severities that distinguished his career. "*Il était si doux,*" was the invariable reply of the girl where he lodged, to every accusation that was brought against his memory.

APPENDIX I

THE OPERA (I)

THE articles in this volume on Lord Mount Edgcumbe's *Musical Reminiscences*, and *Bellini*, would suggest even to a reader unfamiliar with the *Memoirs of Shelley* that Peacock was an interested and regular patron of the opera. He was also a professional critic. Among Mrs. Clarke's papers is a sheaf of newspaper cuttings of the years 1830-34; each is neatly dated, and the name of the paper is added where necessary—*i.e.* on the extracts from the *Globe and Traveller.** These are only three in number (June 18 and 21, and August 9, 1830), but it is very unlikely that Peacock did not write other opera notices for the *Globe*, to which he had already contributed verses; he was certainly writing them for some paper in the previous year, or earlier, for Hazlitt's article on *The Utilitarian Controversy*, in the *Atlas* of July 19, 1829,† refers to him as a dramatic and operatic critic. Hazlitt is attacking the policy of repression which he discovers in the sermons of the Rev. Edward Irving and the articles of the *Westminster* reviewers ; he objects to " privations made of

* Those from the *Examiner* retain the heading of the " Theatrical Examiner " column.

† This article has recently been reprinted, from a complete file of the *Atlas* now at Yale, in Mr. P. P. Howe's valuable volume of *New Writings by William Hazlitt*, pp. 171-8, from which the quotations in this paragraph are taken.

APPENDIX

the most trifling and innocent amusements, which, for no other reason than because you like them, the votaries of spiritual pride and presumption resent and denounce as incurring the loss of heaven and the vengeance of the Most High " ; and he complains that the Utilitarians " are seized with the same *hydrophobia* of music, painting, and poetry, as their pious predecessors." This brings him to a string of rhetorical questions. " Will Mr. Irving let you go to Covent-garden or Drury-lane ? No more will the *Westminster*, unless Mrs. Chatterley should act, ' who in herself sums all delight, so absolute she seems ' to Mr. P——. Will Mr. Irving send you to the opera to hear sounds from Madame Pasta ' that might create a soul under the ribs of death ? ' No more will the *Westminster* ! P——, poor fellow ! dare no more show his face there than his own Sir Ourang-Outang ! " So far as such a passage can be reduced to mere fact, it seems to imply that Hazlitt knew Peacock both as an enthusiastic critic of certain actresses and singers, and as a *Westminster* reviewer—and found the positions incompatible.

Hazlitt's allusions, and the existence of the cuttings, made it desirable to attempt to establish a canon of Peacock's operatic notices for the press, and the result will be found in the second section of this Appendix, a third section being devoted to quotations. It was necessary to limit the number of these, for though some of the notices are highly characteristic, others are commonplace, many passages are of ephemeral interest, and the total bulk is very considerable. It would not, therefore, be advisable to print them all, but it is clearly essential to place on record the dates and extent of the cuttings preserved, with all details necessary for their identification. In a few cases, where there is reason to doubt the ascription of a notice to Peacock, foot-notes have been added.

With the object of securing any further recognizable

403

APPENDIX

pieces for the canon, and of obtaining, if possible, some light on Hazlitt's remarks, Mr. C. E. Jones undertook an examination of the operatic and dramatic notices in the *Globe and Traveller* from January 1, 1825, to May 31, 1831 (except those of December 1830, which are not available in the British Museum), and in the *Examiner* from January 1815 to December 1837 (except the years 1820 and 1823). The results, for the *Globe and Traveller*, were disappointing ; the only reference to Mrs. Chatterley which is not brief and commonplace, is very severe,* and Hazlitt's allusion to her remains unexplained. There is a certain amount of not very distinctive writing of which the general tenor agrees with Peacock's views, and there are occasional notices of the King's Theatre in 1830 which might be accepted as his if any external evidence were available, but can seldom support a definite claim on their own merits. Such are the lively attacks on the representation of the third act of Rossini's *Guillaume Tell*,† and on the appearance of the Ghost of Ninus in his *Semiramide*.‡ The two most tempting notices are a typical encomium on Malibran, § and a typical onslaught on the usual handling of the close of Mozart's *Don Giovanni* :—" The curtain fell amidst a shower of hisses, a well-merited compliment to the more than usual bungling of the paltry *diablerie* at the end, to which Mozart's own magnificent conclusion has been so strangely sacrificed." ‖ Peacock frequently attacks the introduction of stage devils at the close of this opera,¶ and both the opinions and the style of these

* " Mrs. Chatterley played *Miss Hardcastle* in a style which would not have done honour even to a boarding-school miss displaying her talents at a Christmas breaking-up. In the lady she wanted even the grace and dignity of the bar-maid ; and in the bar-maid we could recognise neither the assumed manners of the servant nor the real manners of the lady . . . " [Notice of *She Stoops to Conquer*, November 3, 1828].

† 8.3.30.   ‡ 24.5.30.   § 2.8.30.   ‖ 5.7.30.   ¶ See pp. 238-9, 432.

APPENDIX

two notices show a likeness to the rest of his criticism which is much too strong for mere coincidence.* Also, they fall within the brief period of the three authenticated cuttings from the *Globe*.

With the *Examiner*, better results were obtained. Mr. Jones has formed a definite opinion that from January 1815 to 13 February 1831, and from January 1835 to December 1837, nothing can be claimed for Peacock, but in the intervening period there are fifteen notices (apart from those preserved in the family cuttings) of the authenticity of which, from internal evidence of style, subject, and treatment, the editors are convinced. All of them fall within the period covered by the *Examiner* cuttings, and the authorship on all counts is so clear that it seems unnecessary to adduce detailed evidence (such as a reference to Lord Monboddo,† or to the Ionic *à minori* metre ‡) for each article.§ They have accordingly been used, for quotation and illustration in this Appendix, as freely as those preserved by Mrs. Clarke, from which, in the list of Peacock's writings in Section II., they are distinguished by enclosure in square brackets. In the theatrical criticism of the *Examiner* there is not only no trace of Peacock's hand, but there is an apparent continuity which strengthens the impression that he limited his work to the opera.‖

* They have been included, within square brackets, in the list given in Section II.

† 2.6.33. ‡ 7.8.31.

§ Several of the articles are also authenticated by references in or to those preserved by the family. Those of 17.7.31 and 8.7.32 are claimed in the notice of the preceding and following week respectively; that of 2.6.33 refers back to the notice of 31.7.31 (" We then characterised the opera as . . . "); that of 5.6.31 is mentioned later on 10.3.33 (" We said two years ago . . . ").

‖ For instance, on 2.7.37 (p. 422 of the *Examiner*) a writer, certainly not Peacock, dealing with *The Bridal*, refers to his own notices of 1834, pp. 693 and 709.

APPENDIX

As early as 1817 Peacock had been attempting to educate Shelley in the theatre ; his failure with comedy was complete, but he believed that Miss O'Neill's performance in Milman's *Fazio* * had some influence on the character of Beatrice in the *Cenci*, and he succeeded in making Shelley " an assiduous frequenter of the Italian Opera " from 1817 until his final departure from England. Shelley was brought to share his friend's appreciation of Mozart ; they saw *Don Giovanni* together in May, 1817, and the *Nozze di Figaro* (probably more than once) in the opening months of 1818. Peacock's tastes and habits were early formed and enduring, and his published criticism of the opera of a dozen years later is full of characteristic prejudices and appreciations. He liked to see a performance in comfort, and the protests on this score in his review of Lord Mount Edgcumbe † were preceded by various outbursts in the *Examiner* against " the conduct of the vandals whom they [the management] let loose on the civilized portion of the audience." ‡ He refused to admit any " necessary connexion between liberal opinions, and a rough great coat redolent of cigars, or a pair of dirty boots, ostentatiously displayed, as we have sometimes seen them, on the seat-cushion, the wearer sitting on the rail, with a hat on his head." § And still more was he disturbed by that " irremediable total eclipse of the stage, behind some of those walls of gauze, lace, silk, velvet, or plumage, which some women, with a selfish disregard of the comfort of others, are in the habit of building on their heads : to say nothing of an occasional square foot of tortoise-shell, professing to be the top of a comb. We derive a malicious pleasure from seeing a female, thus equipped, deprived of the opportunity of annoying. We have surrendered a seat to a simply apparelled head, but never to one of

* Seen by Peacock, Shelley and Mary on 16.2.18.

† Pp. 226, 248-9 of this volume. ‡ 29.6.34. § 5.2.32.

APPENDIX

these : they deserve no courtesy. It is curious and true, as we have ascertained by repeated observation of the phenomena, that the volume of the head-dress increases in mathematical proportion with the ugliness of the wearer." *

Certain features of the performances also displeased him. The gesticulations and *tapage* of conductors are frequently reprehended ; the article on *Musical Reminiscences* gives no names,† but in the *Examiner* the offender was always Signor Costa, who was accused, on June 2, 1833, of having " literally beaten a hole in the top of his copy of the overture to *Tancredi*," and was requested to " be satisfied with subjecting the irresponsive air to his ' unavoidable battoon '." For a time Peacock thought he saw symptoms of amendment, but by July 28 Costa was " rapping his book as offensively as ever. He does not beat time ; he threshes it. We almost expect to see the notes leaping from the page under his baton, ' like chaffy grain beneath the thresher's flail '." ‡

Another continual grievance was the mutilation or combination of operas. The notices of *Gli Arabi nelle Gallie* and *La Straniera*, in the *Examiners* of 20.5.32 and 1.7.32, exactly illustrate the account of the maltreatment of those pieces given in the review of *Musical Reminiscences*,§ and are therefore quoted in full.‖ It would be easy to add half-a-dozen other

* 22.5.31. The version printed above is found both in the British Museum copy and in Mrs. Clarke's cutting. The copy in the London Library, however, contains curious variations ; instead of " which some women, with a selfish disregard of the comfort of others," it reads " which women, with that selfish disregard of the comfort of others, which characterises so large a portion of the fair sex," and instead of " deprived of the opportunity of annoying " it reads " standing all the evening." It seems probable that the more savage version was the earlier, and that Peacock repented of it in time to modify his phrases in the later-issued copies of the paper.

† Pp. 226, 248.   ‡ See also the notice of 15.6.34, p. 426.
§ Pp. 236-7.   ‖ Pp. 421-3, 424-5.

407

attacks on this practice,* the neatest perhaps being
that of 27.5.32, which concludes :—"We wish the
management would call things by their right names ;
Lucus à non lucendo would be an excellent general
title for the entire performance ; but as variety is
desirable in titles, it might make out its bills something in this way :—' This evening, an *imbroglio* of
music, from Pacini and others, called *Senza capo e
senza coda ;* with fragments of an old ballet, deranged
into a divertisement, called, *Que diable allons-nous
faire ?* ' " In fact there is only one notice in which
Peacock even for a moment condones any tampering
with the complete score of an opera. This is his
account † of the Elsler sisters' benefit performance at
the King's Theatre on June 26, 1834, when he saw
" the two first acts of *Otello*, a divertisement, and the
masked ball of *Gustavus*," and thought that " the
arrangement of the whole was so admirable, that it
must have been the work of the Elslers themselves.
No one else, now about the theatre, could have done
it. If we could tolerate mutilations, we should bear
as patiently as with any, with the omission of the third
act of *Otello*, which is dramatically offensive and
musically superfluous. The series of music is complete
without it. We almost think it as much improved by
the cutting off its third act as Lord Monboddo's original
man was by losing his tail. We are inclined to sym-
pathise on this occasion with our old friend, *Manager
Mist*, who, having received only four acts of a manuscript tragedy, determined to perform it as it was,
on the principle of the less of a bad thing the better.
But *decipit exemplar vitiis imitabile*, therefore, we will
tolerate no mutilations, because we cannot confide
such a discretion to the sorts of heads which usually
manage this theatre."

Another practice which Peacock vigorously opposed

* *E.g.* 29.5.31, 26.6.31, 3.7.31, 7.8.31, 13.5.32, 27.5.32.

† 20.7.34.

APPENDIX

was the temptation of so many stars from the opera to the concert room. " This same concert singing," he wrote in March 1832, " is the bane of all our great theatrical singers, male and female, at this time of the year. They come forward on the stage with their voices in full freshness, fix their reputation, are immediately in general requisition, drive about from concert to concert, public and private, and sing morning noon and night, till their once sweet voices are only redolent of weariness : and the moment their stage performance shows symptoms that they are tired of their parts, their audiences grow tired of them." * And he returned to the charge in one of the latest and neatest of his notices :—" there is no time for rehearsals, and the company can only perform in parts with which they were all familiar beforehand. ' It was ever yet the trick of our English nation, that when they had a good thing they made it too common : ' but the dozen captains, who ran about Eastcheap to knock up Sir John Falstaff, are nothing to the dozens of concerts, morning, noon, and night, that knock up our Italian singers, and leave us, season after season, to the eternal repetition of the same half-dozen operas." †

Readers of the article on Lord Mount Edgcumbe's *Musical Reminiscences* will remember that it severely criticises " the signal failure of a professing reformer " of the Italian Opera in the season of 1832, and the enormous rent exacted by the proprietors of the theatre to the ruin of the lessee.‡ The whole story of Monck Mason's unfortunate management of the King's Theatre in that year can be traced, by the student of operatic history, in Peacock's references in the *Examiner*, of which we may give a rapid summary. They open on 5 June, 1831, with a vigorous attack on the " estate " of Chambers and Co. for " exacting

* 3.6.32.   † 18.5.34.
‡ Pp. 223, 247, 250-1 of this volume.

APPENDIX

for the theatre about three times as much rent as it ought to pay." Monck Mason's season began in the following February, and Peacock's first notice of it, on the 12th, while giving him credit for " high character . . . ability to select well, and inclination to perform faithfully," showed an obvious suspicion that the traditions of the theatre would be too much for him. In less than a month a severer tone was thought necessary ; the " Theatrical Examiner " of 18 March begins :—" Everybody knows Boileau's epigram on Corneille—

> ' Après l'Agésilas,
> Hélas !
> Mais après l'Attila,
> Holà ! '

It is time to cry *Holà !* to Mr. Monck Mason." And later in the notice Peacock adopted Jeffrey's famous opening :—" This will never do, Mr. Mason."

From this point he became less and less hopeful of amendment. On April 29 he wrote that " according to Mr. Mason's shewing, every thing that has been done ill in his theatre, has been done by somebody else. If so, somebody else must have been very busy all the season, in the place of the manager." This was followed on May 27 by a complaint that " the management goes to work with an opera as a cook does with a chicken ; cuts off its head, plucks off its tail, takes out its interior, flattens its breast, and trusses it up into the smallest possible compass " ; though " the simile does not hold good in this, that the cook retains of the chicken all that is worth keeping, which is very much the reverse of this management's dealing with an Italian opera, to which head and tail are essentials." A week later, Peacock airs the grievances of the subscribers ; on July 29 his " patience is exhausted with seeing all our old favourite operas seized on by this Mohawk management, and subjected, one after another, to the scalping-knife and the

APPENDIX

tomahawk "; and on August 5 he pronounced a funeral oration on the management :—" Nothing was wanting to it but the great *desideratum* of all governments,—brains at the head of affairs . . . The theatre closed last night ; and the season, viewed from first to last, remains, as far as respects the Italian Opera, the most barren of valuable novelty, and the most conspicuous in mangling, garbling, and bungling, of all descriptions, of any season within our recollection." *

Even if none of the *Examiner* notices had been preserved as Peacock's, there are passages in them which would have betrayed the author of subsequent phrases in the *London Review*. The remark, on page 250 of this volume, about " heroes of one string, and heroines of one toe " would present no difficulty in itself, but its precise application can be traced back to the *Examiner* of 12.6.31 (Paganini's " performance on the single string " †), and that of 20.4.34, where the King's Theatre notice concludes :—" The Elslers have returned. Fanny is much improved, and will soon outshine all Europe in the art of pirouetting on one toe." The saying of Catalani's husband, " ma femme, et cinq ou six poupets," ‡ had already appeared on 15.5.31 as " M. Valabreque's impertinent axiom," and on 13.5.32 as " M. Valabreque's maxim " ; and the emphatic eulogy of vocal expression as " the one all-pervading and paramount quality, without which

---

* Peacock gives an interesting summary of the financial results of Monck Mason's management on 10.3.33 ; he paid £16,050 in rent, and remained in debt (to tradesmen, artists, etc.) £17,471. Debts recoverable, and properties, it was hoped, might reduce the season's loss to £11,317. " If so, and if the theatre had been managed, as formerly, by a proprietor, and not by a lessee, the proprietor would have had £5,000 profit, and the artists and tradesmen would have been paid. As it is, according to Mr. Mason's statement, the proprietors receive £16,000, and the artists, tradesmen, &c. lose £11,000. We ask, is this right ? "

† P. 444.   ‡ P. 242.

411

dramatic music is but as a tinkling cymbal," * had been foreshadowed in the *Examiner's* comment on Madame Lalande :—"her singing, though highly skilful, has little of the soul of music, expression." † The very phrase, "la Déesse de la danse," applied to Taglioni on p. 251, had already been given her in the same notice, and the Ionic *à minori* metre had been discussed, before its appearance in the article on *Bellini*,‡ in a paragraph of the "Theatrical Examiner."§

As a critic of the opera, Peacock has many virtues ; his wide reading continually appears in the turn of a phrase, in references to great authors, or in judgements which remind us that Shelley owed much of his knowledge of Greek and Elizabethan drama to his friend.‖ The makeshifts of slipshod stage management were abhorrent to him, and often gave scope for such reviews as that of *La Donna del Lago* :—"The curtain rising, discovered some Scottish peasants, armed with two hay-rakes amongst them all, who informed us, in a chorus, that they were going to stir up the wild boar. This prepared us for a deep tragedy, as it was quite clear that, if they accomplished their purpose so equipped, they would never return to tell the result of their exploit. However, they escaped with the loss of their hay-rakes only, and lived, without any other change in their equipment, to typify the court of Scotland in the last scene." ¶ On bad performances he could be extremely caustic, and also on bad criticism, which he assailed with a formidable conciseness ; when the *Times* critic professed to have seen the whole of Rossini's *Tancredi* (though only the first act had been

* P. 225.   † 17.4.31. See p. 318.

‡ P. 333.   § 7.8.31 ; *v. infra*, p. 436.

‖ A good example is his comment on the story of Iñez de Castro ; *v. infra*, p. 430.

¶ 1.6.34. A good example of Peacock in this mood is the notice of Spontini's *Vestale* (*v. infra*, p. 427).

APPENDIX

played) without hearing a word that was spoken by Laporte (though Peacock, at the very back of the pit, had heard every syllable most distinctly), the comment is merely that " Hearing nothing may be a fair set off against seeing double." * Peacock's appreciation of music never overcame his sense of humour ; when the German opera † began its season in 1833, he praised Madame Pirscher's voice, but found her, in appearance and action, somewhat large and ungraceful ; and after comment on the voices of the tenor and the bass, he observed that " these two Herr'n, and the lady already mentioned, would have pleased Julius Caesar, who liked to have those about him that were fat. Little Nina Sontag, (as *Annchen*,) with her pretty slim figure, and with her otherwise fair cheeks daubed over with a deep brick-red, looked like the spirit of scarlet fever flitting among the plethoric." ‡

But when he discovered an artist, whether composer, singer or dancer, of whose skill he approved, no man could praise more warmly, and it would be possible to illustrate at some length, from the *Examiner*, his later appreciative references § to Mozart, Beethoven and Rossini, to Malibran, Grisi and Pasta, ‖

* 7.7.33. Peacock enjoyed a thrust at other press critics, particularly if he detected in them any susceptibility of " paw-paw impressions " (5.5.33). A good instance both of this pugnacity, and of his refusal to taste with a distempered appetite, will be found in the notices of 20. and 27.2.31 (p. 429).

† For his opinions on the German opera, see pp. 241, 422-3, 431-2. ‡ 24.3.33.

§ In the articles on *Musical Reminiscences, Bellini*, and *The Épicier* ; *e.g.* pp. 244, 251, 294, 319-21 of this volume.

‖ His enthusiasm for male voices was naturally less, but one sentence is too good to omit :—" Bulky as Lablache is, he has as much lightness and buoyancy as bulk ; it seems as if no smaller cubic area could contain the immensity of mirth and music that is in him, or give utterance to that stupendous voice, clear, deep, and sonorous as a bell—the Great Tom of the musical stage." (6.5.32.)

APPENDIX

and to Taglioni. The notices now reprinted of these and a few other artists (including Paganini) are necessarily limited in extent, but the selection will be found representative.

Peacock probably ceased to write for the *Examiner* at the end of 1834 ; the issue of December 28 contained a pleasant little discussion of Christmas shows in general, and of the delight they give to children, which is preserved among the family cuttings. But the last of his purely critical paragraphs is that of August 17, which describes in detail " the circumstances of trouble and discomfort, which now attend a visit to the pit of this [the King's] theatre." It may reasonably be assumed that Peacock's career as a critic of the opera ended in that month, and that the final ring of his closing paragraph expressed a definite leave-taking :—" We remember the time, when the pit was comfortable and decorous. We are, in this matter, *laudatores temporis acti*. We seem, indeed, to be admonished in something like the words of Horace :—

" Lusisti satis, edisti satis, atque bibisti :
Tempus abire tibi est ; ne potum largius æquo
Rideat et pulset lasciva decentius ætas."

THE OPERA (II)

This section contains a complete list of the collection of dated articles from the *Globe* and *Examiner* in the possession of Mrs. Clarke. The dates (and, for the *Globe*, the name of the paper) are added in ink (very rarely in pencil) in a contemporary hand which is probably feminine, and is certainly not Peacock's ; but the cuttings were not without his supervision, for one—the tribute to Grisi on April 13, 1834—is dated, and two others are corrected, in his hand.*

* The corrections occur in the *Globe* notice of 21.6.30, where " pleasant " had been misprinted " present " ("the

414

APPENDIX

The cutting of 21.8.31 is the only one which seems, from internal evidence, entirely apocryphal, but in several others it is probable that paragraphs not by Peacock have been included for the sake of retaining the cutting in one piece instead of two. In all these cases a foot-note has been added.

The list has been made, as far as possible, a complete record of Peacock's ascertained contributions to journalism as a regular critic of the opera, by the inclusion of the two *Globe* and fifteen *Examiner* notices, not preserved among Mrs. Clarke's cuttings, which the editors accept without reservation as Peacock's work.* These have been distinguished from the rest by inclusion in square brackets.

The Globe.

18.6.30.	King's Theatre.	" Last night. . . . his best characters."
21.6.30.	,, ,,	" We must protest . . . of the Horatii."
[5.7.30.	,, ,,	" Il Don Giovanni . . . strangely sacrificed."]
[2.8.30.	,, ,,	" On Saturday evening . . . in this theatre."]
9.8.30.	,, ,,	" On Saturday evening . . . claimed her much more."

present imitation," five lines from end of notice), and in the close of a brief notice of *Anna Bolena* in the *Examiner* of 14.8.31 :—" This opera has been for Madame Pasta the great triumph of the season ; and it is well that her leave taking remains associated with the most splendid exertion of her genius." The printer had turned " exertion " into " portion."

* See Section I of this Appendix, paragraphs 2-4.

APPENDIX

* The cutting includes also the notices of the Haymarket and Queen's Theatres, but they are written in a style which is certainly not Peacock's.

† This is a long notice of a drama entitled *The Evil Eye:* The style is not distinctive, and serious doubt of Peacock's authorship of the notice is aroused by the sentence :— " particular persons are supposed to possess this gift or curse of bringing calamity on the objects of their dislike ; and many have been pointed out to us in various parts of Sicily, as well as of Greece, to whom the power was attributed."

‡ The *Adelphi* notice is the only long one, and contains a characteristic objection to sitting in the theatre behind " a phalanx of bonnets . . . like the *testudo* of the ancients." But there is nothing in the two short notices to cast doubt on Peacock's responsibility for them.

APPENDIX

18.12.31. Drury Lane.
25.12.31.   ,,   ,,

22.1.32. Covent-Garden.   Italian Opera.*
 5.2.32. King's Theatre.
12.2.32.   ,,   ,,
26.2.32.   ,,   ,,
 4.3.32.   ,,   ,,
18.3.32.   ,,   ,,
 1.4.32.   ,,   ,,
 8.4.32.   ,,   ,,
29.4.32.   ,,   ,,
 6.5.32.   ,,   ,,
13.5.32.   ,,   ,,
20.5.32.   ,,   ,,
[27.5.32.   ,,   ,,   ]
 3.6.32.   ,,   ,,
17.6.32.   ,,   ,,
 1.7.32.   ,,   ,,
[8.7.32.   ,,   ,,   ]
15.7.32.   ,,   ,,   Covent Garden.†
22.7.32. Covent Garden.
29.7.32. King's Theatre.
[5.8.32.   ,,   ,,   ]

* These notices, with an intermediate one on the *Olympic Theatre*, occupy the greater part of a double column page of the *Examiner*. The section has been cut out in one piece, but the *Covent-Garden* and *Italian Opera* notices are each dated at head in ink ; the *Olympic Theatre* notice is not dated, shows no trace of Peacock's manner, and has evidently been preserved merely by the accident of its position between the others.

† The cutting from the " Theatrical Examiner " of 15.7.32 contains three consecutive notices ; one of the *King's Theatre*, which has been dated at head ; one of the *Covent Garden* theatre, which has " Taglioni " written at head ; and a third of the *Haymarket*, which has no characteristic features, and was probably preserved, with other matter, merely by the accident of being printed on the back of the *King's Theatre* paragraphs.

APPENDIX

10.2.33.	Drury Lane.	
24.2.33.	King's Theatre. [Olympic.] *	
3.3.33.	,, ,,	
10.3.33.	,, ,,	
24.3.33.	,, ,, †	
31.3.33.	,, ,,	Covent Garden.‡
14.4.33	King's Theatre.	
21.4.33.	,, ,,	
28.4.33.	,, ,,	
5.5.33.	,, ,, §	
12.5.33.	,, ,,	Drury Lane. Olympic.
		Adelphi.‖
19.5.33.	Haymarket Theatre.¶	

* Two cuttings of this date have been preserved, but both contain the *King's Theatre* notice only, without the *Olympic*. It would appear, however, both from the cookery reference in the latter, and from the concluding sentence of Peacock's *Drury Lane* paragraph of 16.2.34, that the *Olympic* notice is also his.

† Two cuttings of this date have been preserved; one contains the *King's Theatre* notice only, the other has also the subsequent notices of *Drury Lane* and *The Minors*; but these latter are almost certainly not by Peacock, and owe their preservation in the larger cutting to a desire to keep the *King's Theatre* notice in one piece.

‡ The *King's Theatre* notice is certainly Peacock's, and there is nothing in the *Covent Garden* one either to prove or to disprove his authorship.

§ Two cuttings of this date have been preserved; one contains the *King's Theatre* notice only; the other has also the subsequent notices of *Covent Garden* and the *Adelphi*, neither of which is at all suggestive of Peacock's manner.

‖ The *King's Theatre* notice is unquestionably Peacock's, and there is nothing to show that the other three in the cutting are not his.

¶ The cutting of 19.5.33 contains, after the *Haymarket* notice, a long paragraph on Kean, headed KEAN IS DEAD. This was probably preserved out of interest in the subject; the continuity of tone in other theatrical notices, certainly not of his authorship (*e.g.* 14.3.30, 6.3.31 *D.L.*, 10.6.32, 24.6.32 *Haymarket*, 31.3.33 *C.G.*, 30.10.36 *D.L.*), militates strongly against the ascription of this obituary to Peacock.

418

APPENDIX

2.6.33.   King's Theatre.* [Drury   Lane.   The
          German Opera.]
9.6.33.   King's Theatre.   Drury   Lane.   English
          Opera (Adelphi).†

23.6.33.   „   „
7.7.33.   „   „   ‡
14.7.33.   „   „   §
28.7.33.   „   „   followed, after a short
                           printer's rule, by a
                           general notice (three
                           paragraphs, without
                           heading) of theatrical
                           affairs for the week.

[18.8.33.   King's Theatre.]

26.1.34.   First two paragraphs of the "Theatrical
           Examiner." ‖
16.2.34.   Drury Lane.
[9.3.34.   King's Theatre.]
16.3.34.   „   „
30.3.34.   „   „
13.4.34.   „   „
20.4.34.   „   „

* The cutting is misdated 26.5.33, and ends with the words
"unavoidable battoon." But it is indubitable that the next
paragraph, and the notices of *Drury Lane* and *The German
Opera* which follow, are also Peacock's.

† The first two notices are typical ; the third is only six
lines long, but contains nothing to warrant its rejection.

‡ The cutting is misdated 30.6.33.

§ The cutting is misdated 7.7.33.

‖ These paragraphs, on performances at the *Olympic* and
the *Adelphi*, though not remarkable, may well be Peacock's ;
the remaining part, in smaller type, of the "Theatrical
Examiner" in this number (two paragraphs of theatre
announcements, and some gossip about a "row" between
Malibran and the King of Naples) is certainly not his. But
the cutting could not be kept in one piece without them, and
other (non-theatrical) matter is preserved in it for the same
obvious reason.

419

APPENDIX

11.5.34. King's Theatre.
[18.5.34.   ,,   ,,]
25.5.34.   ,,   ,,
1.6.34.   ,,   ,,
15.6.34.   ,,   ,,
29.6.34.   ,,   ,,
20.7.34.   ,,   ,,
27.7.34.   ,,   ,,
17.8.34.   ,,   ,,
28.12.34. " Theatrical Examiner."

THE OPERA (III)

It is evidently desirable that two or three *Examiner* notices should be reprinted in full, and others at greater length than was possible in the first section of this Appendix. For full quotation, three typical examples have been chosen ; those of Pacini's *Gli Arabi nelle Gallie* and of Bellini's *La Straniera*, which explain the allusions on pp. 236-7 ; and that of Rossini's *L'Assedio di Corinto*, which illustrates Peacock's opinion of Rossini, Costa and Grisi, and his habit of literary allusion. A fourth extract of some length, the first paragraph of a notice of Spontini's *Vestale*, has been added for its characteristic liveliness and vigour ; and the rest of the section consists of critical passages of general interest, removed from their setting in the journalism of the theatre to form a permanent record of Peacock's opinions of music and the stage.

The headings in the following pages have been supplied for convenience of reference ; the original notices in the " Theatrical Observer " column appeared under the names of the various theatres, as shown in Section II. Names of persons were printed in roman capitals, which have not been retained.

420

APPENDIX

PACINI's GLI ARABI NELLE GALLIE*: AND THE
GERMAN OPERA (DER FREYSCHUTZ).

Prime donne pass over this stage like *Banquo's* line
of kings. Two more appeared on Saturday the 12th
—Signora Grisi, a soprano, and Madame Mariani,
a contralto. The latter has a fine, powerful, and
flexible voice, correct intonation, good taste, and just
expression ; and is an effective and intelligent actress.
Of Signora Grisi, we cannot speak so highly on any
of these scores ; but we may make deductions on all
of them, and much praise will still remain to her.
In personal appearance she has greatly the advantage.

The piece chosen for their *debuts*, was a sort of
pasticcio, made up apparently by picnic from the
portmanteaus of the performers, with a *libretto* put
together by the printer's devil, in which one thing was
read while another was sung ; and with scenery,
let down at random, at the convenience of the scene-
shifters, and happily consistent throughout in consummate inappropriateness. This curious *mélange*
was called, in the bills, Pacini's *opera seria, Gli Arabi
nelle Gallie.* The chaotic atoms of the representation
jumbled themselves into something like the following
story :—A king of France has been murdered ; his
son has escaped, and turned Mussulman. He comes
back, not to regain his crown, but to subject France
to fire and sword. He takes a knight prisoner ; and
is going to kill him, when a lady (to whom the knight
has been previously making love in front of a castle)
comes out from a mosque, which stands in the back
ground, with Roman temples and rostrated columns
at the side scenes, and which personates a French
convent in the mountains. She intercedes for the
knight, and the Mussulman makes her a present of
him. Then the Mussulman finds out that the lady
had been betrothed to him in his infancy, and tells

* See pp. 236-7.

APPENDIX

her that he is *Prince Clodomir*. She tells him, he lies ; on which he vows to set France on fire. After which, he and the knight meet in a cellar, and swear eternal friendship. Then the lady comes in by herself, in front of a Grecian arch, with a piece of Babylon in the back ground, and sings an air, to the effect that she is very uncomfortable ; and so ends this strange eventful history, in which all that is intelligible, is the curious historical fact, that when the Arabs marched into France, they carried Mecca with them, and picked up Rome and Babylon by the way.

The stage-manager has evidently been selected on *Dogberry's* principle, as " the most senseless and fit man." Perhaps, indeed, he is only paying court to his audience, and propitiating the aristocracy by typifying virtual representation. So much for the reform of the musical stage, which, after going on for three months, has been brought as near to perfection as if it had been taken in hand by the great Captain himself.

The German opera is quite another thing. It has a real company, with an excellent, intelligent, and well-organized chorus. *Der Freyschutz* is in truth the first performance of this year, which has been really given as a drama. It is, throughout, well acted and well sung ; and the whole of the music is performed with religious fidelity, excepting the unjustifiable liberty taken by the *Max*, (Herr Haitzinger) of opening the third act with an air of Bellini's. Madame de Meric, in *Agathe*, puts forth new claims to approbation. She delivers the exquisite *scena* in the second act, as if her voice were a perfectly-tuned instrument, through which the mind of the composer was pouring forth its own inspirations.—Mademoiselle Schneider raises the character of *Annchen* into an importance unknown to the English versions of the opera. Her voice has good tone, and flexibility, with considerable powers of execution. Her action is delightful : we

APPENDIX

cannot describe it better than in Pigault Le Brun's favourite phrase : *rayonnante de joie et d'amour*. The tenor (Haitzinger) and the bass (Pellegrini), deserve no measured praise, for the strict correctness of their entire performance. Without any qualities to dazzle or surprise, they do all they undertake thoroughly well. In short, here is a perfect company, without any thing that in theatrical parlance is called a star—-Here is an admirable opera, well performed in all its parts : and the crowded audiences which attend it may teach the manager, that this is the sort of performance to draw the public to his doors, and not a paltry *imbroglio*, jumbled together without any semblance of design, but that of showing off individuals.

[*King's Theatre*, 20.5.32.

[Peacock gave equally high praise to the German opera in the following week, in a paragraph following that which we have quoted * on Beethoven's *Fidelio*, contrasting the company very favourably with the Italian opera under Monck Mason's management. The contrast was doubtless still in his mind when he wrote the passage on p. 241 of this volume. In 1833 he also praised the German singers,† but in 1834 the verdict had changed :—]

The German opera has progressively degenerated. The first year it was excellent in principals, chorus, and orchestra. The second, it was excellent in chorus alone. The third, which is the present, it is excellent in nothing, except the tenor, Herr Schmetzer. We have an orchestra, consisting chiefly of recruits, with some of whom we scarcely think Spagnoletti would fiddle through Coventry ; and a chorus, remarkable for nothing, but the heterogeneousness of its composition, and the independence of proceeding asserted by its constituent voices.

[*King's Theatre*, 25.5.34.

* See pp. 432-3.   † See pp. 431-2.

APPENDIX

BELLINI'S LA STRANIERA.*

Bellini's most celebrated opera, *La Straniera*, has been performed with indifferent success. The truth is, it was not a performance, but a rehearsal, and a very imperfect one. For example, there is a hunting chorus, which we know, from other sources, to be a pleasing composition, but which, as it was given here, would have puzzled Œdipus, turned musician for the nonce, to decipher the composer's design. It resembled nothing earthly but the concert for which Rousseau had set down notes at random : *jamais on n'avait entendu un semblable charivari :* and this was not the only instance in which the orchestra and the chorus were, like the hunters themselves in the forest, seeking each other in the dark. Tosi and Tamburini, who have performed in this opera abroad, were perfect in their parts : Donzelli was nearly so : but Tamburini omitted his first air, and Donzelli sang something else instead of one that belonged to his part. We see in Tosi the remains of many excellencies : she is a good actress, and an accomplished musician : but her voice has no music in its tone : and here, tone is indispensable, whatever it may be in Italy, where they seem to be satisfied with tune and power. There were other essential drawbacks on the musical effect of the performance : but we have said enough to shew, that *La Straniera* may possibly deserve its continental reputation, notwithstanding any evidence to the contrary, in the showing of these deponents of the King's Theatre.

Signora Tamburini is a passable *seconda donna*. We hope she will rest contented in her natural station.

The *libretto* is an interesting tragic melodrama, and the poetry is above the common order. The scene is in Brittany, in the thirteenth century ; and the story has the air of being taken from an ancient *fabliau*.

* See p. 237.

APPENDIX

It has all the character of the tragic tales of the period, and those who are familiar with them will find nothing in it incongruous or unintelligible, as some of the diurnal critics have done.

The stage manager was at his usual tricks. Tamburini, having to be wounded and fall into a lake, was obliged, in the character of a man run through the body, to climb over a wall before he could tumble into the water. *Bottom* knew better than this, when he got up *Pyramus and Thisbe*: he would not allow *Wall* to walk on " before his cue."

[*King's Theatre*, 1.7.32.

ROSSINI'S L'ASSEDIO DI CORINTO.

Rossini's tragic opera, *L'Assedio di Corinto*, was produced last Thursday week for the benefit of M. Laporte, and repeated on the Saturday and Tuesday following. This opera was first brought forward in Italy, in 1820, under the title of *Maometto Secondo*; and in 1826, a *rifacciamento* of it was produced by Rossini in Paris, at the Académie Royale, and called *Le Siège de Corinthe*. This *rifacciamento* consisted chiefly of the addition of a third act to the original two. The characters, who had been killed at the end of the second act, were kept alive to the end of the third. We are not sure that it would not have been better to adopt the scheme of Manager Mist, in his tragedy of *Gulliver the Great*; when, having killed off all his characters at the end of the first act, he introduced, in the second, their executors, administrators, and assigns. The whole of the composition was at the same time retouched, on the principle of firing off the greatest possible volleys of sound, in conformity with the established taste of the Académie Royale.

Our first impressions from the first representation were unfavourable. We thought it improved on

APPENDIX

repetition. But it wants two essentials of an effective opera—an interesting *libretto*, and rememberable melodies. From a little after the rise of the curtain to the close of the first act, there is little but braying of trumpets, beating of drums, clashing of cymbals ; the whole of the orchestra playing *fortissimo ;* the whole of the performers, principals, and chorus, roaring like Bottom's nightingales ; and, in the centre of the tumult, Signor Costa belabouring his book with his *baton* as a thresher belabours a wheatsheaf, and keeping up an uninterrupted and most merciless *tapage*, which penetrates through the hurly-burly like the eternal mill-clack through the roar of a mountain-torrent. In the second and third acts there are some subdued passages ; but, generally, the characteristics of the composition are

> Bombalio, stridor, clangor, taratantara, murmur,
> Cum strepitu et crepitu, cum fremitu et gemitu.

And all this was exaggerated and made offensive by (to borrow a word of Aristophanes) the perpetual *phlatto-thratto-phlatto-thrat* of the aforesaid Signor Costa, who has become altogether a nuisance that must positively be abated.

In the progress of the performance, the first thing that struck us as worthy of notice was Grisi's execution of a rapid and impassioned passage, *La data fè rammento*, standing with a dagger in her hand, drawing up her fine symmetrical figure, and throwing all the energy of feeling into her beautiful and eloquent features, like a model for Melpomene, or, rather, like Melpomene herself, newly descended from the sky.

A situation, in which the heroine recognizes her lover in the invader of her country, who has her father prisoner, is the subject of a *trio*, which has some fine passages, but which is too like many things in Rossini's former compositions. At the beginning of the second act, Ivanhoff sings a very pleasing air, *Oh come risorgere.*

APPENDIX

Then comes Grisi with an air interpolated by Signor Costa, a mere music lesson, all shakes and roulades, and running up and down the chromatic scale ; very suitable for an introduction into the second act of *Il Barbiere,* but totally out of place for a tragic heroine in the climax of distress and difficulty. This affair is applauded ; of course for the sake of Grisi. It certainly served to exhibit all the wonders of her voice and skill. She went through the semitones in strict accordance with the nicest division of the monochord ; and her voice, considered merely as an organ, as it must be considered in the execution of an air, which is thoroughly inexpressive and a mere piece of musical trickery, demonstrates, at least to our satisfaction, that it is the most pure and perfect soprano voice ever heard within our days in this theatre. We may praise a duet of Grisi and Tamburini, especially in the passage, *Vieni, Pamira, all'ara ;* a solemn chorus which follows it, *Divin Profeta ;* an air of Rubini in the third act ; and a prayer by Grisi towards the end, in which, however, there is more credit due to her than to the composer, who has produced much better things of the same kind. The destruction of Corinth at the close is cleverly managed.

[King's Theatre, 15.6.34.

SPONTINI'S VESTALE.

" *Exit Crusoe, and enter several savages, dancing a saraband,"* says the stage direction of the would-be dramatist baronet, in Foote's farce of the *Author.* " *Exit Numa Pompilius, and enter Mademoiselle Fourcisy, spinning a pirouette,"* say, not in words, but in substance, the stage directions of the management of this theatre, in the performance of Spontini's *Vestale.* The opera is quite bad enough in itself, without the astounding trumpery that is foisted into

427

APPENDIX

it under the misnomer of "appropriate divertise-ments." The story is drawlingly told, in villanous Italian verse, modelled upon French metres, with music (excepting here and there, where the orchestra and the chorus together strike up a preposterous noise, putting to sudden rout many a comfortable nap), dull, dismal, and monotonous, like an eternal funeral march ; passionless, melodyless, and un-rememberable. We have heard a story of a German Baron in Paris, who, emulous of the vivacity of his new acquaintance, exercised himself daily with setting all the chairs in his room in a circle, and jumping over them in succession, till he was out of breath ; and who, on receiving from his unhappy under-lodger a visit, to inquire what ponderous merchandise was perpetually lumping over his head, answered, as he stood glowing with perspiration in his doublet and drawers,—" *Sh'apprends être fif !* " Some genius of this description has been making Spontini *vif*. Fancy the palace of *Numa* in the back-ground : before it, a military band, in which the most conspicuous figure is a long trumpeter, leaning on his *trombone ;* with the Vestal Virgins on one side of the stage, and the High Priest of Jupiter on the other, superintending the execution of a series of the most common-place steps of the modern French school of dancing, which have no more connexion with the story, no more reference or resemblance to the remotest shadow of classical antiquity, than a dance of Esquimaux : unless a fertile imagination can make any thing classical out of a set of very indifferent female dancers, called, Heaven knows why, " *coryphées*," beating tambourines abominably out of time. It would be more " *fif*," more amusing, and quite as appropriate, to introduce *Mr. Jonathan W. Doubikins* " larruping his nigger " round the Temple of Vesta. The interior of the said temple, by the bye, is a very accomodating scene : it does duty as a drawing-room

428

APPENDIX

in *Elisa e Claudio ;* and, being neither a temple nor a drawing-room, it serves equally well for both.
[*King's Theatre,* 1.4.32.

THE BALLET AND THE PRESS.

The Morning Herald has begun canting about the dresses of the female dancers. *The Times,* according to custom, will not begin canting till after Easter, when it will be sure of the largest audience.
[*King's Theatre,* 20.2.31.

We adverted last week to some newspaper cant about the dresses of the female dancers. We do not hear of any proposal to change the style of dancing at this theatre ; therefore we must have *pirouettes,* and the ladies must make some exhibition of under drapery. This is most commonly a sort of elastic fawn-coloured pantaloons, of tolerable substance, which at the most, gives a flying glimpse of something like a Venus, sculptured out of the same sort of stone as Tam O'Shanter and Souter Johnny. The only alternative is in volumes of white muslin drawers, which set forth the shadowy semblance of something like a Dutch farmer's wife skating to market in a high wind. On the score of taste we prefer the Venus, not to say that the more cumbrous drapery renders grace and good dancing impossible. As to the influence of either costume on the *morale* of the spectator, it seems to us to be absolutely nothing— unless perhaps, in the case of such imaginations as Tiberius liked to have about him in the island of Capreæ. [*King's Theatre,* 27.2.31.

INES DE CASTRO.*

Ines de Castro is a ballet in five scenes : the first almost all dancing, the four last all tragic action,

* The story of Don Pedro of Portugal and Iñez de Castro was told, more than a quarter of a century later, in *Gryll Grange,* Vol. V. pp. 298-300 of this edition. See also *supra,* p. 412.

APPENDIX

rhythmical action, action literally set to music, and measured out in bars . . . .

The story of *Ines de Castro* is one of the most striking in history ; but its great and leading feature, the passionate and long-enduring love of her husband, which led him to pursue her murderers through the world, and when he ascended the throne of Portugal to have her body disinterred and crowned by his side, does not, perhaps, admit of stage representation. We say perhaps, because we think our old English dramatists would have told the story from first to last, and concluded it with the coronation ; but this is a flight of too great boldness for the modern Melpomene.

[*King's Theatre*, 9.6.33.

MOZART.

[Peacock's admiration for Mozart, briefly expressed on pp. 237-9, 244, 294 and 321 of this volume, and in *Gryll Grange* (Vol. V., p. 142), had been more fully shown in the *Examiner*, where he wrote (in a notice of *Don Giovanni*, 10.2.33), " There never has been any thing perfect under the sun except the compositions of Mozart." We reprint one complete notice, and append to it Peacock's comment on the only occasion when he saw the close of *Don Giovanni* performed to his liking.*]

There is nothing perfect in this world except Mozart's music. Criticism has nothing to do with it, but to admire. Whatever is is right. Mozart cannot even be disparaged by comparison with himself—the detractor cannot say, " How inferior this thing is to that ! " for every composition seems to have a peculiar appropriateness to the occasion, and it is impossible to conceive any thing more suitable. There is nothing of mannerism in Mozart's music, and yet it cannot be mistaken for any other, or any other for it—it is peculiar in its excellence. The signature of the master is in an exalted sweetness of turns. In

* See pp. 237-9, 404.

430

APPENDIX

Mozart's operas there is every variety of style and expression, each having a marked style to which the varieties within it are subordinate and tributary. *Don Giovanni* and the *Zauberflöte* are both romantic operas, but of what different characters ! In each the grandeur is relieved with gaiety ; and here again how different the gaiety ! In *Giovanni* it is touched with riot, in the *Zauberflöte* it is all fanciful and cheery. As wide a distinction is to be marked between the gaiety of *Figaro* and of *Cosi fan tutte ;* the first is of enjoyment, the other the light laugh of the world coming more from the brain than the blood. The expression of the serious passions has as much variety in the works of Mozart as the comic. The simple sustained style of the *Clemenza* has no likeness in any of the solemn passages of his romantic operas, and the grandeur of the *Zauberflöte* is as distinguishable from the grandeur of *Giovanni*, as the devotional from the terrible. In the expression of tenderness there is most sameness in Mozart's compositions ; and how could it be other than same while true to nature, which, in all states, shows herself much alike in the melting mood ?

The *Zauberflöte*, which has not for many years been performed in this country, was produced on Monday at Covent Garden by the German Company. Most of the beauties of this opera are, however, already familiar to the English public ; and we heard several persons expressing their surprise at meeting with their old acquaintance, the *Manly Heart*, in the German guise. To many a known song in a fine opera is as acceptable as a known face in a strange land. They are glad of something to recognise when their faculties have been on the stretch to admire what they cannot understand. As a drama, the *Zauberflöte* is extremely heavy and stupid. The actors, however, do all that can be done to carry it off. Both musically and dramatically there is nothing wanting on the part

431

APPENDIX

of the principal performers. Madame Devrient plays *Pamina; Tamino* is played by Haitzinger, and *Papageno* with great spirit by Uetz ; Schafer did full justice to the part of the Chief Priest. So far as this cast is concerned the opera is well performed ; and having said that, those who have any relish for the exquisite music of it, will understand the gratification which is in store for them.

[*The German Opera*, 2.6.33.

The carrying-off of *Don Juan* was managed by the same identical red-and-yellow gauze-winged devilry, which we described last week in our account of *Macbeth*. The machinists, having got it up, could not get it down, till, after many ineffectual efforts, it was forced, crashing, through the traps, damaged, we hope, beyond repair; for it is worse than superfluous, and we earnestly desire to see it no more. Fortunately, the good sense of the musical management having restored the beautiful conclusion which has heretofore been sacrificed to a dance of devils, the bungling of the stage management was more than redeemed. For the first time within our knowledge the opera terminated as it ought to do. We have more than once required the restoration of the legitimate musical conclusion. We feel grateful to the management for having restored it. It was generally felt and acknowledged, as we were always sure it would be if the experiment were tried, as a great and most essential improvement.

[*King's Theatre*, 15.7.32.

BEETHOVEN.

[There are short but significant references to Beethoven on pp. 321 and 337 of this volume. We quote the first and more general paragraph of a notice of *Fidelio*, an opera whose "intrinsic and indestructible beauty" was also praised in the following year (14.4.33), and to which a much later tribute was paid in *Gryll Grange* (Vol. V., p. 142).]

Beethoven's *Fidelio* is the absolute perfection of

APPENDIX

dramatic music. It combines the profoundest harmony with melody that speaks to the soul. It carries to a pitch scarcely conceivable the true musical expression of the strongest passions, and the gentlest emotions, in all their shades and contrasts. The playfulness of youthful hope, the heroism of devoted love, the rage of the tyrant, the despair of the captive, the bursting of the sunshine of liberty upon the gloom of the dungeon, which are the great outlines of the feelings successively developed in this opera, are pourtrayed in music, not merely with truth of expression, as that term might be applied to other works, but with a force and reality that make music an intelligible language, possessing an illimitable power of pouring forth thought in sound. *Fidelio* is, we believe, Beethoven's only opera. It is the sun among the stars. It is not a step in the progress of dramatic music. It is a clear projection of it, a century in advance of its march.

[*King's Theatre*, 27.5.32.

ROSSINI.

[Peacock had seen the first performance of an opera of Rossini's in England in the month of Shelley's departure, March 1818.* We give here the opening (and general) paragraphs of two of his *Examiner* notices.]

The opera of *Matilde di Shabran* is one of our especial favourites. Rossini's early Italian operas are characterised by invention and simplicity; his later by less invention, and more elaborate and scientific combinations. *Tancredi* is a happy specimen of the first, *Semiramide* of the second, of these classes. *Matilde di Shabran* belongs to the second class, and is, in our opinion, a brilliant, animated, and richly diversified series of dramatic music.

[*King's Theatre*, 10.3.33.

* See p. 244.

433

APPENDIX

If there be any Italian opera (we speak not of those of Mozart) pre-eminently entitled to the appellation of divine, it is decidedly, in our opinion, Rossini's *Semiramide.* It is, however, one that requires very high musical talents in the three principal parts. The *scena* of *Arsace,* beginning *Eccomi alfine in Babilonia ;* the *Bel raggio lusinghiero* of *Semiramide ;* the duet of *Arsace* and *Assur, Bell' imago degli Dei ;* that of *Semiramide* and *Assur, Se la vita ancor t'è cara ;* and that of *Semiramide* and *Arsace, Ebben, à te, ferisci ;* are all severe trials of power and skill. To execute them moderately well is impossible. It is a case in which there can be no more distinction than honest *Dogberry* recognised between "most tolerable, and not to be endured."

[*King's Theatre,* 16.3.34.

DONIZETTI'S ANNA BOLENA.*

"How many things," says Goldoni, who was a good judge of these matters, "are necessary to the success of an opera ! A good drama, good music, good voices, young women, fine accompaniments, scenery, and machinery. And all this is not sufficient, if the *je ne scai quoi* be wanting, which even criticism cannot explain, though every body thinks proper to be critical."

> "Perchè riesca bene un' opera,
> Quante cose mai vi vogliono !
> Libro buono, e buona musica,
> Buone voci, e donne giovani,
> Belli suoni, scene, e macchine.
> E poi basta ? Signor no.
> Che vi vuole ? Io non lo so :
> Ma nol sa nemmen chi critica,
> Benchè ognun vuol criticar."
> *L'Arcadia in Brenta.*

We shall apply Goldoni's tests to Donizetti's opera, *Anna Bolena.* In the first place, there is *buono libro,*

* See p. 319, and *Gryll Grange,* Vol. V. pp. 141-2.

APPENDIX

a well-contrived and well-written drama, with enough of incident and stage-effect to fix an attentive interest in the progress of the action. In the next place, there is *buona musica*, agreeable, varied, and characteristic, though not very original, music. It is of the school of Rossini, as all Italian music has for some time been. The *Times* says, that sometimes Rossini, and sometimes Bellini, is imitated in Donizetti's opera : as if Bellini had a style of his own. It is true, that Bellini professes to be original ; he tries hard to throw off the tyranny of the *Bolognese :* but the extreme limit of his success is to play fantastical tricks with his chains. The very opening of the overture of *Il Pirata* is a striking specimen of these hornpipes in fetters. Donizetti has none of this trickery. He acquiesces in the style, which must be the style of his day : but he has produced a series of music, diversified, animated, impassioned, and, throughout, essentially dramatic. The drama, and the music, together, develope the powers of Madame Pasta more effectively, in our opinion, than any opera in which she has appeared in this country—not even excepting *Medea.* The memory of a first love, sacrificed on the altar of ambition ; the revival of the feeling, with the return of its object from banishment ; repentance, and consequent misery, in the midst of splendour ; mistrust of the *King's* designs ; terror on being entrapped into the semblance of delinquency ; proud indignation at his premeditated injustice ; passionate resentment, followed by affectionate forgiveness, on discovering her rival in her friend, *Jane Seymour ;* alternations of hope and fear, delirious visions of the happy scenes of youth, dissipated by the reality of despair and death, afford, in the part of *Ann Boleyn,* scope for the highest and most varied powers of musical tragedy ; and Madame Pasta displays them all with consummate excellence. . . .

[*King's Theatre,* 17.7.31.

435

APPENDIX

BELLINI *

The genius of Bellini is much better suited to melodrama than tragedy; and accordingly, *La Sonnambula*, which was produced on Thursday, for the benefit of Signor Rubini, is a more agreeable composition than *Il Pirata*. The music is, for the most part, a light and pleasant series of lively melodies. There are some touches of the pathetic, but not many, nor deep : the most striking is Rubini's

"Il più tristo de' mortali
"Sono, o cruda, e il son per te."

But the predominant character of the music is a graceful playfulness. Bellini's is a dancing spirit : we think this would be abundantly manifest, if this music were taken as the accompaniments of the ballet of *La Somnambule*.

[*King's Theatre*, 31.7.31.

There are two very beautiful airs in the second act of *La Sonnambula :* Rubini's "Ah ! perchè non posso odiarti ? " and Madame Pasta's "Ah ! non giunge uman pensiero." The first of these is, perhaps, both in composition and execution, the finest thing in the opera : but our principal purpose, in adverting to them at present, is to notice the peculiar *classical beauty* of the latter. The music is adapted, with singular purity and precision, to the *Ionic à minori* metre.† This metre, we must observe, with all deference to Dr. Burney's antispastic theory, is the true Dionysic metre : the predominant metre of Greek theatrical music. All the choruses of the *Bacchœ* of Euripides, for instance, are resolvable into it. The measure of the air in question is discriminated into Ionic monometers, with an accuracy unusual in modern musical composition, in which everything like poetical metre is generally frittered away. The air

* See pp. 240-2, 315-38, 412, 424, 435.   † See p. 333.

APPENDIX

is sung by Madame Pasta, with a correctness of taste, and a natural grace of action, strictly accordant with its delightful simplicity.   It came upon us as a shadow of the Athenian stage.

[*King's Theatre*, 7.8.31.

Last Thursday Madame Pasta produced, for her benefit, Bellini's opera of *Norma*.   The drama is a tragedy very like *Medea*, except that the scene is in ancient Britain, and that the heroine, after intending to kill her children, alters her mind, and sacrifices herself.   The character suits Pasta admirably, but does not present her in any new light.   *Anna Bolena* and *Medea* together have already presented the proto-types of every striking situation in *Norma*.   The *libretto* is well written.   The subject is not well adapted to the light and airy style of Bellini.   His genius is out of its element, and, in endeavouring to be sublime, he is too apt to become merely noisy. The music has less, and less varied, melody than any of his other operas with which we are familiar ; but he cannot write without melody, and there are many pleasing passages. . . . .

[*King's Theatre*, 23.6.33.

Zingarelli, Guglielmi, Vaccaj, three composers to the worthless *libretto* of *Romeo e Giulietta*, were already at least two too many.   We are surprised that Bellini should have been ambitious of adding a fourth to the number.   Vaccaj called his opera *Giulietta e Romeo*, and Bellini has called his *I Capelletti e i Montecchi ;* but the *libretto* is, with some few differences in the lyrical passages, essentially the same.   It is a dull affair at best.   A dull affair Bellini found it, and a dull affair he has left it.   No genius, indeed, could make much of such a *caput mortuum* as the drama is reduced to in this Italian version : but Bellini has made less of it than either Zingarelli or Vaccaj.   The finale of the first act, the only attempt at concerted

437

APPENDIX

music in the whole composition, is animated and effective : and the air in the third act, *Deh tu, bell'anima*, is a sweet melody. Pasta, De Meric, Donzelli, and V. Galli did their best for it : so did Messrs. Harper, whose trumpets were the beginning, middle, and end of the business of the orchestra : but the curtain fell in silence on the second representation. We may, therefore, consider it condemned.

[*King's Theatre*, 28.7.33.

MALIBRAN.

[The article on *Bellini* contains high praise of Malibran * ; we add here part of a notice of the performance of " a fragment of *Otello* " (given for Laporte's benefit) from the *Examiner* of 7.7.33, and the conclusion of an even fuller tribute to her interpretation of the characters of opera, from that of the previous month.]

Benefit nights are privileged : and moreover, with all our dislike of scraps, we cannot quarrel with any arrangement that gives us even a glimpse of Malibran where she would otherwise not be seen at all. When it was first announced that Pasta and Malibran were to appear on the same evening, we hoped it would be together in one opera,—*Semiramide*, for instance : in this we were disappointed : but it is much, and very much, to see Malibran on this stage in any thing. Her *Desdemona* is a combination of all that is beautiful, impassioned, and intrinsically real in action, with all that is skilful in musical execution, and all that is true and touching in musical expression. No character in the range of the lyrical drama misbecomes her. As every situation of real life was becoming to Aristippus, so every situation of mimic life is becoming to Malibran. Still there must be a more and a less even with her universal genius. She clothes every part she assumes in as much ideal

* See p. 319.

APPENDIX

beauty as is consistent with its dramatic truth, and, therefore, appears to greater advantage in proportion to the greater degree of ideal beauty that belongs to the poetical conception of the dramatic character.

[*King's Theatre*, 7.7.33.

Her acting and singing combined are almost a demonstration of Lord Monboddo's proposition, that " music is more natural to man than speech." * She makes the music of her part seem an essential constituent of its reality. Her voice is of extra-ordinary richness, sweetness, compass, and power, and, in its lower notes especially, instinctive with the very soul of feelings which " lie too deep for tears." Her musical skill is consummate ; and in the very exuberance of her ornaments there are always meaning, appropriateness, and a regulating judgment which brings her down in safety from those Pindaric flights into " Cecilia's world of sound," which few could take and not fall like Icarus. But the spirit of music, in the voice of Malibran, soars on " native pinions," and not on " Dædalean wings."

[*Drury Lane*, 2.6.33.

GIULIETTA GRISI.

[The occasional references to Grisi in the body of this volume (pp. 242, 251, 294) hardly indicate the degree of admiration for her performances which Peacock had expressed in the *Examiner* of the previous year. We quote two examples † (the former from an account of her appearance as Ninetta in *La Gazza Ladra*).]

Transcendently fascinating is Giulietta Grisi. We almost fear to speak of her under the influence of first impressions, lest we should run into exaggeration, which, nevertheless, we can scarcely think possible.

* See Peacock's note to Chapter VI. of *Melincourt* (Vol. II., p. 58, note 1).

† See also pp. 421, 426-7.

439

APPENDIX

We are, indeed, in the condition of travellers in the Arabian desert, lighting unexpectedly on a green oasis, with a well of sweet water, and a canopy of palms. The spot would be beautiful anywhere; but allowance must be made for the charm of contrast. Yet, take away the contrast, the elements of beauty remain; the water, the verdure, the sunshine, and the shade. So with Giulietta Grisi: take away the contrast with her predecessors of this season, there will still remain all the charms with which nature and art, in their most lavish combinations, can adorn a *prima donna;* a lovely, amiable, and intelligent countenance; a full-formed and symmetrical figure; a bust, such as Canova would have desired for a model; a simple, easy, and natural carriage; action, combining the simplicity and reality of native impulses, with the effects of a regulating judgment, surprising in one so young: a voice, a most pure and perfect soprano, sweet, clear, flexible, powerful, unerringly in tune, and responsive to every gradation and change of feeling, however impassioned or however subdued: execution, developing all the resources of science, in conjunction with the truest and most touching expression. This is a " catalogue of perfections; " and, nothing being perfect in this world, it follows that she must have some faults, which it is an important part of critical duty to discover. We shall bestow all diligent investigation on this point, and when we have found a fault in Giulietta Grisi, we shall lose no time in publishing the discovery.

[*King's Theatre*, 13.4.34.

Giulietta Grisi has appeared as *Anna Bolena*, a part written for Pasta, both poetically and musically. Pasta had identified herself with it. It was, in truth, *Anna Bolena*, in the character of Pasta; for the matronly dignity with which the great actress invested the part belonged to herself, and not to the

APPENDIX

historical Anne Boleyn. Giulietta Grisi presented us
with the heroine, as she might really have been, in
all the splendour of her youth and beauty. It seems
to us preposterous to say, as some have said, that
she copied Pasta. She had reminiscences of Pasta,
but did not turn aside from her own course, either to
imitate or avoid them. Her singing was all her own :
on this point there is no difference of opinion—the
most beautiful of voices, guided by the truest feeling,
and the most consummate skill. Her *sotto voce*
singing, in the prayer in the last scene of this opera,
as that in *La Gazza Ladra*, is pure, sweet, uniform,
distinct, and thrillingly pathetic, to a degree unequalled and unsurpassable.

[*King's Theatre*, 20.4.34.

PASTA.

[Peacock's high opinion of Pasta might be gathered from a
single line of his article on *Bellini*,* and though his references
to her are not of the full length devoted to Grisi and Malibran,
they are generous enough to justify Hazlitt's allusion.
Peacock speaks of her, on 3.7.31, as showing " a degree of
comic talent which has really surprised us," but he more
often refers to her " fire " (29.5.31), or to those " powers which,
when she was last among us, placed her above all who had
then preceded her in lyrical tragedy " (15.5.31). Two years
later he thought her " still the queen of lyrical tragedy,"
and found that " Her singing has all its varied, deep, and true
expression, and her action all its picturesqueness and vivid
reality, regulated by consummate judgment." † We quote
below a brief passage from a notice of Rossini's *Semiramide*.‡]

We have seen in print, and heard still more frequently in conversation, the opinion that Madame
Pasta has fallen off. We cannot assent to this
opinion. In the ordinary compass of the *mezzo
soprano*, her voice was always full, sweet, and powerful :
in *contralto* parts her lower notes were always husky ;

* See p. 320. † 5.5.33.

‡ Other references to her in this Appendix will be found on
pp. 403, 435-8, 440-1.

APPENDIX

in *soprano* parts her upper notes were always shrill. She always sung and acted with taste, judgment, simplicity, and feeling : but in six characters only : *Medea, Semiramide, Desdemona, Nina, Tancredi, Romeo.* Whether she can sustain any others, remains yet to be seen. Her *Zerlina* is " most tolerable, and not to be endured." But in all the points we have enumerated, she seems to us scarcely changed.

[*King's Theatre*, 19.6.31.

TAGLIONI.

[Peacock had an extraordinary admiration for his " Déesse de la danse." * Only once, in a notice of 27.7.34, did he speak of her without high praise, and then it was to find fault with the staleness of the entertainment provided, which kept her " dancing night after night the same eternal steps, of which, if there be twenty persons not heartily tired, we are not among the number. *Toujours perdrix !* "]

But Mademoiselle Taglioni, the star of stars, " *la déesse de la danse,*" how can the cold language of criticism satisfy those who have seen her, or pourtray her to those who have not ? Sculpture and painting cannot fix her thousand graces, nor poetry do justice to their infinite succession. Faultless symmetry, perfect grace, unprecedented power with unequalled ease, unerring precision in time, and inexhaustible variety in action : let the imagination make of these elements what it may, the result will still fall short of the reality of Taglioni.

[*King's Theatre*, 17.4.31.

Mademoiselle Heberlé, who made her first appearance on the same evening, in a divertisement between the acts, is a dancer of transcendent excellence. She has not the absolute grace of Taglioni : that indescribable flow of form, which carries with it the instantaneous conviction that it is the ideal beauty of

* See p. 251.

APPENDIX

motion : but with this reservation, we have never seen anything that, in the conception and execution of the beautiful and brilliant in dancing, and the graceful and expressive in pantomime, surpasses Mademoiselle Heberlé.

[King's Theatre, 29.4.32.

We are not addicted to praise the *spirit* and *enterprise* of Managers, which terms ordinarily signify no more than that they bestir themselves actively in expedients to fill their houses, and most commonly by ministering to the coarsest tastes of the town. Let us, however, see a Manager proposing to gratify the more elegant tastes, and we will cordially give our applause to the taste and boldness of his design ; and such is the merit of Laporte. The performances at Covent Garden Theatre are exquisite treats. One night the beauties of Paganini—of his wonders we speak not ; another the grace of French comedy, the incomparable Mars, and Taglioni in ballet, whose art wants a name, and transcends description. If we call it dancing, the practice which has hitherto been so called should have another name, for the first thought which strikes us is, that we never saw dancing before. Dancing, as we had before seen it, we now perceive to have answered to Ovid's description of " beating the ground alternately with the feet." If such has been dancing, Taglioni's is flowing into attitudes of grace, and making sensible the loveliness of motion,—it is on the music she seems to move, sporting (as Gay's song has it) " on seas of delight," waving, buoyant, and sparkling.

[Covent Garden, 15.7.32.

Taglioni, as usual, came bounding before us—as the Shepherd boy pipes in the Arcadia—as if she would never grow old.

[Covent Garden, 22.7.32.

APPENDIX

Paganini is the great wonder of the day. It is a dispute among the learned (for which we refer to divers tractates *De Musicâ Veterum*), whether the tensile instruments of the ancients were all played by the hand, or whether some of them, of which the form seems well adapted to the purpose, were not played by the bow. We have hitherto been sceptical on this point : the evidence adduced by the partizans of the ancient bow has appeared to us shadowy and inconclusive : but, having heard Paganini, we are now satisfied that Orpheus and Amphion played on the violin, and that Paganini, having launched his bark into " Cecilia's world of sound," has discovered, what is to us a new land, but in truth only the lost land of the ancients, the Atlantis of musical magic.

Paganini draws forth from his instrument notes and combinations which (in the modern world) none before him have produced or dreamed of : wild and wonderful alike in the strongest bursts of power, and in the softest and sweetest touches, air-drawn and evanescent as the voices of distant birds. The triumph of mechanical skill, astonishing as it is in itself, is the smallest part of the wonder. The real magic is not the novelty of the feat, but the surpassing beauty of the effect. It is the same with his performance on the single string (the fourth, or G string), as with his performance on four. New and surprising as is every part of the process, none of the phenomena of his execution appear to be exhibited for the sake of their own display : they appear as means, not ends. Novelty, of course, enters into the charm of the effect : but the great charm lies deeper than novelty : the perception of surpassing beauty would remain, if that of rarity and strangeness were withdrawn. It is this transcendent beauty and effect, that hushes his crowded audiences into an attention more profound

444

APPENDIX

than we ever witnessed in this usually gossiping theatre. The stillness was so deep, on the night of his first concert, that a single piece of wax, dropping from the side of a candle on the stage, had an effect absolutely startling : and this silence, contrasted strangely with the equally unprecedented tumult of applause, which burst forth at the close of his performance, accompanied by the unusual spectacle of the flourishing of hats, and the waving of handkerchiefs by ladies in the boxes.

Paganini is, to appearance, about forty-five ; in person tall and thin, with long arms and long fingers—long black hair, parted on the forehead, and flowing back on the shoulders : small, and usually half-closed, eyes ; a stupendous Roman nose ; a tapering chin ; a narrow and pale face, bearing traces of long and habitual ill-health ; a figure that would be uncouth, if copied : manners that would be grotesque, if imitated—but both agreeable, and even graceful, from their natural and unaffected simplicity. He stands up, between the lamps and the orchestra, which is arranged on the stage, and plays, without written notes, music of his own composition, which seems to be the result of the inspiration of the moment, and which is replete with intellect and feeling—as if his mind were an inexhaustible treasury of deep thoughts and thrilling emotions, which he was pouring forth through the medium of " all sweet sounds and harmonies."

[*King's Theatre*, 12.6.31.

APPENDIX II

GASTRONOMY

READERS of *Crotchet Castle* and *Gryll Grange*, to say nothing of *Maid Marian*, cannot long remain in ignorance of Peacock's lively interest in his food, and it may be doubted whether any author of the two centuries in which he lived can match him for a drinking song. He was a discriminating epicure, prepared to take some pains to secure the gratification of his tastes, which were not unlike those of Doctor Opimian. " Mrs. Opimian," it will be remembered, " was domestic. The care of the Doctor had supplied her with the best books on cookery, to which his own inventive genius and the kindness of friends had added a large and always increasing manuscript volume." Such a volume, similarly increased, has survived from Peacock's own household; it is written on one side only of forty-two folio leaves, or half-leaves, of blue foolscap (unwatermarked), and almost all of it is in Peacock's autograph, written, probably for the press, in a larger and clearer hand than was usual with him. It was recently in the possession of a bookseller,* who has supplied it with a modern binding and a MS. title-page bearing the date 1849-50. This ascription is likely enough to be correct; Peacock probably wrote out his receipts for the benefit of his daughter, Mary Ellen Nicolls, who was keeping house for him

* It is now in that of Mr. C. E. Jones.

446

APPENDIX

at Lower Halliford until her marriage to George Meredith in August 1849. The volume opens with a title, *The Science of Cookery*, and some prefatory paragraphs covering two pages and a half, all in her hand, but evidently the work of her father. Peacock's practical receipts then follow ; the first page of them has been cut in two by the binder, after the instructions for " Sir-Loin of Beef " and " Ribs of Beef," in order to make room for another page, in George Meredith's hand, containing considerable additions for inclusion under both these headings. After this the MS. continues in Peacock's autograph, with an occasional sentence added by his daughter, who has also written the five receipts on the last page and a half.

It seems probable that the volume belongs to the period of the article on *Gastronomy and Civilisation* (printed in *Frazer's Magazine* for December 1851), and that it was designed for publication as a cookery book ; this is suggested not only by the introductory paragraphs, but by such sentences as " Friendly Reader, your Oracle cautions you to Buy no Leg of Pork which is slit at the Knuckle," or "The boiling of Bacon is a very simple subject to comment upon,— but our main object is to teach *Common Cooks* the art of dressing common food in the best manner." *Gastronomy and Civilisation*, though obviously the work of her father, was published over the initials of M.[ary] M.[eredith], and probably *The Science of Cookery* was also undertaken on her behalf. It would certainly have made a pleasant little volume. It opens with a significant quotation from Sylvester's *Philosophy of Domestic Economy* :—" If science can really contribute to the happiness of mankind, it must be in this department ; the real comfort of the majority of men in this country is sought for at their own fire-side ; how desirable does it then become to give every inducement to be at home, by directing

447

APPENDIX

all the means of Philosophy to increase domestic happiness." Peacock follows up this general statement by an equally characteristic touch of literary reminiscence :—" The Cook in Plautus * (*Pseudol.*) is called *Hominum servatorem*, the preserver of mankind ; and by Mercier, *un Médecin qui guérit radicalement deux maladies mortelles ; la Faim et la Soif.*" And then, after quoting at length from the Encyclopædia Britannica on Food, he comes to the purpose of the book :—

" It is said there are *Seven* chances against even the most simple dish being presented to the mouth in absolute perfection ; for instance a Leg of Mutton.

    1st. The Mutton must be *good,*
    2nd. Must have been kept a *good* time,
    3rd. Must be roasted at a *good* fire,
    4th. By a *good* Cook,
    5th. Who must be in *good* temper,
    6th. With all this felicitous combination you must have *good* luck, and
    7th. *Good* appetite.—The meat, & the mouths which are to eat it must be ready for each other.

" It is only by considering the impediments to be foreseen, guarded against and overcome that the young housekeeper can so thoroughly master the theory herself as to be able to detect the practical omissions of her cook and so instruct her as to ensure regularity and perfection in her future operations. To such the minute directions given will not seem unnecessary or trivial, and by giving them her studious attention she will acquire a knowledge of all those delicate distinctions which constitute all the difference between a common & an elegant table, which can only be otherwise learnt from the scattered com-

* The volume is popularly intended, but the author could not quite renounce the classics, and the receipt for " Hare " is headed by Martial's " Inter quadrupedes gloria prima lepus."

448

APPENDIX

munications of others or through her own dearly-bought vexatious and tedious, if ever acquired experience.

"Let any one reflect on the differences in the dressing of the same plain joint on different occasions and they will be convinced that as the process of boiling & roasting can & ought to be always the same it must be from inattention to the rules of time, temperature, distance, basting or covering that such extreme variations arise."

The receipts fill the rest of the volume, and two of them are printed as specimens at the end of this Appendix—those for " Mutton, Venison Fashion " and for " Lamb " ; they are chosen not so much on account of *Maid Marian*, or of Doctor Folliott's enjoyment of " a slice of lamb, with lemon and pepper," as for the characteristic comments by the author. Peacock could not write even a cookery book impersonally ; the dislike of bad cooking, which must have made him a somewhat formidable guest, is not limited to a distrust of " Grass Lamb " on Easter Sunday, but appears up and down the book in such remarks as " Ham is generally not half soaked, as salt as Brine, and hard as Flint ; and it would puzzle the stomach of an Ostrich to digest it " ; or the advocacy of " The Western Pigs, from Berks, Oxford, and Bucks," which " possess a decided superiority over the Eastern, of Essex, Suffolk and Norfolk ; not to forget another qualification of the former, at which some readers may smile, a thickness of the skin, whence the Crackling of the roasted Pork is a fine gelatinous substance, which may be easily masticated ; whilst the Crackling of the thin skinned breeds is roasted into good block Tin, the reduction of which would almost require Teeth of Iron."

There are plenty of such turns of phrase to enliven the ordinary run of receipts ; " A Sucking Pig, like a young child, must not be left for an instant " ;

449

APPENDIX

or again, " Some Epicures like the bird very much underdone, and direct that—a Woodcock should just be introduced to the Cook, for her to shew it to the fire, and then send it up to Table." But the author's most conspicuous qualities are practical experience and sound common sense.* It is evident that he knows his subject thoroughly, and has satisfied himself of the best methods for obtaining the desired results. He will take nothing merely on trust, and maintains, for instance, that Michaelmas Geese, in spite of their reputation, are by that time too full grown " for those who eat with delicacy." In fact he is always peculiarly careful about the choice of season, and says elsewhere that " Pigeons are in the greatest perfection from Midsummer to Michaelmas ; there is then the most plentiful and best food for them, and their finest growth is just when they are full feathered. When they are in the penfeathers they are flabby ; when they are full grown, and have flown some time, they are tough. Game and Poultry are best when they have just done growing, *i.e.* as soon as Nature has perfected her work.

" This was the secret of Solomon, the famous Pigeon feeder of Turnham Green, who is celebrated by the poet Gay, when he says,

' That Turnham Green, which dainty pigeons fed,
But feeds no more—for Solomon is dead.' "

It is a pity that the book was never completed for the press. So far as it extends, it deals with the cooking of joints, game and poultry, in three sections : Roasting (which opens well with " the noble Sir-loin of about fifteen pounds "), Boiling and Frying ;

* There is no point too small for his care ; in very cold weather the Turkey must be brought into the kitchen the night before it is roasted, for " many a Christmas dinner has been spoiled by the Turkey having been hung up in a cold larder, and becoming thoroughly frozen ; Jack Frost has ruined the reputation of many a Turkey Roaster."

450

APPENDIX

but it is certainly not complete, for there are no receipts for fish, and only a few incidental directions for sauces ; and Peacock was learned in both these subjects.

Here, however, it is possible to supplement the contents of the folio volume from other material. Peacock's granddaughter, Mrs. Clarke, recalls that when she lived with him at Halliford he used to do all the housekeeping himself, and would go down every morning to the yard gate to meet the fishmonger or the greengrocer or the butcher, would choose the food that he wanted, and would himself take it in to the cook and write on scraps of paper his instructions for preparing it. More than forty of these scraps are still in existence ; most of them are evidently blank pages (or smaller pieces) of letters ; one is part of an envelope posted to Peacock on March 5, 1861 ; half-a-dozen of the slips contain watermarked dates, 1853, 1857 (two), 1859 (two), 1860. In choosing a few of these receipts for the press, it seemed only courteous to pay some heed to the opinions of those admirable judges of gastronomy, Doctor Folliott and Doctor Opimian. The former, who admitted on one occasion that Mr. MacQuedy's country was " pre-eminent in the glory of fish for breakfast," was enthusiastic over a Thames salmon, and believed that " the science of fish sauce is by no means brought to perfection ; a fine field of discovery still lies open in that line." * It is true that he spoke of the cruet sauces, " where the quintessence of the sapid is condensed in a phial " ; but he might have found something to his taste in Peacock's receipts for " Spitch-cocked Eel " and " Sauce for Eel," for " Slice of Salmon," and for " Cold Salmon." Doctor Opimian's championship of fish is also well known, but as Mrs. Clarke's papers contain a receipt for " Bream Pie " (with the watermark 1857) and another

* *Crotchet Castle*, pp. 16, 47, 50.

451

APPENDIX

for " Stew for Bream," it is worth while to recall the Doctor's speech in favour of bream at the dinner-table of Mr. Gryll, who had aspersed that fish. " On the contrary, sir," said Doctor Opimian, "I think there is much to be said for him. In the first place, there is the authority of the monastic brotherhoods, who are universally admitted to have been connoisseurs in fish, and in the mode of preparing it ; and you will find bream pie set down as a prominent item of luxurious living in the indictments prepared against them at the dissolution of the monasteries. The work of destruction was rather too rapid, and I fear the receipt is lost. But he can still be served up as an excellent stew, provided always that he is full-grown, and has swum all his life in clear running water." *

Finally, in order that fish may not monopolise these later extracts, a sauce " For Roast Mutton " and a promising receipt for a " Small Pie " are added.

MUTTON, VENISON FASHION

Take a Neck of good four or five years old Southdown wether Mutton, cut long in the bones ; let it hang (in temperate weather) at least a week; two days before you dress it, take allspice and blackpepper, ground and pounded fine, a quarter of an ounce each, rub them together, and rub your mutton with this mixture twice a day ;—when you dress it wash off the spice with warm water, and roast it in paste like Haunch of Venison. Rub a large sheet of soft white paper all over with butter and cover the Mutton with it, having first rubbed the joint perfectly dry. Make a paste with flour and water, a pound or a pound and a half of flour, roll it out three quarters of an inch thick ; cover the Fat side entirely with this paste, and over that put three or four sheets of strong white paper ; tie it securely with packthread, have a strong close fire, baste it as soon as it is put done [sic], and keep it basted all the time. A quarter of an hour before it is done, cut the string, remove the paper and paste carefully, baste it with butter, dredge it with flour and when it is nicely frothed and is of a light brown colour take it up and dish it. Garnish the Knuckle bone with cut paper. Serve Currant Jelly Sauce, and strong but unseasoned Mutton Gravy with it.

* *Gryll Grange*, p. 7.

APPENDIX

Obs. Persevering and Ingenious Epicures have invented many methods to give Mutton the flavour of Venison ; some say that Mutton, prepared as above, may be mistaken for Venison,—others, that it is full as good ; the refined palate of a Grand Gourmand, (in spite of the Spice and Wine the Meat has been fuddled and rubbed with) will perhaps still protest against " Welsh Venison "—and indeed we do not understand by what conjuration Allspice and Claret can communicate the flavour of Venison to Mutton ; we confess our fears that the flavour of Venison (especially if it is fat) is inimitable—but believe you may procure Prime eight toothed* Wether Mutton, keep it the proper time, and send it to table with the accompaniments usually given to Venison, and a rational Epicure will eat it with as much satisfaction as he would " feed on the Kings Fallow Deer."

LAMB †

Is a delicate, and commonly considered Tender meat,—but those who talk of tender Lamb—while they are thinking of the Age of the Animal, forget that even a Chicken must be kept a proper time after it has been killed, or it will be tough picking.

Woeful experience has warned us to beware of accepting an invitation to Dinner on Easter Sunday, unless commanded by a thorough-bred Gourmand, our Incisores, Molares, and Principal Viscera, having protested against the Imprudence of encountering young tough stringy Mutton under the Misnomen of Grass Lamb. The proper name for " Easter Grass Lamb " is " Hay Mutton."

To the usual accompaniments of Roasted Meat, Green Mint Sauce, & a Salad, are commonly added ; and some Cooks, about five minutes before it is done, sprinkle it with a little fresh gathered, and finely minced Parsley ; Lamb and all Young Meats ought to be thoroughly done ; therefore do not take either Lamb or Veal up till you see it drop with white gravy.

N.B. When green mint cannot be got, Mint Vinegar is an acceptable substitute for it ; and Crisp Parsley on a side plate is an admirable accompaniment.

* An earlier passage on Mutton explains this phrase : " If you wish to have Mutton tender, it should be hung almost as long as it will keep : and then good eight-tooth, *i.e.* four years old Mutton, is as good eating as Venison, if it is accompanied by Ragout Sauce, and Currant Jelly Sauce."

† Mary Ellen Peacock has written, at the sides of this title, " Grass Lamb is in season from Easter to Michaelmas, House Lamb from Christmas to Lady Day."

APPENDIX

SPITCHCOCKED EEL.

Turn the eel round and skewer it.
Rub it over with the yolk of an egg.
Strew over it fine bread crumbs, pepper, salt, nutmeg, grated lemon-peel, & chopped parsley.
Broil it before the fire.

SAUCE FOR EEL.

Mix with a breakfast-cup-full of good Beef Gravy :
  A table-spoonful of Mushroom Ketchup,
  A table-spoonful of Onion Vinegar,
  A mustard-spoonful of Mustard,
  A dessert-spoonful of Shalot Wine,
  A dessert-spoonful of Anchovy Sauce,
  A dessert-spoonful of Worcester Sauce.
When warm put in a dessert-spoonful each of
  Sweet Marjoram
  and Parsley :
mixed as fine as possible.
  Serve in a sauce tureen.

SLICE OF SALMON.

Oil.
Parsley leaves ⎫
One gherkin ⎪
One shalot ⎬ minced fine.
One anchovy ⎭
Half a tea-spoonful of cayenne sauce.
Mix these with the oil, and rub over both sides of the fish.
Wrap the slice in buttered paper, and bake.

COLD SALMON.

Two table-spoonfuls of liquor boiled in.
A table-spoonful of Salad Oil.
A dessert-spoonful of Chili Vinegar.
A dessert-spoonful of Cucumber Vinegar.
A tea-spoonful of Capers minced fine.
A tea-spoonful of Anchovy Sauce.
Mix these well together. Separate the salmon in flakes, and lay them in the mixture, to soak about two hours. Take them up separately, and lay them in the bottom of a scollop. Mix what is left of the sauce with enough bread-crumbs to give it consistence, cover the fish with it and warm it in the American oven.

454

APPENDIX

BREAM PIE.

Lobster : small quantity :
Anchovy : one :
Sweet herbs :
Lemon-peel : small quantity :
Yolks of two hard eggs :
One onion :
Minced fine and mixed up with butter.
Laid in layers with pieces of fish.
Gravy, Ketchup, & Cayenne Sauce or Lea & Perrin : poured
over, before baking :
Filled up with after baking.

STEW FOR BREAM.

Gravy.
Lea and Pērrin.
Ketchup.
Anchovy.
Capers.
Green Onion.
Parsley.
Blood of fish.
Port Wine.
Garnish with horse-radish and slices of lemon.

FOR ROAST MUTTON.

A glass of Port Wine :
Two table-spoonfuls of Reading Sauce :
A tea-spoonful of Onion Vinegar :
Four table-spoonfuls of gravy from the dish :
Made hot together, and served separately in a tureen.

SMALL PIE.

1 lb. rump steak.
2 kidneys.
    Half a Spanish Onion } chopped.
    One pickled Walnut
    A Salt-spoonful of black pepper.
    Half a Salt-spoonful of Salt.
    Mixed and laid under, between,
    and over, the pieces of meat.
The fat on the top.
A little made Gravy, with
    One table-spoonful of Mushroom Ketchup.
    One dessert-spoonful of Walnut Ketchup.

BIBLIOGRAPHICAL AND TEXTUAL NOTES

The nine articles in this volume were written for the magazines from 1827 to 1851. Four of them appeared, without indication of authorship, in the *Westminster Review* from 1827 to 1830 ; four more, over the initials M. S. O., in the *London Review* for 1835-6 ; and the last, *Gastronomy and Civilization*, in *Fraser's Magazine* for December 1851, over the initials M. M. [Mary Meredith].

Moore's Epicurean was the fourth article in the October number of *The Westminster Review* for 1827 (Vol. VIII, pp. 351-384). The review title at its head is ' *The Epicurean*. By Thomas Moore.' The running title (on every page) is ' Moore's *Epicurean*.'

Moore's Letters and Journals of Lord Byron was the first article in the April number of *The Westminster Review* for 1830 (Vol. XII, pp. 269-304). It is headed by a full review title (relegated to the foot-note to p. 71 of this volume). The running title (on every page) is ' Moore's *Letters and Journals of Byron*.'

Jefferson's Memoirs was the third article in the October number of *The Westminster Review* for 1830 (Vol. XIII, pp. 312-335). It is headed by a full review title (reproduced in the foot-note to p. 143 of this volume). The running title (on every page) is ' Randolph's *Memoirs, &c. of Thomas Jefferson*.'

456

TEXTUAL NOTES

London Bridge was the tenth article in the same number (pp. 401-415). It is headed by a full review title (reproduced in the foot-note to p. 191 of this volume). The running title (on every page) is ' *London Bridge.*'

Lord Mount Edgcumbe's Musical Reminiscences was the eighth article in the April number of *The London Review* for 1835 (Vol. I, pp. 173-187). It is headed by a full review title (reproduced in the foot-note to p. 223 of this volume). The running title (on every page) is ' LORD MOUNT EDGCUMBE'S MUSICAL REMINIS-CENCES.'

French Comic Romances was the third article in the October number (Vol. II, pp. 69-84). The title (repeated as a running title on every page) is ' FRENCH COMIC ROMANCES.'

The Épicier was the fourth article in the January number for 1836 (Vol. II, pp. 355-365). The title (repeated as a running title on pp. 356-362) is ' THE EPICIER.' The running title on pp. 363-5 is ' THE PHYSIOLOGY OF THE EPICIER.'

Bellini was the tenth article in the same number (pp. 467-480). The title, ' BELLINI.', is also the running title on every page.

Gastronomy and Civilization was the first article in the December number of *Fraser's Magazine* for 1851 (Vol. XLIV, pp. 591-609). The title is repeated as a running title on left hand pages, but the running titles on right hand pages (indicating the contents) are :— *Social Habits of the Greeks, The Feast of Trimalchio, Festal Amusements among the Romans, Eastern Banquets, The Feasts of our Ancestors, A Feast in the Time of James the First, Gastronomy in France,* and *Modern English Cookery.*

In reprinting articles published in different magazines over a period of more than thirty years,

TEXTUAL NOTES

it becomes necessary to make certain adjustments in details of typography and punctuation, in which the methods of the original printers would present a disconcerting variety. To indicate quotations, double quotation marks have been adopted, in accordance with Peacock's practice in the novels, with single marks for a quotation within a quotation, while no marks at all have been used for verse quotations, or for passages of prose introduced in smaller type. Peacock's formula for referring to the pages of works cited was, for a two page reference, pp. 41, 2, or pp. 41, 42 ; for a longer reference, pp. 41-8, or pp. 41-48. This was usually followed by his magazine printers, but a few exceptions (41-2, or 41, 8) have been corrected. In the introduction of quoted paragraphs, he uses colon with dash, colon without dash, dash without colon, comma with dash, or no intermediate stop at all. Most of these variations have been retained, as conveying shades of expression, but there seemed to be no good reason for differentiating between colon with dash, and colon without dash ; they frequently occur, through the carelessness of author or printer, in precisely similar contexts, and on the same page. The dash, when omitted, has accordingly been added to the colon. The dash without colon is much less frequent, and has its uses ; at the foot of p. 353, for instance, it allows the construction of the sentence (though in a different language) to remain continuous.

In the use of italics, the original articles varied. In the present reprint, names of operas will be found in italics not only in the account of Bellini, which had them originally, but in the review of Lord Mount Edgcumbe, which had not ; and italics have also been supplied for the names of a few works of fiction in *French Comic Romances*. In the printing of foreign words, the original article has been followed except where it contained manifest inconsistencies ; for

TEXTUAL NOTES

example, in *The Épicier* the words *épicier, corbleu, fiacre, boutique*, occurring in both roman and italic type, have been uniformly italicised, carrying with them single instances of *gendarme, centime, diable, allons*, and *fête champêtre*. On the other hand, Peacock systematically printed Italian words and phrases in the review of *Musical Reminiscences* (mostly, no doubt, as current terms of English musical criticism) in roman type, which has been retained.

A few trivial misprints have been corrected; *e.g.* p. 101, *Smectymnus*, p. 159, thoughout, p. 244, spirit-stiring; and a few obvious adjustments have been made, such as the transference of the comma on p. 166 l. 4 from 'would' to 'world', and the substitution of square for round brackets on pp. 77 l. 10, 382 l. 20.

While the present volume was going through the press, an original list of *Errata* was discovered at the end of the October number of *The Westminster Review* for 1830 (page 522). It is introduced by the paragraph: "In the article on Jefferson's Memoirs and Correspondence, there are several typographical errors, the sheets having been inadvertently printed without having passed under the proper revision. The following corrections are the most essential." There follows a list of twelve misprints, the last six of which have been corrected in the present volume, which had been printed off, when the list was discovered, only as far as the end of sheet L. Unfortunately, as the first six misprints occurred before that point, it has not been possible to correct them in the body of the article, and the following original errata will therefore be found in the present text :—p. 154 l. 25, 'was' for 'were'; p. 155 l. 24, 'Government' for 'Governments'; p. 161 l. 7, 'first' for 'final'; p. 163 l. 8, 'Figure to yourself apart' for 'Figure apart'; p. 165 l. 6, 'Waden' for 'Warden'; and p. 168 l. 27, 'dollars on' for 'dollars annually on.'